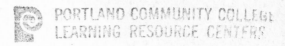

THE SOVIET MAFIA

THE SOVIET MAFIA

Arkady Vaksberg

Translated from the Russian by
John and Elizabeth Roberts

ST. MARTIN'S PRESS
NEW YORK

First published in the United States of America in 1991

Printed in Great Britain by Butler & Tanner Ltd
Frome and London

ISBN 0–312–07135–3

Library of Congress Cataloguing-in-Publication Data

Vaksberg, Arkadii.
    The Soviet Maria/Arkady Vaksberg: translated
from the Russian
  by John and Elizabeth Roberts.
        p.   cm.
    Includes index.
    ISBN 0–312–07135–3
    1. Organized crime—Soviet Union–History.
    2. Soviet Union—Politics and government—1953–
1985.
    3. Soviet Union—Politics and government—1986–
    I. Title.
HV6453.S73V34   1991
364.1'06'0947—dc20   91–26569
                                              CIP

Contents

Illustrations

All illustrations supplied by the author

Between pp. 150–151

Two 'heroes' – Leonid Brezhnev and Sergei Medunov
Behind the scenes of a meeting held in Sochi: Churbanov, Medunov,
   Naidenov, Razumovsky
The city fathers of Sochi at play
Militia pictures of Voronkov after his arrest
Gold jewellery taken as bribes by Voronkov
The Sochi–Krasnodar party mafia on a picnic
Money, valuables and bank account books confiscated from party
   mafiosi in Krasnodar and Sochi
Arkady Vaksberg and Yevgeny Bogat interviewing Nikolai
   Shcholokov
Shcholokov greets the Chief Justice of the US Supreme Court
Chief Justice Burger at a meeting with the Soviet militia
Chief Justice Burger in a children's prison camp
Sharaf Rashidov, Yuri Churbanov and one of the leading officials
   of the Union of Writers, Yuri Verchenko
The rebellious investigators: Telman Gdlyan and Nikolai Ivanov
Yuri Andropov
Yuri Churbanov under a portrait of his father-in-law
Kunaev with his wife and the present president of Kazakhstan,
   Nursultan Nazarbaev

Chapter One

'We Have No Mafia in the Soviet Union'

It was May 1980. In the far south, in the mountains surrounding the Black Sea bathing resort of Sochi – the Nice of the Soviet Union – they were shooting an insignificant film. Insignificant, that is, for everybody but me, because this was the first feature film to be shot using a script of mine. Practically every day I would have a telephone call from the director with news of how work was proceeding. It was one bit of alarming news after another: suddenly one of the actors fell ill; worse, it looked as if he would be off sick for some time. Some of the scenes in which his character appeared had already been shot, but filming couldn't be held up until he was back. The rest of the team had to move on to a location beyond the Arctic Circle before summer ended. There was only one way out: to make some urgent changes in the screenplay – to write the sick actor's part out of the script. The director, on the verge of tears, begged me to fly down, even for two or three days.

This didn't fit my schedule at all. There were endless telephone calls. The situation was becoming more and more difficult. In the end I yielded.

The flight was due to leave for Sochi at 7.30 am. I ordered a taxi for six. But at five the phone rang. It was not the taxi driver. The familiar-sounding man's voice was dry and impersonal. I noted straight away that there was not even so much as a 'good morning', let alone an apology for ringing at such an ungodly hour.

'You're about to fly to Sochi?' said the voice at the other end of the line.

'Who's speaking?' I said by way of a reply.

1

'Naidenov . . . ' said the voice.

Now I remembered who the voice belonged to. That's who it was – Viktor Vasilievich Naidenov, Deputy Prosecutor-General of the USSR, in charge of investigation work in all prosecuting departments throughout the Soviet Union. In the course of my work he and I had met fairly often, as will become clear, but our relations weren't close enough for him to phone me at home in the early hours. I remember the thought flashed through my mind: how could he have got to know about my trip to Sochi? But I didn't manage to put the question.

'It would be better for you not to go,' he said with almost military curtness and decisiveness, without further elaboration.

'Is somebody out to get me?' I said jokingly, not quite grasping what he was trying to say.

Naidenov didn't take it as a joke. 'I don't think they will go as far as killing you,' he said.

I began to realize at this point that he was in deadly earnest and must have had to think very carefully before making this dawn call.

'Would you please explain what this is all about?' I said.

I detected more than just the dry tone in his voice – there was weariness and even despair now. Despair at the slow-wittedness of the person for whose sake he was revealing an official secret – confidential intelligence, in fact.

'You're going to be framed on a charge of attempted rape. The victim and five witnesses are already waiting for you at the hotel where a room has been booked for you. They have a medical expert waiting at the end of a telephone who will come immediately he is called. The trap is set for this evening.'

'This is like something out of a cheap detective novel.' I laughed in disbelief.

'You'll have to make up your own mind about that,' said Naidenov, back in his dry prosecutor's voice. 'You can get on a plane to anywhere you like, I'm simply warning you. Obviously, we're not going to let you be arrested, but . . . ' There was an over-long pause.

'But what . . . ?' I repeated impatiently.

'But as a journalist and a person in public life you will be finished. Your reputation will never recover. The plan is not to have you put inside. The plan is to compromise you once and for all. They've had enough of you. The plan will be carried out, whatever lengths they have to go to.'

He hung up without even saying goodbye and not specifying who was meant by the mysterious 'they'. The obvious thing was to take the flight and treat the whole thing as an experiment. And I might get some sensational material for the newspaper. I am ashamed to admit that I couldn't summon the courage. I went downstairs and paid off the taxi driver when he came. I sent a telegram to the film director saying that I had been taken badly ill. I hated myself: why on earth had I been such a wimp?

Later events were to show that I had made the right decision.

The unexpected information from the Deputy Prosecutor-General had come as a shock, but was not entirely a surprise. I still naively wanted to believe that such things simply could not happen. Later I was to discover that the action planned against me was an innocent prank compared with what they'd already chalked up.

The organizer of the operation could only be someone who wielded total and unrestricted power within the territory under his control, a dictator who was afraid of nothing and nobody. This person was Sergei Medunov, who had for seven years held the post of First Secretary of the Krasnodar regional committee of the Communist Party of the Soviet Union. In other words, a governor endowed with untrammelled power over a territory almost the size of Spain.

Moreover, it is not a question of sheer geographical size: until very recently, any first secretary was complete master of his domain. But the Krasnodar district is a special case. I have already mentioned Sochi which is situated within its bounds – the 'All-Union Spa', to use traditional Soviet terminology. What is more important for the purposes of this story, countless government dachas are to be found in this corner of paradise beloved in his time by Stalin himself. It was from here in October 1964 that Nikita Khrushchev was taken to the historic and literally fateful meeting of the Central Committee – already in effect overthrown by the plotters against him. These same dachas then became the favourite summer residences of the new barons – members of the 'Leninist Politburo' – such as Leonid Brezhnev, although he, it is true, rather preferred the former tsarist estates to the west in the neighbouring Crimea.

In the wake of these topmost VIPs followed slightly lower-level bosses – though still very high up – and after them came those slightly lower still. Lower, but none the less top party people. Even if on health grounds not every one of them should have come to luxuriate in this area of maximum humidity and low atmospheric pressure (in tsarist times, it was considered to be a godforsaken place, suitable only for disgraced exiles) they migrated here in order to be close to those who were higher up the pecking order.

Spa life was conducive to relaxation, working relationships imperceptibly shaded into friendships, everything favoured easy intimacy. In order for this fantasy world to be realized, the right comforts were needed. There had to be a level of service undreamed of in the Soviet world, worked out to the last detail and drawing into its orbit thousands of workers to satisfy every conceivable need. This provided a life virtually cut off from reality – not quite up to Western levels and not even Western at all, but no longer Soviet, having nothing in common with the life led by tens and hundreds of millions of Soviet citizens. Thus, without having even the faintest idea of how the inhabitants of these government dachas, special sanatoria, special guest houses and special hotels would spend their days and nights, a mass of holidaymakers from all over our great country would come to Sochi, a city of dreams. In their ordinary lives, cheated, robbed and soiled by the daily grind, they would throng here in order to spend a few days or even weeks under the illusion of comfort and material well-being, to liberate themselves from the monotonous greyness of their drab existence and to breathe the same air as those 'servants of the people' who are separated from the people by a high wall.

The case that became known amongst journalists as the Sochi Affair was not given much publicity. There was no 'hype'. The newspapers carried correspondents' reports consisting of a few lines cleverly written so that the whole thing seemed a bit of a yawn. Something boring, and banal ... someone had done something to somebody ... in the depths of the provinces ... a bribe had been passed ... the affair had been exposed ... the guilty punished.

Nothing much there to excite a Soviet citizen! However, when I met Viktor Naidenov in the corridor of the Supreme Court of the USSR, he asked me with studied casualness: 'Have you seen that report in the paper?' It wasn't immediately clear to me what he was talking about: a thirty- or forty-line newspaper report on a criminal case which had left no trace in my memory. Naidenov noticed the puzzled expression on my face, smiled, said nothing and passed on.

I realized that his question was quite deliberate. I shall pass over the extremes of cunning involved then – as now – in penetrating court archives. I shall only say that it would have been impossible without people who secretly shared one's own deep beliefs and sought to unmask as fully as possible the masters of our lives. One way or another, two weeks later I was sitting in the offices of a member of the Supreme Court of the Russian Federation with sixty volumes of transcripts of court proceedings on the table in front of me. I was locked in from outside – was this to stop me taking the documents home? No, it was to prevent anybody knowing that I was reading them. There were spies and informers everywhere.

I spent several days reading the documents. There was enough material for ten or twenty novels. Now I knew what was behind that cunning smile on the face of the Deputy Prosecutor-General.

These sixty volumes were more of a sideshow to something far bigger that became slangily known to lawyers as 'The Fishy Business' or 'Ocean'. This was the name of a firm which operated hundreds of shops all over the country selling sea products – not only fresh and frozen fish, but mainly salted and smoked produce, those most highly prized delicacies to the Russian palate. And, even more important, black and red caviar. All these goods had long since been in short supply and in reality no longer appeared on any fishmonger's slab. However, the Ministry of Fisheries of the USSR held significant reserves of these delicacies and had the right to distribute them via the chain of Ocean shops which came under its control. In conditions of extreme shortage of supply, caviar, crab, sturgeon and salmon became like hard currency and, more than that, a key which could open any desired door. The racket worked as follows: top officials in the ministry would reach an agreement (naturally, for a consideration) to open a branch of Ocean in some town or other. Local officials would appoint (naturally for a consideration) people to run it. The ministry officials would (naturally, for a consideration) fulfil an order (naturally, for a consideration) from the local officials for a supply to their Ocean shop of additional quantities of caviar, crab and other special seafood. These supplies, it goes without saying, would never appear on the counter. Apart from a tiny quantity, they would all be swallowed up by underground dealers at five or six times the official price. Roughly a third of the

5

money would be appropriated by those immediately involved in the operation; the rest would go in bribes to those capable of guaranteeing complete protection of the criminals – not only their job security but also their future careers.

Such was the racket whereby vast sums of money were regularly made without any serious effort. This formed the basic capital of an illegal Sochi bank. There were many such banks in various cities, and all of them could be provided with 'hot' money, again with no effort but a stroke of the pen of the Deputy Minister of Fisheries of the USSR, Rytov.

It is perfectly possible that the racket would have gone on for much longer, but Rytov and his partners in crime were too cocksure and blew it. They were caught out not on their home ground but in connection with their foreign dealings. Under an agreement reached (naturally, for a consideration), thousands of tins of caviar would be sent to foreign trading partners labelled as sprats in tomato sauce or herrings in brine. The price difference would be divided amongst a vast army of accomplices but the sums involved, both in roubles and in foreign exchange, were such that there was plenty for everyone. Only a combination of colossal ignorance and sheer impudence could lead a Deputy Minister and his valiant crew to carry out such a risky operation. Did they really believe that amongst the thousands involved, there would not be a single person with a sense of civic duty? There are plenty of informers in the Soviet Union as well as abroad.

I refer to the collapse of Okean because it is essential to an understanding of how one of the first and most powerful of the Soviet 'mafias' came into existence, was organized and grew, drawing into its vortex all branches of the Soviet political structure including the most faithful of all Leninists – namely, the head of the Communist Party and of the Soviet state. Sochi, let it be remembered, is not simply a town on the map, a town like hundreds and thousands of others. Sochi is unique in our country – unique and unrepeatable. Those responsible for hosting 'honoured guests' from the highest echelons of power were able to borrow without limit. Top local posts were filled exclusively by those best capable of both pandering to the grandees from Moscow and at the same time profiteering from them during their Black Sea sojourn.

One of these was Vyacheslav Voronkov, the mayor of Sochi. Not yet thirty and an able civil engineer, he had begun to rise quickly to senior posts in various building enterprises. Unlike other Soviet towns, the country's leading spa resort was expanding. Good technicians were in demand and, at this stage, the young engineer's career duly flourished. Nobody was surprised when, still only thirty-two, Voronkov was appointed deputy mayor of Sochi with responsibility for construction. In this job it was natural for him to have meetings once a month at the very least with the regional overlord, Medunov. Medunov himself had made his career in Sochi, having been Party First Secretary for the city. Voronkov seemed to Medunov to have the right potential, so that the way was open for his career to take off once again.

For this sort of thing, it was sufficient in Stalin's day just to be loyal. If the 'leader and teacher' entertained no doubt about a person's absolute loyalty, then that person could count on blessings from on high. This tradition continued under Khrushchev, but with an added nuance: the declared devotees were by no means always devout in their actual doings. As we know, without blinking an eyelid they would derive ecstasy and delight from deceiving their 'beloved Nikita Sergeyevich'. At the beginning of the seventies, under Brezhnev, this well-organized system for advancement was updated: an oath of loyalty was now invalid unless supported by its expression in material terms. Thus, Voronkov, sensing that his master looked on him with favour and not missing the hint that his status could possibly change for the better, had now to offer proof that he could be useful in a more exalted post and that he would never forget a favour done to him.

It would be a mistake to think that these multiple chess moves were made plainly and in the open. Of course, nobody would dream of extracting a bribe, of setting conditions, offering to do this in return for that. Instead, a new ritual of 'party relationships' was elaborated and put into daily practice. Exact observation of this ritual went hand in hand with accepting the rules of the game and becoming one of the chosen people.

The most important move in this chess game was the first one: that is, the presentation of a token gift. God forbid something of value should be given to begin with, gold or silver or, worse still, money. That would constitute the crudest breach of etiquette and lead to a career nosedive, even to prison. The infuriated party magnate would strike a proud pose and denounce the attempt to buy him. Remembering the party's sacred tablets, and even the criminal code, he would, needless to say, take the appropriate steps.

Yet, if he were to be offered – 'out of the purest of hearts' – a small selection of fine brandies or a basket of fruit 'from Grandfather's orchard', that would be considered normal, and fitting, and in accordance with the best traditions. A modest gift of this sort would act as a litmus paper. On the one hand, it obligated no one: a senior party functionary was not being 'bought'; you couldn't buy the boss of a whole region for an apple or a peach! On the other hand it served as a coded signal: the donor indicates that the peach could be followed by something more substantial; the recipient, by accepting the gift rather than throwing the donor out on his neck, indicates that a relationship has been established and may be allowed to continue.

However, no senior functionary had a salary large enough to cover casual purchases of brandy, let alone a more substantial gift, nor, clearly, was there a grandfather with an orchard. Nevertheless on such functionaries depended the entire fate of innumerable subordinates. On the deputy mayor depended chiefs of administration in the construction field, directors of whole industries, managers of wholesale warehouses, garages and so forth. The same unwritten rules of the game governed in their turn their relations with people lower down, deputies and departmental heads, and their relations with their subordinates, right down to the ordinary chauffeur who valued his job. For in the USSR the possibility of making it rich (at worst, making life bearable) is available not only to those at the helm of the ship of state but also to the driver at his steering wheel.

Soon Voronkov became mayor. On the same day, he found on his desk a selection of brandies sent by anonymous 'friends'. When he got home, he found the fruit and caviar from 'friends' also too modest to give their names. The trap was set, the nooses of reciprocal obligation had been tied.

I wrote all about this in a full-page article entitled 'The Screen' in *Literaturnaya Gazeta*. It tells how – with incredible rapidity – the mayor became an inveterate bribe-taker. Raking in many thousands for various services rendered, he was nevertheless happy to accept small considerations for getting an otherwise unobtainable airline ticket or a room in a good seaside hotel at the height of the season.

The actual process of publishing my article was not unlike a detective story in itself. In a weekly newspaper the columns are typeset in advance; you can look at them not only in the typesetters' room, but also pinned up in the offices of the editor and his deputies. On this occasion, we took precautionary measures: my columns were not pinned up anywhere. Instead, in order to put even our own colleagues off the scent, we put up pages from another article not destined for publication. At the same time, we put a rumour around the editorial offices that publication of my article had been stopped by a phone call from some mysterious member of the Politburo. On the other hand, we informed our editorial censor, who was obliged to alert the authorities about any suspect article, that, although the editor himself was firmly set against publishing the article, some unnamed member of the Politburo for some reasons unknown to us was insisting on it being published: apparently a reshuffle was about to take place and it was not our business to poke our noses into Kremlin intrigues. Having pulled the wool over everyone's eyes and encouraged hundreds of informers to relax their guard, we entered the finishing straight, and at this point a rather strange visitor came to see me. Young, pleasant, with a nice smile and well-mannered, he said that he was a friend of a long-standing fan amongst my readers and, winking meaningfully, said that he knew about the forthcoming article and was looking forward to it, but that there were others who were neither looking forward to it nor wanted it to appear. Moreover they were prepared to express their *appreciation* to me if I would *temporarily* withhold publication.

'How much?' I asked straight out.

The young man winced. 'Why be so crude? Come down to Sochi, have a rest, relax a bit, now that spring is here.'

True, it was spring, and spring in Sochi is beautiful, and I had no doubt that a royal welcome would await me.

Two days later the article was published and created a sensation. Since that day, I have kept away from Sochi.

Reaction to the column came not only in the form of thousands of letters to the editor, but in commentaries in many Western newspapers, including *The Times*, the *Daily Telegraph*, the *International Herald Tribune* and *Le Monde*. Recently, I found a strange document in our editorial archive. It was entitled simply 'Memorandum'. There is no date on it, no signature. But, to judge by its contents, it came from somewhere 'up top' – or 'sideways' from one of the secret agencies. The document says: 'As can be seen from comments in the bourgeois press, the article ."The Screen" is being taken as evidence of a struggle alleged to be taking place within the Soviet leadership, where one "group", in an attempt to get the upper hand over another "group", is trying to discredit it, libellously accusing it of "corruption" and "contacts with the criminal world".' It goes on to allege without proof that 'the article was set up "by one group against the other" and the newspaper in question is therefore the mouthpiece of one faction within the leadership of the party and state. These fantasies are harmful to the authority of the Soviet state ... therefore the publication of the article in question must be acknowledged to have been an error.'

There had been no such speculation, of course, in the 'bourgeois press'. This was simply the normal routine, crude and long-established, with the 'relevant agencies': to compromise anybody they thought needed it.

It is a curious fact that the arrival of this 'memorandum' which would seem to concern me above anybody else had not been brought to my attention. When at an internal meeting mention was made of the importance of the publication of 'The Screen', one of the editorial staff (naturally unaware of the high-level implications) said that the article would 'deal a blow to the Soviet mafia', the then editor of the newspaper, Alexander Chakovsky, interrupted the speaker, and said decisively, 'We have no mafia in the Soviet Union, get that into your head.' We duly did. It was 1980.

What was so threatening about my article – and who was threatened? Who sent that go-between with the seductive offer, in effect, to join the mafia, which 'we do not have'? Who wrote that hostile memorandum, clearly a warning against any repeat of such wilful impertinence?

The answer to all these questions became obvious to me when I read those sixty volumes of criminal proceedings, and tried to understand why they – although on the face of it completely run-of-the-mill – were given top security treatment. It was clear even to the untrained eye that the unmasked mayor and the directors of several shops and restaurants arrested with him were not just a tight little circle of functionaries found guilty of embezzlement: the connecting threads led further and further and higher and higher. But then they were inexplicably severed in a very clumsy, crude way. For example:

when there is a serious discrepancy between missing valuables or money and what is actually found on the person arrested, any experienced investigator obviously asks where the rest has gone – what was the money spent on, or to whom was it given? The answer may be false, but in any case it is essential for the investigator both to put the question and get an answer. But the record of this case showed that such questions were not even put, although the investigation was carried out by the most experienced detectives in the country.

A second example: many bribes were given in order to secure appointment to senior posts in the city and the region. But a significant proportion of these posts were not in the mayor's gift. In other words, it was clear that he would have to share the money he received with more highly-placed colleagues. The investigators, exhibiting an astonishing lack of curiosity, chose not to follow that up. However, the seniority of the investigating team was so high that there could have been no question of neglect due to sheer indolence. It could only have been deliberate: either under pressure or, more likely, on direct orders from above. They could not find a single judge clever enough to put the right question. When one of the defending lawyers nevertheless asked his client whether he had been forced to share the proceeds with anybody, the judge hurriedly disallowed the question as 'having no bearing on the matter'.

The powerful figure of the uncrowned king of the region, Sergei Medunov, stood out all too clearly amongst those who were hiding in the shadows. That was obvious even to those who were trying to close their eyes to reality. But outside the confines of the courtroom, people were not so blind. The flagrant and cynical conduct displayed by Medunov and his cronies had long since been food for gossip amongst friends. Thousands of letters had been sent to the Kremlin in Moscow to that warmly loved and deeply respected figure, comrade Brezhnev. Each of these letters spoke of law-breaking, extortion, misappropriation of state property, summary justice dealt out to anyone that crossed the authorities, and in every letter the finger of guilt pointed at Medunov. These letters would be 'lost' en route, and, if they did get to the Kremlin (many people, fearing the local postal censor, would send their letters from adjacent regions or even have them posted in Moscow), they would lie around on desks or be sent back to Medunov for action. And he would take

11

action: hundreds and thousands of people looking for justice were removed from their jobs, had fabricated criminal charges brought against them, or were left to rot in jails, camps and psychiatric hospitals.

But even Medunov was not at the top of the heap up which progressed the gifts collected by Voronkov and his gang. The gifts reached up into those greater heights commanded by Brezhnev and the members of his clan. Thus Sergei Medunov felt invulnerable, protected as he was by the head of state himself. Fate had already caused my path and Medunov's to cross seven years previous to this. Although the contact was at a distance, it was nevertheless hostile. I had no idea to whom I was throwing down the gauntlet, so I cannot boast of any heroism in the resulting confrontation. Who could have thought that a simple, everyday journalistic assignment which promised no clash with the authorities, just a reasonably interesting newspaper article, could lead to such consequences?

In the city of Krasnodar there is a medical school, and one with very ancient and proud traditions. The chair of epidemiology at the school was held by Professor Z, a scientist with a solid reputation and widely respected not only in the USSR. He had been awarded several honorary degrees, diplomas, prizes and medals. Not long before the events described, he had played a prominent role in saving the country (his region, at the very least) from the consequences of an outbreak of cholera, not far from Krasnodar in the Black Sea port of Novorossisk. And then, suddenly, this worthy scientist who had worked there for decades and nurtured thousands of young doctors, was fired from his job and expelled from the party. By the standards of the time, that was severe punishment because it effectively made his life impossible. They even began moves to rescind not only his awards but also his title of professor. What was he guilty of? The fact was that his two sons, aged thirty-three and thirty respectively, had got into drunken company and raped some ladies by no means in their first youth. I had then, and still have, no desire to say anything in their defence. The whole episode struck me, frankly, as sordid. But I was appalled at the father being punished as well as those guilty of the assault. The question of whether the measures taken against the father were in any way defensible was the basis of the newspaper article I wrote.

By a strange chance, this was the only time that I bowed to the wishes of my editors and signed off the article with a pseudonym. One might ask why a well-established journalist and author should be asked to use a pseudonym, but *Literaturnaya Gazeta* in those days – and even now under perestroika – was scared of accusations of being pro-Jewish. The paper was headed by Alexander Chakovsky (a Jew); his first deputy editor, Vitali Syrokomsky, had a Jewish wife and had been brought up in his Jewish stepfather's family. Many of the journalists working on the paper were of the same 'infamous race' and amongst its staff correspondents were people with 'unfortunate' surnames. The fear of being accused of being part of a 'Zionist nest' hovered constantly over the management and sometimes prompted them to do stupid things. They often suggested I should drop my real name. I turned them down flat. But in this particular case, I had agreed to it. Intuition? The hand of God? Who knows ... Three weeks later a letter came from the editor of *Pravda*, every published word of which was still regarded as holy writ, inviting Comrade 'Rozanov' (this was the name under which my article had appeared) for an interview. It would be forbidden to conceal my true identity from the 'central organ of the party', and so I went.

The majestic party lady, Nina Matveyeva (recently editor of *Pioner-skaya Pravda* – the main printed medium for the disinformation of millions of Soviet children), rearranged the silver curls bestowed upon her in the Kremlin salon and stared at me like a boa constrictor at a rabbit, anticipating a tasty dinner. Next to her sat a young colleague who today occupies a senior post on *Pravda*, Oleg Matyatin.

'Who were you trying to get at, Comrade Rozanov-Vaksberg?' was the first smooth question put to me with evident self-satisfaction by Madame Matveyeva. Straight away, her young colleague started making notes on his pad.

Who had I been trying to get at? Of course, the professor could only have been sacked from his job and expelled from the party with the agreement of the regional committee of the Communist Party. Who had taken personal offence? And why? I really couldn't answer the question.

'So you don't know then?' said the party lady even more smoothly. 'In that case, there is nothing more for us to discuss. Thank you for coming.' She stood up and nodded curtly. The audience was over. The meeting had lasted exactly five minutes.

13

How could I not understand – I was not a novice. There was
no mistaking why that charade had been necessary. According to
pseudo-democratic, immutable Soviet rules, not a single critical
word can appear in a newspaper without there being a chat beforehand with the victim of the criticism. This applies, like it or not,
even more if the victim is one of your own colleagues. The interview
they needed was a pure formality. Now all I had to do was to
wait for the article in *Pravda* destroying me. It would reveal the
pseudonym, just as in the unforgettable years of the 'struggle against
cosmopolitans'. They needed to destroy not only the mythical
Comrade Rozanov, but the flesh-and-blood citizen Vaksberg with
all the inevitable consequences. One didn't argue with *Pravda*. Even
now not many people dare to.

Back at my newspaper office I went straight to the deputy editor.
I had hardly started my story before he got the picture and immediately went to the editor. A minute later, Chakovsky flew out of his
office, putting on his coat as he went. Despite his sixty years he did
not wait for the lift, but rushed down the stairs, taking them two at
a time. I remained behind and about three hours later my office door
flew open. Never before had the editor-in-chief bestowed a visit
upon me. Now he stood in the doorway with his coat unbuttoned,
his scarf awry, an extinct cigar clamped between his teeth, sweat
beading his forehead. 'If you knew how sick and tired I am of you,'
he growled and slammed the door. That meant that he had saved
my bacon.

What had happened? It goes without saying that the editor was
not concerned for my fate. He was alarmed about the prestige of his
newspaper. Without wasting his time on lesser fry, he had gone
straight to Suslov.* The latter could not refuse to see him. Chakovsky's personal relationship with Brezhnev and the favourable opinion
of him held by the 'true Leninist and leader of the world communist
movement' were common knowledge. Suslov only had to press a
button on his desk to establish that the article attacking me would
be published in *Pravda* the next day.

But it did not appear either then or later. Comrade Suslov decided
that my article was too insignificant a matter to make into a public

---

* Mikhail Suslov, chief party ideologist and 'eminence grise', number two in the party and
the state under Brezhnev.

issue, especially as *Literaturnaya Gazeta* was a paper that carried political weight in the world at large.

There was no warning of this. They preferred to hush the matter up, but the grounds, as it turned out, were by no means insignificant. I discovered that only two or three years later, when I was lunching in the Union of Journalists restaurant in Moscow, and a stranger came up to me and introduced himself in an unusual way: 'I have a bone to pick with you.' It turned out that he had been *Pravda*'s correspondent in the Krasnodar region. It was he who had written the article denouncing me which had not appeared and, because it had not appeared, he had been thrown out of Krasnodar by Medunov himself. As if he, or anyone else for that matter, could have gone against Comrade Suslov's decision.

Then I understood what mechanism had been set in motion against me and what people were drawn into this intrigue, invisible to the world at large. But what had set it in motion? I couldn't get out of my head the reaction to what was really a trivial incident. I again sought out the professor, who had fled from Krasnodar, having spent his whole life there, and was now resettled in Odessa. It took a long time to persuade him to talk to me. Fear of considerably more frightful consequences, and a feeling of helplessness in the face of powerful and vengeful forces, had sealed his lips. Somehow or other I had saved him from complete demise: he retained his professorial title, he had a chance to recover. So he decided to talk but made me swear to keep silent 'for a minimum of ten years'. Twelve years have passed and so my vow of silence can be lifted.

What was the secret that the Professor revealed to me?

By that time it had become routine practice for students to be enrolled in 'prestige' institutes on orders from above, and this had ceased to surprise anybody. Institutes were considered 'prestigious' if they guaranteed a good career, or a good income. The pride and joy of the Soviet system – free medical care – had, under conditions of total shortage and complete state indifference to the individual, made the medical profession hardly the most rewarding. Only if you had a deep purse could you allow yourself to be ill. Otherwise you had to rely on God or a certain death.

University administrators quickly became used to receiving from higher authority lists of school leavers to be accepted, and to the conventional signs which gave the admissions panel guiding hints as to whom to 'plough' in the examinations and who should be awarded good grades. It was considered that high party comrades knew better than professors who should be a doctor, lawyer or teacher. But then, at the beginning of the 1970s, the 'right' ideological qualities and untarnished family background alone were no longer enough as an entry pass to the temples of learning. Party bureaucrats turned the recommendation process for admission to further education into an underground auction. Every recommendation cost money, and this tax tended to increase since it had to be shared with colleagues, from the very top of the administrative ladder down to the very bottom.

Because of its geographical position, boobies and dolts from the various rich neighbouring republics – Georgia, Armenia, Azerbaijan, Dagestan and Northern Ossetia – all headed for the Kuban Medical Institute in the town of Krasnodar. Was it only because of its geographical position that they all headed that way? No: the rumour that the area committee of the party would take bribes spread throughout the Caucasus. A place in the medical institute cost 4,000–6,000 roubles, sometimes as much as 10,000. No small sum for those days, though now it sounds laughably little. The number of hopefuls who brought money in their pockets rather than knowledge in their heads was so great that there were no places left for mere mortals, and the so-called competitive entrance exam became an auction. Those who paid the most became students, or those with the most powerful protectors. Occasionally a high official, unaware of the rapidly-changing circumstances, took less than a junior manager. There would be squabbles in the wolf pack – dumping prices threatened to upset the reasonably smooth workings of the market.

So, did Professor Z also occupy a modest place in this 'market'? I will not venture an opinion, since I have no facts. But whether for professional reasons motivated by purely honourable considerations, or perhaps because he was driven to it for other reasons, Z decisively opposed the admittance of certain school leavers. As he explained to me: 'These young people were totally outside the acceptable range: judged by minimal objective criteria, they were not even worthy of a primary school certificate.'

The poor professor did not know that the first secretary of the district committee of the party, Sergei Medunov himself, had agreed to fix the admission of these ignoramuses from a fraternal Caucasian republic! As fate would have it, within a few months the professor was to give bottom marks to a student who had been admitted to the institute as a nominee of the same regional boss. When the student took the exam for the second time, the situation was repeated: the illiterate would-be doctor could not answer a single question.

This began to look like defiance. When Medunov was told about the obstinate professor, he treated his actions as though they were aimed at him personally. Of course, he could not sack the professor for it. He waited for an opportune moment. The professor's sons obliged: their arrest was a happy coincidence. And here is a curious detail. I asked my colleague at our meeting in the Union of Journalists what he could have accused me of in the article that had not appeared in *Pravda*. 'It's very simple,' he replied. 'That, in defending the professor, you were protecting your own interests.' These people at that time measured everyone by their own impoverished standards. That I could be acting from any other motive would be beyond their comprehension. This was the best their brains could think up, but any charge would do (if I had thought of defending myself in a court) because the courts were under their control.

Bottomless greed and pig-ignorance formed the perfect partnership. And so, after the incident with the professor only a few years previously, I had once again dealt Medunov a blow, straight to the heart, by guessing with deadly accuracy where the threads from the Voronkov affair must lead. And Medunov was naturally convinced that not only did I realize this but also had knowingly aimed straight at him. At that moment, without being aware of it, I had become his sworn enemy. I lived and worked, unaware what a web of intrigue was being woven around me and what a cunning plot was being planned to put paid to me once and for all.

But other forces were waiting in the shadows and, at great risk, were preparing a counterblow, carefully watching every step of the Medunov clan. Their secret agents had informed them of the trap being set to catch me. I was not necessary to these forces, though they had no wish to reveal themselves by saving me from falling into a trap. But of course they could not allow a completely innocent man who was in fact on their side to fall into a trap. These loyal party troopers and disciplined functionaries remained, however, loyal to their professional duty. That is why Deputy Prosecutor-General Naidenov decided to make that unthinkable telephone call. Saving me, he in some way saved their whole operation.

What kind of operation were they setting up?

Chapter Two

Brandy for Brezhnev

Perhaps it is wrong to go into such detail about Medunov, now a political corpse thrown into the rubbish bin of history, but that corpse was until quite recently a sinister reality, with an often tragic influence over people's fate – due to his closeness to Brezhnev and his circle. This gave Medunov for a certain time more influence than any other member of the Politburo. Secondly, what happened under his leadership in the Krasnodar region exemplifies, as if in a laboratory, how the cancerous tumour of the Soviet model of socialism develops, takes hold and spreads throughout the whole country. That cancerous growth bears the all-embracing, familiar name 'mafia'. Mafia! Under socialism? Under Soviet power? Is that possible? Strange as it may seem, the answers to these questions are both 'yes' and 'no'.

Yes, on the one hand it is possible, because the Soviet mafia is a reality, supported by factual evidence, established by official investigations, acknowledged by politicians and academics of both the left and the right, supporters of Gorbachev and opponents of Gorbachev. Everyone agrees!

No, on the other hand, because the whole political regime of the country – in all its guises – for the last seventy years is itself a mafia: a despotic totalitarian regime cannot be otherwise. Thus, those structures and phenomena which we call 'mafia-like' today, which we recognize as illegal, criminal, anti-state, are in fact very simply the natural outcome of a system of this type, expressing itself in various ways at various stages of its existence.

Leninism–Stalinism established a regime of political tyranny.

Khrushchevism, sensing its dangers, took steps to soften that regime and prepared the ground for the transformation into its new shape. Brezhnevism, yearning nostalgically for the days of Stalin, completed this process, finding support for political gangsterism in economic gangsterism, knitting both strands closely together: power and criminality mingled, the rulers of the country became not figuratively but quite literally criminals, although they were criminals who were also the leaders and rulers of a country. American Presidents, British Prime Ministers, French politicians shook them by the hand, those common thieves, swindlers, bribe-takers, keepers of disorderly houses ... I repeat the word 'common' – because they did not differ greatly from other gangsters in the amounts they pocketed. The only uncommon thing was that they were people who had managed to acquire state and party positions.

Stalin and his circle had no need of money: everything which in those days was considered desirable, prestigious and attainable only by the few could be had without money – by the very fact of belonging to the party elite and through the benevolence of the beloved father of the workers of the world. Money itself meant nothing, therefore it was not and could not be the aim of life or the means for attaining an end. Hence the sham asceticism of the Stalin era and of its namesake, the leader of all peoples and for all time. Correct, Stalin did not appropriate millions of roubles; he was entirely content with the millions who perished in his name. This 'income' was far more useful to him and gave him far more pleasure than banknotes, gold or diamonds. His legal heirs (children and grandchildren) were left nothing but badly printed illustrations torn out of old copies of *Ogonyok*, whereas his political heirs were left an enormous country with its untold wealth and tens of thousands of slaves. While the country stirred from its long and painful slumber, while new generations slowly freed themselves from the ideological poison introduced into their genes, his political heirs managed to squander their inheritance, completely ruining the country in the process.

Another distinguishing feature of the Brezhnev regime was that the people who came to power were ignorant cynics, incapable of dissimulation, vulgarian self-seekers. The many years of Stalinist repression had annihilated the whole of the professional elite in the upper reaches of power, so the country had to rely for a certain time on specialists of a different cloth. Practical work had given them some experience but 'revolutionary idealism' had completely given way to a cheerless, dry but businesslike pragmatism. The new leadership, with relentless deliberation, forced these people off the road, starting with Kosygin. Even functionaries such as these, completely dedicated, were no longer any use to anybody, and their places were taken exclusively by members of the new clan, namely the celebrants in the all-round and ongoing festival of plunder.

It is sometimes claimed that the new leadership were, to begin with, not completely lacking in ideals or morals but under the influence of the growing mafiosi became degraded and slipped into the bog of corruption. But you can only be degraded and fall if you have at one time been upright. Voronkov, in his extravagant declarations in court of repentance for his misdemeanours, harped on about how tragically he had degenerated: he had fallen into the clutches of the trading mafia – and crashed. It might be asked: what was there to boast about in that? He had became a degenerate, bribe-taker and thief ... But only a man *who has once been something else* can degenerate.

Can these people ever have been 'something else'?

Sergei Medunov bore an old grudge against *Literaturnaya Gazeta*. Many years earlier, he had sworn to get even with it and with everybody working on it. That was after we published Aleksei Kapler's article 'Trampling on Feelings'.* Today that article would seem an innocuous pinprick, but at the time it was bold and caused a stir. It told how the Sochi chief of police had dealt with a completely innocent young worker, putting him away in prison for an invented crime, simply because he had the misfortune to catch the fancy of the police chief's daughter. Fearing that a girl of a 'big noise's' family might marry a 'boy from nowhere', the all-powerful father did not spare his daughter either: he had her virginity publicly tested in front of friends and relations.

---

*Aleksei Kapler (1904–79), screenwriter of films well-known in their day, such as *Lenin in October* and *Lenin in 1918*, which fully reflected the Stalinist version of the Bolshevik Revolution and inter-party conflicts. Kapler was first love of the young Svetlana Alliluyeva (Stalin's daughter), as she recalls in dramatic detail in her *Twenty Letters to a Friend*. Having paid for his 'sedition' with many years in the camps, Kapler returned after his rehabilitation more to journalism and television reporting than to screenwriting. We worked together on *Literaturnaya Gazeta* and for some years were neighbours in the same writers' apartment block.

Kapler had a particular affinity for this story, as, in a way, it reflected his own. In publishing the article, the paper assumed it was throwing down a challenge merely to someone in the lower reaches of the militia. It turned out, however, that the real challenge was to the first secretary of the Sochi party committee – the then unknown Sergei Medunov. The girl's father and the overlord of the country's leading spa were in the same business ring, which years later would become known as the Krasnodar mafia. Indeed, this was its embryo. But the paper knew nothing of this. We thought we were simply handling an isolated story on a moral theme.

All this was in 1962. The country was still basking in the euphoria of the Khrushchev thaw, and no one was bothered about a telephone call from the secretary of the Sochi city council, complaining to our editor that 'the article had not been agreed with the party'. 'He reckons he's the party' was the editor's jocular comment. It was too soon to be making jokes. The first call was followed by a second, third and fourth one. The fourth was from within Moscow. These calls came at higher and higher levels, as did their vocal pitch. There was clearly somebody else behind the 'military governor' of Sochi.

'Brezhnev,' said Kapler confidently. 'They will have got to know each other either at the bank or on the beach.'

Brezhnev, at that time chairman of the Presidium of the Supreme Soviet of the USSR was not yet party general secretary. We weren't dealing with Khrushchev! And maybe that was why the paper was let off with only a mild scare: for a long time Kapler's pieces could not be published, and colleagues who had helped prepare his article were penalized in various ways. Moreover, the newspaper *Sovietskaya Rossiya* (even then noted for its exemplary 'democratism'!) gave us a cudgelling entitled 'Trampling On A Flea'.

Some years later, Kapler and I were strolling near our apartment block. Recalling the episode, I asked why there had been such a high-level fuss about a small-time official. After all, viewed from the Kremlin heights, the Sochi police chief must seem a mere hillock. Kapler smiled and gently chided me for my saintly naïveté and sang a couplet from a trite ballad of yesteryear:

'Money, money, my friend, everywhere.
Without it, you never get anywhere.'

I laughed, assuming he was joking to avoid giving me a serious

21

answer. It was some more years before I realized that he had, in fact, given me a straight and unambiguous answer. To recapitulate, the Sochi bosses were trampling on anyone who got in their way as early as 1962, and fleecing them at the same time. All this came out much later, but it is worth stressing that even then, before Brezhnev ascended the Russian throne and before Medunov became known outside a narrow circle, the two of them were already in cahoots, and the basis of their alliance was no great secret.

It is clear that the key position of local police chief could only be held by somebody belonging to a tight circle of close and mutual trust. Very soon, wherever there was the smell of money, of 'special facilities' or career enhancement, you only found so-called 'reliable' people. The overwhelming majority of these had started life in the Komsomol youth movement of the party. At booze-ups there, they would make friends, get used to each other, and from there begin to push their own kind into the cushy jobs. When Brezhnev became sovereign master of the country, and made Medunov party first secretary for the whole region, the latter, operating as a regional Brezhnev, moved with astonishing speed to get rid of anybody in a potentially useful job if he did not trust them. He replaced them with his own team of people who shared the same aims. They were shaped by a new phenomenon which had then appeared in society.

Nowadays this new phenomenon is known by its proper name, the black economy, but in those days the name did not exist. Few realized that behind the separate sets of circumstances that came to their attention lay a powerful new force just beginning to gain its place in the sun. Alongside the legal equivalent, for example, there was hidden underground manufacturing, followed by mis-appropriation of so-called 'reserved' goods belonging to the state (and therefore to nobody), the use of state (therefore nobody's) facilities for the production of unrecorded goods and their disposal 'on the side', a developing turnover of massive sums of money, nonexistent on paper but none the less real – there was none of this under Stalin's totalitarian rule. Now that the screws have been loosened a bit, the black economy has fallen like an avalanche onto the official one. By the way, why should it be called 'the black economy'? Would it not be more appropriate to apply that epithet to the exhausted economy of 'real' socialism which has been con-ducting its crazy experiment on people for the last seventy years in an attempt to bring about the Marxist–Leninist utopia?

Is it possible to go on forever using administrative measures wilfully to suppress or break effective economic laws? If such laws exist, as they undoubtedly do, nobody can tell them to go away. If they are suppressed, they simply go underground. Thus, is it simply not the case that all that acquired the name 'the black economy' is the natural and inevitable consequence of subjective interference with objective processes? And is it not more accurate to consider it a good thing (judged by economic rather than emotional criteria) for there to be a spontaneous tendency for a distorted economy to straighten itself out and bring itself into line with those laws, the brazen violation of which only leads to poverty and destitution?

One way or another it now seemed that the old saying 'money isn't everything' was slightly off the mark if taken literally. When dismissal could be followed by a camp sentence or 'elimination', money certainly wasn't everything. Even ordinary retirement promised apparatchiks comfortable state provision, in contrast to the poverty experienced in old age by the majority. Now there is no real threat of a camp sentence, even for those overthrown or removed from highest party circles, often at a moment's notice at their master's whim. But, finding themselves free and not fearing a bullet in the neck, today's retiring apparatchiks realize they have lost all their usual material blessings. What can they fall back on? Each of them may have felt the insecurity of his position, but that position, while he held it, opened the way for easy material accumulation. Simple worldly logic dictates: you must exploit your position to the maximum, and hurry, hurry, hurry . . .

Thus, the natural processes going on in the economic sphere began to converge with the interests of the new political class (to use Milovan Djilas's label). Wherever the newly-emerging Soviet businessman found support from party and state functionaries, both sides flourished. If separate groups of clever dealers were bold enough to try to operate independently, not sharing with or relying upon the ruling elite, they usually got it in the neck. The violence that was meted out in these cases seemed to the uninitiated both strange and incomprehensible.

It is sufficient to recall the unparalleled persecution under Khrushchev and later under Brezhnev of organizers and participants in unregistered workshops and the shortages that were the natural outcome of that policy. It was then that the fiercest sanction, the death penalty, was introduced for economic crime. One really ought to put quotes here round the word 'crime'. A normal sense of justice – as distinct from one ideologically poisoned – could hardly accept that normal business activity constituted the gravest crime against the state. But the depths of shamelessness were further plumbed and international opinion outraged by the retrospective application of this draconian law. Dozens of people were executed whose acts when they were committed were neither subject to the death penalty nor even listed as punishable under the criminal code.

There was world press coverage of this campaign, waged under the banner of Khrushchevian, and subsequently Brezhnevite, 'justice'. It was seen that the campaign, accompanied as it was by the baying chorus of the Soviet press, both metropolitan and regional, bore an openly anti-Semitic character. It was indeed the case that the vast majority of those who were wrongly executed were Jewish, and that the Soviet papers assiduously underlined their nationality, making offensive play with their non-Russian names (as in our day do those newspapers and journals sympathetic to the notorious 'Pamyat' society). This was done deliberately to play on the basest instincts of a certain section of the population so as to enlist the 'support of public opinion'. This campaign of vilification demonstrated that the illegality and immorality of their actions, and their continuing pig-headedness, was evident even to the Soviet leadership themselves.

The anti-Semitic taint of these unforgettable acts was not the main purpose of the exercise. Not for the first time and not for the last the 'Black Hundreds' were invoked simply to put the frighteners on those who were yearning for freedom and independence, because economic freedom is a first step towards freedom in general. And that is something a totalitarian government cannot allow. The embezzlement of state property was fine in itself, as was stealing from your neighbour. Neither caused the authorities so much as a blink. There was one indispensable condition, however: that the embezzler should co-opt into his band of accomplices and protectors one or preferably more – and ideally more senior – persons from among those in power. 'Cut them in', in the language of the underworld. And if an intelligent and flourishing embezzler happened to be Jewish, his high-placed patron would still protect him, putting aside his ineradicable anti-Jewish phobia: the old Russian saying 'money doesn't smell' (to use an old saying once again) became a guiding principle of the activities of the new Soviet mafia.

Those sixty volumes of transcripts of court proceedings mentioned earlier are supplemented by a quantity of photographs. That whole multi-volume dossier is like a gripping thriller with brightly coloured illustrations. They are, in fact, colourful thanks to the wonderful scenery against which they are taken. Our heroes had a burning need to record for posterity on film the very sweetest moments of their *dolce vita*, and these were, of course, the picnics with their favourite barbecues (especially in the south) and finest brandy. And beautiful girls. More of them later.

The picnics used to be organized at the most picturesque spots, and the imported photographic film with which these high-placed VIPs loved to record themselves conveyed the surrounding landscapes and the picnics in all their magnificence. That is not their main interest, however. The picnickers never dreamed, of course, that these photographs would end up adorning a police file rather than the family album. Nor could they imagine for a moment that they themselves would be easing the task of future criminal investigators by providing concrete evidence of their complicity and documentary proof of their accomplices' identity.

One might ask: what is criminal about a few colleagues getting together in the open air? What is wrong if regional and city leaders were seen in the company of waiters from local hotels, barmen, butchers, masseuses and hairdressers? Should the party comrades have kept themselves apart from ordinary people such as these? Why should they not have relaxed with simple Soviet sons and daughters of toil? And whose business is it who eats and drinks what, with whom and where? After all, these VIPs were the lords of creation now and forever more.

But, leaving aside the landscapes, it is not only the drunken faces against the background of snowy mountains that are of interest. This same dossier contains other photographs, all of a kind, which look rather like poor-quality adverts for jewellers' shops. These were not taken by the picnickers, but by criminal investigators, and what was there recorded was hardly for the purposes of advertisement. Hundreds of rings and signet rings, brooches, pendants, knives and forks, sugar bowls, vases and goblets, all of them either gold or silver. Not one of them had had the price tag removed; none of them had ever been used. These valuables were discovered during searches of the offices of city and regional party secretaries, of mayors and their deputies and of various other regional authorities. They were never intended for use. Their purpose was to turn valueless roubles into inflation-proof objects, put away 'for a rainy day'.

One might say that this was a natural precaution for anybody who has the capacity to think ahead. But in this case it was clear and convincing evidence of the process taking place in Soviet society. These thieves, once independent – even frightened – of each other, were joining in a quasi-legal, well-organized system, not requiring major efforts to conceal it. The system was clearly intended to last and develop over a long period. The owners of these spoons and pendants were convinced that, sooner or later, the time would come when they could be exchanged for money which had real value and thus assure the owners a guaranteed standard of life, regardless of their shaky foothold on the slopes of the party Olympus.

I well remember two episodes from when I was still a young man working as a lawyer. A perfectly ordinary, run-of-the-mill band of thieves had been caught in Central Asia. They were members of a village consumers' cooperative. In the pitiful mud-walled hovel where one of them lived, packets of half-rotten, worm-eaten bank-notes had been found in the cellar, hundreds of thousands of roubles, in fact. Fearing discovery, this cooperative worker and his family lived in horrifying poverty and squalor in order to create an image of being practically beggars, while their ill-gotten wealth was rotting away uselessly underground.

A few years later, I came across an absolutely identical situation in Moscow itself. They had arrested the manager of a butcher's shop. He was remarkable for his irreproachable, almost fanatical frugality and honesty. He would severely punish his workers if they were found to have cheated a customer by as little as five kopeks. He never went to a restaurant, preferring to enjoy a thin sandwich in front of his staff, which he would bring from home, washing it down with a mug of watery tea out of a thermos. When his daughter married, he gave poverty as an excuse not to provide a proper wedding, but instead counted out a hundred roubles to enable the young couple to go to Leningrad for the weekend. The lost hundred roubles made such a dent in his budget that for the following week the manager's lunchtime sandwich became even thinner.

The search of his house revealed a cache of 240,000 roubles bricked up in a wall. In today's terms that would have a purchasing power of many, many millions. All the notes had rotted away and could not possibly be paid in to the bank. The 'certificate of destruction of material evidence' is still in my archive.

Such was the morality of that period, when there were thieves but the mafia had not yet appeared on the scene. There were loners and tiny groups of thieves who carefully masked their criminal activity and feared a detective behind every bush. There was nowhere to put the money safely. If you put it into a savings bank, you gave yourself away. It was impossible to put it into a business, because business did not exist. It was also dangerous to store up expensive objects. Given the pokiness of Soviet flats, there was nowhere to hide such things. And finally, one would have to hide them from members of one's own family because the memory of the thirties was still too acute, when children would ecstatically inform on their parents, wives on husbands and sisters on brothers.

As time went by, the situation changed completely. The criminals began to make common cause with the people in power, and depended on their protection. There was no further need to hide the proceeds of their crimes. If some overzealous idiot lawyer began to take an interest in the sources of their wealth, there were plenty of ways of cooling his ardour from above. The illicit profits, however much they were being eroded by inflation, could be ploughed back into business deals. The so-called 'black economy' provided plenty of opportunities. The upper levels of the mafia pyramid took on the difficult but not impossible task of protecting the accumulating wealth in conditions of fierce inflation.

The traditional Russian merchant thought it chic to spend his money lavishly, and this habit was copied by those who 'made' the money, but not by those who collected it in: the highly-placed mafia godfathers from the upper echelons of power were distinguished by their excessive meanness. They were not only ready to get out of bed for millions; they would willingly accept a cut amounting to as little as ten or even five roubles. Among the valuables collected by the mayor of Sochi, Voronkov, there were in his Aladdin's cave, alongside the gold and diamonds, pairs of three-rouble cufflinks, two-rouble tie pins, also still bearing their price tags. All these godfathers required a daily supply of free groceries: cheese and sausage, ham and salami, apples and grapes, wines and brandy – all delivered to their houses with clockwork regularity. The managers of shops and the managers of refrigeration units, waiters and barmen – all of whom depended for their positions on the mayor – were dutifully fulfilling their obligations to him.

However, they continued to observe the ceremonial niceties of party practice in their relations with each other, keeping up a kind of theatre as if that somehow elevated what was going on. At one time, for instance, the keeper of one of the Sochi shops got fed up with having to take his daily tribute of groceries to the first secretary of the city council, Alexander Myerzly, and said to him pettishly: 'Why on earth don't you just take money from me?'

'Don't cheapen our friendly relations,' replied the party worthy gruffly.

Everything depended on the level of those 'friendly relations', on degrees of intimacy. From other people, highly-placed mafiosi took money quite willingly. It was well known throughout the area, for instance, how much a party membership card cost.

A little further explanation is necessary at this point. Although the 'soldiers of the party' number about twenty million – there has never been such an army, in any other country in the world, whether armed with ideas or any other kind of weapon – it was by no means easy for any old Tom, Dick or Harry to enter its glittering ranks. For a blue-collar worker it was not too difficult. For an agricultural labourer who worked with a plough or a tractor, it was also reasonably easy. But they weren't exactly queuing to join up. It is a long time since anyone joined the party out of intellectual conviction. They just joined to help their career. What other reason could there be? The special instructions of the Central Committee, specifying the various quotas 'by social class', called for resistance to the onslaught of high-minded careerists. It was particularly difficult for a member of the retailing trade to join the party: that particular 'class element' was not considered the most desirable.

Strictly speaking, there was no need for a shopkeeper or a snack-bar attendant to have a party card, but not belonging to the party was a hindrance to career advancement. You could not become the director of a shop (or a restaurant or a café) or any sort of section leader or divisional head without a party card. Because the quota for admission to the party for service-sector workers was so small, getting into the party meant virtually automatic promotion. There was as short a supply of party cards as there was of sausages, Lada tyres and tape-recorders. And they cost even more.

There was one more significant difference: at the end of the day, the small matter of a spare tyre could be dealt with without involving the party apparatus, or the mafia. But getting a party card could only be fixed through the good offices of the party bosses within the mafia, because literally every place in the party for workers in the retail trade was on a special list, kept under the vigilant, even supervigilant surveillance of the top party leader in the district, city and finally, region. In Krasnodar, the last word was Medunov's. The power of veto was his for a very respectable reason, namely, concern for the purity of the party ranks! And, for the same reason, he might remark, 'That's a man worth watching,' about a comrade who showed promise and about whom authoritative and well-trusted party workers had given positive references. 'He's worth watching' amounted to an instruction to accept the person into the party.

To judge by various indicators in the court files, the going rate at that time and in that part of the country for membership of the party was 3000–3500 roubles. The highest figure I came across was 6000. In the economic circumstances then prevailing that is a perfectly possible figure.

Obviously, the whole amount would not go to one man. Sharing the spoils was the rule within the mafia, even in the Soviet one. One can also be quite sure that those at the top of the party hierarchy would not receive their cut directly from those working the rackets. Although 'gratitude' got through to them, it had to go through several filters and only the most trusted people would be granted responsibility for handing over the relevant share to people on the highest or second-highest rung of the ladder.

To penetrate through to the heart and mind of the Master, it was sometimes necessary to take bold, albeit undesirable, decisions. The secretary of the Sochi party committee, Alexander Myerzly, obliged his wife Valentina, until then a cook in one of the city restaurants, to become Medunov's mistress. Putting business first, she agreed. It was no mean undertaking. Only extreme necessity could possibly have brought her to it. The twenty-stone 'wild boar' (that was the nickname the locals gave Medunov – he was so corpulent, he could not even tie his own shoelaces, for which purpose a special 'adviser' was employed) was physically repulsive. However, the affair earned Valentina Myerzlaya a key job in the commercial system of the whole Sochi spa region, plus the honorific title 'the Shah's Queen', kindly bestowed on her by the people. Now the Sochi mafia, with her husband at its head, felt totally secure, because Myerzly had thus cut out all those standing between him and direct access to the Master, Medunov. Money was no longer dissipated en route to the top, but remained 'in the family' and within a narrow circle.

The barefaced luxury in which the Sochi city fathers began to live is astonishing even now, although we are no longer easily stopped in our tracks by amazing revelations. Using his income from bribe-taking, Mayor Voronkov built himself a house unusual even by European standards, and to Soviet eyes it was Buckingham Palace itself. He brought his own architect from Yerevan just to install a singing fountain for him in the entrance hall. When the jet was at its highest it poured forth as a tenor, and when it was at its lowest, it would drop into a bass. Everybody in town knew about the fountain. Probably before long they would have begun arranging tourist excursions to see it.

The spiritual poverty, the worthless 'cultural' level (is it appropriate to use the word 'culture', even in quotation marks?), the code of behaviour in the circle from which they sprang, drove these lords and masters to public display to satisfy their vanity. To have power and money and not show it off in front of people – such self-denial would dent their sense of achievement. From time to time they needed to salve their consciences, within their limited range, by the occasional gesture. On one occasion party secretary Myerzly was having a night out with a minor member of the mafia, a habitual criminal working at the time as somebody's runner. At a nearby table, some tourists from the German Federal Republic were having supper. Myerzly whispered to his companion, 'Valera, let's show them how we Russians live. Let's order up some jars of caviar for them – and some of those special decorated spoons.' A few minutes later, three large jars appeared on the Germans' table, each containing about two kilos of black caviar, and the feasting started. The Germans obviously thought that this was indeed how Russians live. They could not have guessed that this was simply the party mafiosi showing off, because they didn't know what to do with their money.

Indeed, if you think about it, what *could* they do with their money?

A multitude of similar examples could be given, not interesting in themselves, but witness to the fact that a completely new phase had been reached in the establishment and growth of the Soviet mafia. This was evident in their triumphant and open self-assurance, having emerged from the shadows, in demonstrating their full and uncontested seizure of power.

It is obvious that this phase could not have come about at all unless each member of the ruling clique of one of the most powerful and widespread mafiosi clans had not felt that his rear was fully and reliably protected. Behind the spa bosses stood Medunov. But even that could not give a fairly experienced apparatchik sufficient guarantee of invulnerability. They knew very well that a lot of top jobs both in the city and the region were held by people who belonged to different mafia gangs: rivals, their overt or covert enemies, or people who were not in the mafia at all and therefore despised the Medunov gang even more implacably. They also knew that thousands of protest letters were going to Moscow; at least one might slip through the protective net. They also knew perfectly well that at the very top not everybody had been bought or corrupted, that there were some bold spirits willing to say aloud what others preferred to keep quiet about. Regardless of everything, the mafiosi continued to take millions in bribes, to steal everything that came to hand – food, building materials, clothing, shoes, video and sound equipment, wine and fruit. And to deal in flats, washing machines, holiday bookings in sanatoria and rest-homes, hotel rooms, airline and train tickets ... They took, stole and dealt, fearing nothing and nobody. Not just for a day, a week or a month, but for years and years.

How could this be? There is only one possible answer. They knew for sure that Medunov also had a powerful protector. And that person was an even bigger fish. There were no enemies that could frighten them. For this to be so, there had to be two conditions: one, that Medunov had a personal stake in the security of each member of the gang (if one fell, it would bring the whole structure down round their ears); two, that Brezhnev himself had to have a personal stake in Medunov's immunity (this had to be more than just a friendly interest, because one faithful comrade in arms could easily be replaced by another).

Then came some desperately bad luck for Medunov. The doctors forbade Brezhnev to take his holidays on the Black Sea coast of the Caucasus. To be more exact, they advised against it, and so the 'hero of Malaya Zemlya'* was deprived of the on-the-spot opportunity of shedding a sentimental tear about past victories. For Medunov it was a much greater loss. No longer would he be able to fawn on his protector in the relaxed atmosphere of the Soviet Nice, to extract new benefits and sort out personnel placements.

For any mafia clan, such placements are, of course, vitally important – getting one's people into the right jobs, not only at regional level but also in Moscow, and, on the other hand, removing outsiders who might get in the way.

Brezhnev was, of course, the Godfather and knew very well what Medunov's role was in the 'family'. He knew where the gifts came from. But the surface formality of party ritual was maintained, even in their personal relations. For example, Medunov could never pick up the phone and simply and without ceremony suggest to Mafioso Number One that he should remove or appoint so-and-so – not even if it was in Brezhnev's own interest that he should do so.

So it was only here, under the beach awning shading them from the hot Caucasian sun and enjoying the sea views, or in the white marble sauna much beloved by Red leaders, great and small – only in such an atmosphere was it possible to get from Brezhnev necessary decisions in the quickest possible time, bypassing the intermediary power structures. Here, between the first and second plunge or, more expeditiously, between the toasts which followed each other thick and fast at table, people were hired and fired – people not known to the outside world, but very well known bigshots within: ministerial functionaries, KGB and MVD generals, as well as party

* Malaya Zemlya is the name given to a small bridgehead outside the Black Sea port of Novorossisk, not far from Sochi. This bridgehead was captured by Soviet forces in February 1943, and was held for about seven months. In this operation, which was insignificant in terms of the whole course of the war, a very modest part was played by Brezhnev, a political commissar at the time. Soviet falsifiers of history obligingly made this out to be one of the most fateful turning-points of the war, and Brezhnev its hero. Decades later, he was given the highest military award, the Victory medal, making him once and for all a laughingstock for the entire people. By a curious twist of fate, Medunov had also been at Malaya Zemlya. The political commissar and the junior officer had probably not even met during this trivial incident, but now, years later, relaxing over a bottle of wine on the terrace of a government dacha, they would drool like old comrades in arms, remembering joint exploits.

secretaries at local level. Here also in a matter of minutes the delivery of additional illicit goods in short supply would be agreed and new working units set up, credits and permits to build construction projects of national significance.

Now, that possibility had disappeared and all such business was henceforth finally handled in the Crimea, where Medunov was not the amiable host but just another ordinary supplicant, one of many. Or not even that, because he was not always invited. In any case, you didn't go to see Brezhnev with a bottle or even a case of cognac. The whole exercise had become immeasurably more difficult. To make up for it, the Medunov clan switched its attention to eminent guests of the second, third or even fourth rank. They were not to be neglected. In the Soviet hierarchy, even those lower down the scale have their uses. Members of the Brezhnev family now appeared extremely rarely in Sochi. The spa capital began to wither and decay, rather like Moscow dimming at one point of history before the growing brilliance of St Petersburg.

Medunov issued an instruction that contact should be made with the notorious Fourth Principal Department of the Ministry of Health of the USSR (its earlier name – the 'Kremlin Health and Recuperation Administration' – gave a more accurate description of its functions). The purpose was to obtain advance information of the names of senior political figures who were planning to grace the pearl of the Black Sea coast with their presence. All the managers of rest-homes and sanatoria and hotel directors were further instructed to make a daily report about targetable guests of whose arrival there had been no advance information. In front of me I have one such list of visiting notables, supplied to Medunov by the Sochi KGB: the head of the agricultural department of the Central Committee, Vladimir Karlov; the minister in charge of the water industry of the USSR Yevgeny Alekseyevsky; the Minister of Higher and Secondary Specialist Education, Vyacheslav Elyutin; the chairman of the executive committee of the Moscow regional council (i.e. the prefect of the whole area surrounding the capital), Nikolai Kozlov; the Soviet ambassador to Czechoslovakia, Vladimir Matskhevich, who, until his unexpected switch to the diplomatic service, had served as Minister of Agriculture; the Kremlin's own writers-laureate Nikolai Gribachev and Anatoli Sofronov, who had been inherited by Brezhnev from Khrushchev and Stalin.

A bit of a job lot; that is to say, for middle-ranking mafiosi these 'stars' would be fine for the purposes of organizing and carrying through some reasonable deals, but Medunov operated on a quite different scale. Needless to say, the supply system worked uninterruptedly: the mafiosi – directors of shops and restaurants, all kinds of doctors and 'technical personnel' who had forgotten their medicine but knew how to please their patients – indulged the VIP guests to the utmost. The refrigerators in their rooms would be crammed full of delicacies, and the mini-bars with drinks. Outside, drivers and limousines would be on duty round the clock, and every day there would be new guides and 'consultants' to take the guests on excursions to restaurants and pathetic cabarets, where the local beauties put on a pale imitation of the show at the Moulin Rouge.

There was one more unique 'vaudeville' which we should not be fooled by: the Krasnodar region, on the personal instruction of Medunov, declared war on smoking, the first battle of which was conducted under the slogan: 'Sochi – The Town Without Nicotine'. The sale of cigarettes was severely reduced and smoking at work, on the street or in other public places was punishable by a fine. Both inhabitants and guests of the town were called upon to 'reprimand and publicly shame' those who were given to this disgusting habit, even in their own homes behind closed doors. Naturally, speculation and under-the-counter trading in this semi-prohibited product increased sharply, and likewise the inducements to militiamen with which smokers offered to buy themselves off, and the number of denunciations by militant health campaigners.

But the main consequences – and the whole purpose of the exercise – were completely different. The intention was not so much to divert attention from negative aspects onto the positive, as to create a smoke screen. The newspapers positively writhed in ecstasy, lauding the initiative of the people of Sochi and the Krasnodar region along with Medunov and Voronkov, the papers were constantly full of interviews with them, journalists thronged to the town where a lavish reception awaited them. Their enthusiastic reports were used to counter bureaucrat-bashing articles by more critical journalists.

But all was not going well for them: their day was drawing to a close. The clouds were gathering, the ring was tightening. Medunov, Myerzly, Voronkov and all the other members of that once-powerful clan knew only too well that an attack was going to be mounted against them. The breaking of the Okean scandal in Moscow led to the arrest of the deputy Minister of Fisheries of the USSR and of a large group of senior officials. The threads of the affair led straight to Sochi: the first to suffer would be Mayor Voronkov, that linchpin, the removal of which would threaten the collapse of the whole structure. Medunov did not have the guts to make a stand for Voronkov. Brezhnev did not lift a finger, because by that time he had already lost interest in the 'wild boar of Krasnodar' and now had other toadies and favourites.

The attack on the Medunov mafia came from above and below. His great mistake, the lacuna in his defences, was that he had not contacted and brought into the mafia ranks leading figures in the local militia, the prosecution service and in the organs of state security. However steadfast and upright such people in Sochi and Krasnodar might be, it had been shown in practice that a determined effort to corrupt even a small part of the apparat would be successful. Medunov, oversure of the protection he enjoyed at the highest level, felt that such efforts in his case would be an unnecessary waste of time. And he begrudged splitting the profits. Now he was to pay for his lack of foresight. Against him were ranged the chief prosecutors of the region and of Sochi, as well as the local heads of the KGB and the department of internal affairs.

In Moscow, the enormous investigative team (there were no less than 300 lawyers on the case) had successfully exposed the Okean mafia and thereby gained prestige, medals and even financial rewards. They now wanted to add to their achievements. Like huntsmen scenting their prey, they were able to put two and two together and were setting forth, certain of where the tracks were leading.

It was at the height of these events, brought about by circumstances already described, that I was planning to go to Sochi. At the time, I knew little or nothing of all this. It was completely by chance that my plan to go to Sochi coincided with the critical phase of the affairs of Medunov and his gang. I had no intention of doing battle with the Sochi mafia – my agenda was not journalism, purely my cinema interests. But terror opens one's eyes wide.

In their state of tension, the mafiosi clearly thought that my trip spelled the beginning of an operation and was part of a major campaign organized by Moscow to destroy them, and that the business with the film was a cover for my real intentions. The article I

35

had published a year earlier about Voronkov, where I had displayed knowledge which could only have been drawn from a confidential court file, led them to assume that I was somehow in league with their chief persecutors.

Thus, by raising a public scandal around my name, they would not only avenge themselves but also divert attention from their own illegal activities. That was their calculation when preparing their somewhat risky operation against me. By deciding not to make the trip, I not only saved my own skin but put a spanner in their works, thereby easing the task of those who were trying in difficult circumstances to smash the almost impregnable Medunov fortress.

In Gogol's immortal *Government Inspector* the elders of the town of N took a traveller who chanced to pass their way to be an emissary from His Imperial Majesty. In a similar way, the city fathers of Sochi were not sure who was who and which way the wind was blowing. It was in fact blowing from a totally unexpected direction and from very high up. The whole anti-Medunov operation had been skilfully managed, if not personally handled, by Yuri Andropov. That alone had assured its success ahead of its time.

However, before his final overthrow, but having already lost his best men, Medunov gathered his last strength and took one desperate final step, which gave him breathing space and hope. It did not bring him victory, but it saved him from total destruction.

Chapter Three

Rebellion of the Prosecutors

It is hard to say how effectively the Committee for State Security (KGB) was working at the time. In a country disintegrating rapidly throughout, it is hardly likely that any administrative department could be untouched by the process. In any case, nobody was in a better position to know the unvarnished truth than that all-powerful and secretive Committee. The Politburo was naturally supplied with reports that its members would be pleased to read, or, at least, reports where the facts had been smoothed over or bypassed and in which there was nothing to excite or alarm.

Through his army of informers and his own autonomous control service, and with the assistance of electronic surveillance techniques, Andropov, as head of the KGB, was in receipt of fairly precise information on the activities of the Sochi–Krasnodar mafia. But he could not take them on openly, because he was equally aware of Medunov's relationship with Brezhnev and that caricature of Leonid Ilyich himself – Konstantin Chernenko. The acquisitive psychosis raging in the middle and higher echelons of power was foreign to Andropov's own character. His interests were on a completely different plane, and in this respect one can regard him as more a disciple of Stalin. He loathed thievery and corruption no less than deviation from pure and unsullied Marxism-Leninism. For him acquisitiveness – i.e. mercenary as distinct from political mafia activity – constituted a retreat from an ideology which he regarded as a holy of holies rather than merely as a revelation of literal truth. For this reason alone he saw Medunov, like Rashidov – whose story is still to come – as a deadly enemy.

However, let us not delude ourselves: apart from ideology, Andropov had other reasons, more to do with personal ambition. And these reasons were for him the overridingly important ones. Starting in the mid-seventies, certain changes at the top of the party were in the offing, and Andropov was striving to create the conditions which would facilitate his moving from his key position (but one offering no prospects of further advancement) at the top of the KGB to one of the top posts in the party itself. It was some years before these efforts bore fruit, when, eighteen months before Brezhnev died, he became a member of the Politburo and a Central Committee secretary.

Medunov was also among the likely candidates for the Central Committee apparat. It had been common practice among all Soviet leaders for party first secretaries at regional level to recommend themselves as being the best available candidates for higher party posts. At the time when Medunov's relations with Brezhnev were at their most radiant, he had reasonable chances of preferment. He was not, of course, a direct rival to Andropov, as they were not on the same level. But any move on the Kremlin chessboard could have a decisive influence on the fortunes of either of them. Andropov and Medunov were chess pieces of opposing colours. If Andropov could discredit the Krasnodar mafia, that would give him an important tactical advantage in the complex court intrigues.

Another factor working for Andropov in this hidden world was Suslov's active dislike of Medunov (this dislike, incidentally, worked in my favour as well: when Alexander Chakovsky dashed off to see Suslov, he was aware that the latter's sympathies, even if they remained unspoken, would be with him). Suslov's high-mindedness, ascetic style of living and fanatical loyalty to party dogma were well known to everyone, and he was trying to create a popular reputation for himself on that basis. After pushing Medunov aside, it was he who put his hand to promoting Mikhail Gorbachev.

Suslov was never in very robust health and did not go to Sochi for his holidays. He had always preferred the spas of the Northern Caucasus (Kislovodsk, Essentuki, Piatigorsk, Zheleznovodsk). These spas really had been created for curative purposes and were located not in the Krasnodar region but in the neighbouring Stavropol region where Suslov had been head of the regional party even before the war, the Terror having destroyed all the previous leaders.

It was from here that he was 'elected' to be a deputy to the Supreme Soviet of the USSR. As was customary, Suslov became the patron of Stavropol and took care of his successors and helped their advancement. Likewise according to custom, the head of the party in the region would demonstrate his respect for a VIP guest by spending time with him whenever the latter came to spend a holiday in his territory.

In 1978 Fyodor Kulakov, Central Committee secretary for agriculture and himself a former protégé of Suslov, died suddenly and in mysterious circumstances. He had also been at the head of the Stavropol regional party in the 1960s, when Gorbachev was running Komsomol and other party work there. It was not only for that reason that Gorbachev's chances for appointment to the vacancy were preferred. Medunov's star was no longer in the ascendant. In fact, he was in a permanent state of self-defence, fighting off accusations of corruption which were being laid against one or another of his cronies and every minute expecting a stab in the back. This was no moment for him to come off best in a duel for promotion.

But things were not easy for Gorbachev either. His candidacy was being opposed by Gromyko and – particularly stubbornly – by Grishin and Ustinov (consequently, after Chernenko's death Gromyko expiated his guilt by helping Gorbachev to win against the Grishin–Romanov group). As was always the case at the very height of battle, Suslov preferred to take no active part although his sympathies with Gorbachev were well-known. The decisive role was played by Andropov.

Kulakov had died in July but in September the post of party secretary for agriculture still remained vacant. Andropov was on a rest cure in Kislovodsk; Brezhnev and Chernenko were on an inspection tour of the Northern Caucasus by train; at the railway station of Mineralnye Vody, near Kislovodsk, there took place the now famous meeting of the four party general secretaries who succeeded one another: Brezhnev, Andropov, Chernenko and Gorbachev. Gorbachev was still the party 'governor' of the Stavropol region, where Mineralnye Vody is situated. Today, only Gorbachev could say how the meeting went, but there can be no doubt that it was decisive.

It took another two months to break the opposition of the 'hawks'. Andropov, nevertheless, achieved this with Suslov's support. This meant the collapse of Medunov's hopes because there was a long-established tradition that party functionaries from one part of the country could not be appointed to the highest Central Committee posts too soon one after another. The Stavropol region had won the day and therefore the Kuban (the traditional name for the Krasnodar region) would now have to wait a long time for its turn.

One has to bear all this in mind in order to understand the political background to the battle with the Krasnodar mafia. Let it not be forgotten that this was the first time that mafia had been challenged. Until then it had been gaining strength fearlessly and systematically, putting down roots and creating reliable defences around itself. If the mafia could only operate to the extent that it felt protected, then the opposing forces could likewise only operate if they felt there was someone in power upon whom they could rely.

The Ministry of Internal Affairs (the MVD), headed by one of Brezhnev's closest friends and drinking companions, Shcholokov, was not only unwilling to take on the mafia, but was itself in the person of its minister embroiled in the mafia. Although neither Shcholokov nor his deputy, Brezhnev's son-in-law Yuri Churbanov, belonged to that clan, they successfully milked them. They offered their protection to one and all.

According to the laws prevailing in the 1970s, the KGB had no formal responsibility in relation to these goings-on. It was enough for one of its subsections to take an interest, or worse, show some sign of action, for Shcholokov, who was at daggers drawn with Andropov, to shuffle downstairs in his dressing-gown and slippers to 'Uncle Lyonya' (he and Brezhnev lived on different floors in the same building) and throw himself at the feet of his trusted friend. With a trembling voice and tears in his eyes (he was a master of such monologues) Shcholokov would come out with a tale of how Yuri Vladimirovich (Andropov) was weaving intrigues in a bid for power, that he was trespassing on another department's domain in order to deprive the General Secretary of his true friends, and to cut away at the top leadership, thus easing the way to power for himself.

There can be no doubt, even, that he would gladly stoop to demagogy, threatening Brezhnev with the image of a return to the Terror of the 1930s: Andropov's outfit only had to gather the information and give it to those who could make good use of it. However, leaving Andropov's personal interests to one side, the KGB was profoundly uninterested in the doings of the mafia at that time. It had enough other things to do, because this was the period when witch-hunts were flourishing, when they were looking everywhere for dissidents, and the most powerful secret investigative force in the world was battling not with the octopus of corruption which was sucking the long-suffering country dry, but with writers and readers of *samizdat*.

The Central Committee was likewise obviously unsuitable for the role of campaigner against the mafia. The leader of the party and the country was the friend, benefactor and client of honour of all the mafia clans, Leonid Ilyich Brezhnev. And not a single disciplinary action could be taken against any one of the major functionaries of the Communist Party without the authority of Konstantin Chernenko. All the leading party posts came under him. There remained only one organ which had formally the complete right – to be more exact, the obligation – to take on the mafia. It was not directly involved in high political intrigues, neither was it caught up in the mafia net. That was the prosecution service. This was the case not so much because of the crystalline purity and moral irreproachability of its members, as it was due to gross error and fatal blindness on the part of the not very bright and naturally slapdash bosses of the criminal clan.

After Vyshinsky left the post of Chief Prosecutor of the USSR in 1939 and the era of the great show trials came to an end, nobody at the top took the prosecution service seriously any more, seeing in it only an obedient executor of instructions. Really important decisions were settled in the Central Committee, the KGB or the MVD, and the prosecution service would simply carry out the formalities in the correct professional way, creating an externally legal façade. After Vyshinsky, at the head of the prosecution service there had only ever been second-, or even tenth-rate placemen. Appointment as Chief Prosecutor was an indication that one had been taken out of the running for a major state or party career.

Since 1953 the Chief Prosecutor of the USSR had been Roman Rudenko, an utterly faceless lawyer, deeply indifferent to the world around him and only concerned that nothing should encroach on his peace and tranquillity. His having been chief Soviet prosecutor at the Nuremberg trials added weight and decorum to his persona. In practice, this flabby geriatric took pains to hold back younger and more energetic colleagues from any initiatives whatsoever. With the same pedantic equanimity, he could, if instructed, either send half the country to the camps or release them again. He was neither wicked nor benevolent – he was simply zero.

I never knew him personally, but on my frequent calls at the office of the then chairman of the Supreme Court, Lev Smirnov,* I would find him almost every time on the special Kremlin telephone to Rudenko. These two chief defenders of the rule of law would spend half an hour or a whole hour of working time, showing off their erudition to each other, either about their latest acquisitions from friends in antiquarian book-dealing or about the workings of their insides. The latter topic was one that interested them particularly, and, of course, more so than any court case. Smirnov would carry on quite happily as if I was not there. I would wait patiently until their conversation was finished, and would then immediately try and come to the business which had brought me to the office of the senior judge in the land. It might be a request to reconsider a sentence, or do something about getting an innocent person released. 'Some other time, my dear boy – not now, later perhaps . . .' would be Smirnov's impatient reply. 'You have no idea how busy I am. Snowed under.'

Rudenko was similarly 'snowed under' and thus the least appropriate figure to take on a campaign against the mafia. The latter, knowing the actual as distinct from the pretended function of the prosecution service and of the Chief Prosecutor, saw no way in which a blow could come from that direction. Nor, therefore, did they trouble to protect themselves on that flank. They also failed to take notice of the appointment in 1976 as First Deputy Chief Prosecutor of Alexander Rekunkov, a sickly man despite his athletic build, who had transferred from the analogous post in the prosecution service of the Russian Federation. The Krasnodar region is within the Russian Federation and in his previous post Rekunkov was responsible both for the processes of judicial examination and the administration of justice in Sochi and Krasnodar.

---

* Lev Smirnov (1911–86) began as a detective inspector, and later held senior posts in the prosecution service. From 1957 onwards he was on the bench. From 1972–84 he presided over the Supreme Court of the USSR. He too had taken part in the Nuremberg trials as the assistant to the chief Soviet prosecutor. He came to wider notice as the judge, first, on the case in 1962 of the workers' uprising at Novocherkassk in which he passed several death sentences and, secondly, four years later on the case of Andrei Sinyavsky and Yuli Daniel, which marked the beginning of the long years of persecution of dissidents.

42

He had turned such a blind eye to these things that the mafia had no cause to be even slightly alarmed. Why, therefore, should the promotion of such a non-interfering prosecutor give them a moment's worry?

There was one further transfer in that area off the beaten political track which remained unobserved by the mafia. Rekunkov had brought with him to the USSR prosecution service his deputy from the Russian Federation service, Viktor Naidenov. Both there and in his new position Naidenov was responsible for the administrative supervision and organization at lower levels of the investigation service: such as run-of-the-mill staff deployments which would not have been visible from the distance and blinding sunshine of the Black Sea. Business had never been so good for the mafiosi there. Against that background, what possible interest could there be for them in the tiny triumphs of prosecutors, even if of high rank? A little while would pass and they would realize how fatal had been their lack of foresight. By then it would be too late.

I got to know Viktor Naidenov by chance, and the acquaintance boded ill. This was at the time when *Literaturnaya Gazeta* – to be more exact, some of its staff – hit upon the only possible way of telling at least some of the truth, despite the conditions then prevailing of cover-up and complete suppression of freedom of speech. The country was tormented by the lies, the violence and the summary punishment of people that the regime disliked. People were fed up with the corrupt 'partocracy' which had seized control everywhere – in the centre and in the provinces – knit together by a system of mutual guarantees. In every home, in every family, this is what people talked about. But only behind locked doors and with the telephone unplugged. It was naturally impossible to write about these things. True, the dissident, uncensored *samizdat* did write on these matters. But what could journalists do who, while working on newspapers subject to censorship, wanted to exploit the tiniest possibility of telling the reader that he was not alone, that we saw what he saw and shared his hopes and aspirations? His enemies ... our enemies ... We discovered a very simple, but, as it turned out, most effective modus operandi. What the authorities feared most of all was generalized comment, but they did not interfere with separate, ad hominem, one-off cases of law-breaking by people in official positions. Even separate one-off cases of embezzlement, extortion or fraud. We decided to go along with the game. Can you produce an exceptional case? Delighted to oblige! So we reported on *individual* thieves, *individual* extortioners, *individual* abusers of power. On the instruction of the newspaper's editors and censors each article in the series of exposés was preceded by a special notice to the readers along the following lines: This report from our special correspondent is about an atypical occurrence ... although completely uncharacteristic ... it might nevertheless be of some interest.

We put up no resistance whatever to these idiotic and degrading lead-ins. On the contrary, they became a source of sport. For example, I would often ask for them to be beefed up. Thus: 'an untypical story of a judge taking a bribe' would become 'unique' and 'unprecedented', or 'untypical case of a local official who built himself a palace at public expense and jailed people that had complained' became 'what we are saying here is bound to seem unlikely, unthinkable, perhaps a fabrication, a piece of spiteful slander ...'

Thousands of readers' letters would bear convincing witness that we were on the right track. Others, it is true, swallowed the bait: 'You should be ashamed of yourself,' came a challenge from a reader in the Urals town of Perm. 'According to you, your story was unique. Just come to Perm and you'll see. Exactly the same thing goes on here. And anyway it's pretty clear from your article that the occurrence was one of many.'

I wrote back to him: 'Dear Comrade, If you say it was clear from my article that the occurrence was not unique, that is what you read into it. How I managed to make you see and understand everything correctly is my author's secret.'

A telegram came back from Perm: 'Thanks. Everything understood. Keep it up. Awaiting new articles on unique events ...'

One might be asked: if a simple soul in Perm and thousands of others like him could understand, why was such a primitive ruse not obvious to the powers that be? Perhaps they did realize what we were up to. However, we were obeying the rules of the game and, at that particular stage, keeping to the rules was more important to them than looking at the underlying essence. But it is possible that far from all of them were so sophisticated. As indicated in the first chapter of this book, there were among those in power at that time some irredeemably dim, fantastically stupid people whose insect brains defied belief. What took a street-sweeper no effort to work out was beyond the grasp of those running the country – ministers, Central Committee secretaries and even Politburo members. This may be hard to believe, but I can vouch that it was indeed so. However, I have digressed; back to Naidenov.

I was at the time working on one of those 'unique' articles. It was about a minor event in the Tambov region. The father of a young family had died under the wheels of a lorry. The point was that those involved in running him over were on the 'staff' of the local authority, whereas the dead man had been publicly accusing them of corruption and abuse of power. That was the subject of my piece, and I felt that the local prosecutor was protecting wrongdoers by refusing to take into account certain additional evidence.

Then came the sudden phone call: the deputy prosecutor of the Russian Federation was asking me to go and see him. In a small office I was met by a handsome young man with prematurely greying hair and a dazzling smile. What astonished me straight away was that he seemed to be informed down to the last detail of my writing plans. It was the first time he had seen me, but he was completely open with me – no craftiness, no attempt to conceal anything. No question of 'two for the written record, but between ourselves it will be three'.

'You were planning to expose some local prosecutor' was the way he began, not asking but affirming. 'I think that is inadvisable.'

At the very dawning of Brezhnevism, such open pressure on the press, without any camouflage, was unknown. There were other well-tried, undercover ways of setting the signals at 'stop'. An author often had no idea of the who, how and why of interference with what he had written. And now – this conversation, without any beating around the bush.

'In the present, specific case, the prosecutor has indeed missed a trick. But not because he wanted to meet the criminals half-way. He is devoting all his energy and attention to fighting the local authority. He is one of the few among my colleagues who has had the guts to stand up to the mafia.'

I well remember Naidenov using the word 'mafia'. At the time it was such an unusual word, especially to hear from an official, that I was quite shocked. It may be that it was from Naidenov that I first heard it used at all in the Soviet context.

'Your article will be an answer to their prayers. The regional committee secretary will be simply overjoyed. Your article will be accepted as "correct" and as a result the prosecutor will be fired. Who will be the winner as the result of your work?'

I thought: truth would be the winner, and loyalty to principles which should always be preferred to expediency. It can happen that dishonest people profit when an honest man commits a lesser sin; but should one ignore that lesser sin?

'Trust my experience, and my information.' The sarcasm had disappeared, and his tone no longer seemed to imply that he was giving orders. 'It is too late now to change anything in this matter. All the evidence has been destroyed, a new investigation would reveal nothing. As a lawyer yourself, you don't need me to tell you that. Don't get me wrong: there are plenty of prosecutors who deserve to be thrown out. Don't let's begin with the better ones.'

These were very serious arguments and fears, but I really did not want to become part of a conspiracy, whatever purposes it might serve. 'I appreciate your confidence,' I said as I took my leave, 'but I am not making any promises. We've each got a job to do.'

He objected: 'We've both got the same job to do, but we have to do it using different means.'

That was how we left it. The interview left a bitter aftertaste. There was too much left unsaid, despite the apparent directness. Naidenov was quite obviously an exceptional man. I had never come across anybody like him in the prosecution service, but to withhold from publication an article which seemed to me absolutely justified? Why?

Nonetheless, I did withhold it. I was influenced not so much by the force of the arguments as by the conviction of the person who marshalled them. This in turn gave me confidence but at the same time astonished me.

I rang him to say that the article would not appear.

'Thank you,' he said, without apparent emotion. 'Do call by,' and so I did.

'Why do you waste your time on small fry?' he asked, frowning ironically. '"It's a one-off case – an atypical story. A bit of a laugh!"'

Should I share our little game with him and tell him how much the readers appreciate our 'atypical stories'?

He must have read my thoughts. 'That record is worn out – it is time to put on a new one before the audience gets bored. Can I suggest a case which is right up your street? But only for you – an exclusive. Well?'

I realized that his jocular manner concealed something which was very important to him.

'The case is one of corruption on a massive scale with members of the Central Committee embroiled in it. Well? Are you interested?'

It was so unexpected and so unusual that I lost my presence of mind. I should have said straight away that of course I would take it on, and that I would sort out editorial clearance later. But – and I cannot forgive myself for this – what I did say was: 'I'll have to consult my editor-in-chief.'

'Well, get consulting then.'

And so I went to see Chakovsky. He cut me short: 'You and your Naidenov must have gone out of your minds.'

'The editors have decided against going ahead for the time being' was the more parliamentary language in which I conveyed Chakovsky's answer over the phone to Naidenov.

'Congratulations,' he said sarcastically. 'They got cold feet. I hardly expected anything different.'

Now, years later, I sit pointlessly scratching my head trying to remember what the story was that Naidenov proposed to me. I can remember that the place was the Chechen–Ingush Autonomous Republic, in the network of the republic's granaries. There were gigantic misappropriations of flour, oil and other produce. The money was shared between the local party apparatus, ministers and other 'leaders'. Part of the money found its way to Moscow and that is about all I can remember.

However, two very important details justify these fragmentary recollections: first, this was the time (it was 1975) of the first ranging shots against the mafia; these were indeed fired from within the prosecution service by Naidenov himself and he wanted to get the press on his side. Secondly, shortly beforehand, there had been appointed as head of the Chechen–Ingush regional party committee one Alexander Vlasov, who later became a candidate member of the Politburo, chairman of the Council of Ministers of the Russian Federation, a close colleague of Gorbachev and rival in 1990 to Boris Yeltsin for the post of chairman of the Supreme Soviet of the Russian Federation. Whose side was Vlasov on at that time – was he for or against Naidenov? Why was Naidenov so keen to get the story into print: in order to weaken Vlasov or, on the contrary, to embolden him as a comrade-in-arms?

Alas, that question remains unanswered.

In a system where politics governs the law, the nomenklatura will sacrifice one of their own not because a specific law requires it but only if the balance of political forces at that particular moment does. That is indisputable. The nomenklatura is not a homogeneous entity; within it existed and still exist major opposing forces, not to say hidden hostilities. Thus, when the nomenklatura sacrifices one of its members to the repressive machinery of state, it does so not only on grounds of politics but also on particular personal grounds. Politics are merely a camouflage for an all-pervasive web of intrigue. Besides this, it is occasionally possible to nab a member of the nomenklatura despite the system (but it is quite an undertaking) if individual enthusiasts manoeuvre through the many reefs, at considerable risk to themselves, showing determination, courage and cunning. It can only be done by doing it, just as something can only be written if somebody writes it.

Another powerful stimulus is normal professional ambition – the thrill of the chase and the desire to win. And, finally, it would be wrong to ignore the fact that some lawyers who held important posts in the legal hierarchy did act out of decency, loyalty to the law, and implacable hostility to cynical flouting of the law by those in authority.

Looking back, I am astonished that in the local capital and in practically all the spa resorts on the Black Sea, there were so many leading people in the militia and in the prosecution service who were not neutral but actually fighting the mafia, not afraid to do so although knowing fairly well the extent of its real power and what possible dire consequences could follow from their course of action.

I will only name some of them: the head of the department of internal affairs of the city of Sochi, Valery Yevrushkin*; his deputies

---

* Was expelled from the party by Medunov for 'political unreliability' but Moscow friends helped by getting the punishment reduced to a stern warning. Medunov's friend, Minister for Internal Affairs Shchelokov, had Yevrushkin sacked from his post. Thanks only to old connections with Andropov, Colonel Yevrushkin got a posting to Mongolia, beyond the reach of Medunov, which saved him.

Alexander Udalov*, Anatoly Sysoletin† and Anatoly Churganov; the city prosecutor of Sochi, Petr Kostyuk‡; and the prosecutor for the Krasnodar region, Boris Rybnikov§.

All of them were on the opposite side of the barricades: in effect, a 'fifth column' in a region where the mafia exercised undivided sway. And this 'fifth column' was the more threatening for the mafia because, thanks to their official positions, not only could they keep Moscow informed of what was going on in the region, but they themselves were in a position to take their own measures (even if not against the most highly placed) using their own secret network of informers, spies and electronic surveillance devices. The most astonishing thing is that local prosecutors should be in alliance with people at the top of the local militia who in turn were answerable to Medunov's friends (themselves heads of the even more powerful mafia network), the Minister of Internal Affairs of the USSR Shcholokov and his first deputy Yuri Churbanov, along with their closest colleagues. It is clear that this betrayal, inexplicable in the eyes of the mafiosi, led the Medunov clique to be especially merciless with these 'renegades'.

In order to put the frighteners on these militia 'turncoats', the Sochi city fathers hired recently-released criminals who agreed to kidnap Udalov's little girl for 52,000 roubles. Special agents working for the secretary of the city party committee, equipped with walkie-talkies, acted as lookouts. The headmistress of the little girl's school

---

* On Medunov's instructions, a criminal charge was fabricated against him, he was expelled from the party and arrested. He was rehabilitated after the fall of Medunov, readmitted to the party and was appointed a colonel of militia. At the present time, he is head of criminal investigation for the Turkmen Republic.

† Was sacked from his post and expelled from the party.

‡ Expelled from the party by Medunov; following a 'recommendation' from the Central Committee he was removed from his post for 'having compromised himself whilst holding a responsible position'. His 'crime' was to have sanctioned the arrest of a common thief – in the person of the manager of an ordinary restaurant which was, however, an important link in the mafia network headed by Medunov. Kostyuk escaped from his master's rage in a remote little town in the Soviet Arctic where he found himself a humble job which allowed him to scratch a beggarly living. Even after the fall of Medunov, the authorities did not want to restore his party membership, which would have enabled him to get on his feet again. A particularly fierce opponent of restoring his membership card was one of Brezhnev's favourites, Mikhail Solomentsev, who had been chairman of the Committee for Party Control – the highest 'court' of the Communist Party. Kostyuk was only reinstated in the party in 1990 (when Solomentsev retired to a 'well-earned rest'), well past the normal pension age.

§ Medunov failed to get even with him. The 'case' had been prepared against him, but then Medunov himself fell. Rybnikov remains to this day head of the prosecution service of the Krasnodar region.

kept in contact with them and gave them a tip-off to kidnap the girl in the break between the third and fourth lessons. By complete chance, her father called for her in the break between the second and third lessons to take her to a dental appointment. An hour later, his secret service, which was keeping an eye on all ex-convicts in town, intercepted a strange telephone conversation: the city party secretary's assistant was ticking off in gutter language one of the former jailbirds best known to the militia for having failed to carry out a 'battle order'. In that conversation, the name of the head-mistress was mentioned, as was a schoolgirl called Udalova. The father clicked immediately and the parents smuggled the girl out of town in complete secrecy.

Things went worse for Anatoly Churganov. For a man who worked for the city's department of internal affairs (MVD), he stood out sharply for his vividly expressed social concerns and deep disquiet about everything that was happening in the country. Amongst his colleagues, even among the best of them, he was a *rara avis* indeed.

At the beginning of the 1960s, Churganov had met Nikita Khrushchev when the latter was on holiday at Pitsunde, and similarly the editor-in-chief of the literary journal *Novy Mir*, Alexander Tvardovsky (the pioneering liberal and poet who first published Solzhenitsyn's 'One Day in the Life of Ivan Denisovich'). Later on, he was in correspondence with academician Andrei Sakharov and was a close acquaintance of the well-known historian and political commentator Roy Medvedev and other prominent 'dissidents'. From the outset, all this was known to the central apparatus of the KGB, which maintained a permanent watch on 'troublemakers' in the capital. Having established the identity of the troublemakers' friend in Sochi, the KGB were astonished to discover that he was directly involved in the work of the militia. They sent Medunov an urgent despatch. There was rejoicing in Krasnodar and Sochi: the news that the KGB was after Churganov could not have come at a better moment for them; the boss of all the local detectives had long been a thorn in their side.

One should not be surprised at the KGB being actively and directly involved in pursuing somebody who was fighting the Medunov mafia. It goes without saying that the KGB considered dissidents to be more dangerous to the regime than the mafiosi. Besides, the KGB is not some homogeneous organism, operating logically, consistently and purposefully. Within it are a variety of different departments and, as in all Soviet institutions, the right hand very often does not know what the left hand is doing. The far-sighted strategic thinking of the chairman of the KGB was by no means always known or understood by his colleagues, even senior ones who – each in their patch – operated according to generalized instructions.

The secret services both in the capital and on the Black Sea joined forces to put a stop to Churganov's unmasking of the mafia. When he was in Moscow once on official business, they tailed him when he went to call on Roy Medvedev. There, he made the acquaintance of Craig Whitney, the *New York Times* correspondent. Despairing of ever conquering the mafia by using internal resources, Churganov decided to tell the American journalist about the victimization which he was suffering, only revealing a hundredth part of the dirty tricks the party bosses had been playing on him. On 5 August 1980, the *New York Times* carried Whitney's article 'The State Comes First' which included some of the information Churganov had conveyed. That was enough to get Churganov and two colleagues thrown into prison. They were accused of anti-Soviet agitation and propaganda under the notorious Article 70 of the criminal code, used to send thousands of the victims of the arbitrary Brezhnev–Andropov regime to the Gulag. But this time the main purpose of the punishment was not forcibly to remove one more dissident. Its actual purpose and result was automatically to devalue all Churganov's official reports about the violence and other illegal acts committed by the mafia that he had been sending to Moscow addressed to Naidenov and Rekunkov. 'Members of the Union prosecution service,' thundered Medunov at a meeting of local party activists, 'have been trying to undermine the authority of the party and discredit its finest representatives' – here he must have had himself in mind – 'and do not stop at using the services of malicious slanderers of our country and of our political system, selling out to American and other sworn enemies of communism.'*

* Churganov spent six years in the camps, then was released and rehabilitated under the aegis of perestroika. He remained true to his ideals, continuing after his release to campaign against the highly-placed mafiosi who had still not yielded, having gone way underground. He was heard and seen many times in Moscow speaking at gatherings of thousands in support of Boris Yeltsin and the Inter-Regional Group of Supreme Soviet deputies, and demanding democratic reforms.

The arrests of Udalov and Churganov, and the removal from their posts of other prominent figures in Krasnodar and Sochi seemed a crushing victory for the mafia and a signal for celebration. But it only seemed that way.

Viktor Naidenov had no intention of giving up. The campaign against the mafia continued. It was clear that the contest was not going to end with a knockout. There was only one way forward now: to win on points by slowly but surely advancing bridgehead by bridgehead, capturing more and more territory.

The country's best examining judges were drafted in to the investigative effort. Incidentally, it should be honestly admitted that there were not many of the best, let alone good ones, left. The most able people would already, at the point of finishing university, have been pushed aside by graduates 'recommended' by the party and the Komsomol, and by children and grandchildren of people with fat purses who had simply bought university places for them. Into this category fell practically all the special assignment investigators working for the Prosecutor General of the USSR. Let us note in passing that Telman Gdlyan, who much later made a name for himself as an implacable opponent both of Gorbachev and Ligachev, was not in Naidenov's campaign team against Medunov, although he was already ranked as a special assignment investigator. Naidenov did not take him into the group but put him onto a much less dangerous, lower-profile case. Instead he brought in as assistants to the 'specials' young uncompromised investigators from the provinces: from the north, from the Urals, from Siberia, the Soviet Far East, from the Ukraine and Belorussia. In all, several hundred people. The selection was made in such a way as to exclude anybody who could have the slightest, even indirect connection with the Medunov mafia and its patrons. However widely the mafia cast its nets, it is hardly likely that they would have roped in any rank-and-file provincial Pinkerton whose finest achievement to date might have been the investigation of the theft of a child's bicycle thousands of kilometres away. Now, for these young lawyers who had not dared even to think about rapid promotion, there opened up the possibility of making an unimaginable leap forward, and they were as keen as mustard . . .

The arrest of the mayor of Sochi and his gang had led to new revelations. The trail led further and further, revealing new, enormous realms of extortion and plundering of everything that these people in top state and party posts could lay their hands on. The fear that now seized them spread like an epidemic and took on the character of a collective psychosis.

One of the special assignment investigators, Georgi Efenbakh, called in the mayor of the small spa town of Khost, a satellite of Sochi. Efenbakh had nothing on Loguntsov, but wanted to cross-check some evidence given by Voronkov, the mayor of Sochi. But Loguntsov himself knew what Efenbakh did not, and could see which way the wind was blowing. He went home, rigged up a home-made electric chair by coiling electric cables around his body and turned on the current. Medunov immediately accused Efenbakh of driving the suspect – which Loguntsov was not – to suicide. Following a report from Medunov, Brezhnev's secretariat called for an immediate internal investigation. Efenbakh couldn't stand the pressure and died from a stroke. The mafia's hopes rose once again.

But it was just at this time that another outstanding inspector, Vladimir Kalinichenko, came across one of the major local person-alities, the lady in charge of all the restaurants, cafés and bars in Gelendzhik, a spa district neighbouring Sochi. This was Bella Borodkina, known along the whole Black Sea coast by her nickname 'Iron Bella'. It later transpired that it was Bella who acted as principal banker to the mafia. The very largest sums which formed the basic wealth of the leaders of the clan derived from her. It was later established that they took an average of 250–300 roubles for every visitor to the holiday resort. Amongst these there were many from the north and the Far East who took holidays usually three times a year. They would bring a lot of money with them, dreaming just for once of making a splash without counting the expense. In a year, Gelendzhik would receive about a million visitors, so one can easily calculate Iron Bella's revenues.

Her lover and business partner was the first secretary of the city party committee, Nikolai Pogodin, one of Medunov's most trusted men. In this way, contacts between the Godfather and the chief banker could be maintained without any outsiders being involved, because Pogodin used to fly at least once a week to Krasnodar on party business.

The mafia had already gone over to a war footing, and Naidenov and his team kept up the pressure. Medunov placed his informers everywhere, but his main source of information was from above rather than below. We shall probably never know who all the informers were, but it is possible to name at least two of them from the topmost councils of the land. These are Brezhnev's assistant, Gennadi Brovin (during perestroika he was found guilty of taking millions of roubles in bribes), and Viktor Golikov, the inseparable companion of Brezhnev, who through his whole postwar career dragged him around everywhere like a devoted valet: from Moldavia to Kazakhstan and from there to Moscow. For his slavish loyalty and rare stupidity he took him into the Central Committee. They or somebody else in the know reported to Medunov that Bella was informing on Pogodin and that he himself (the investigators were questioning him as a witness in connection with Iron Bella's case) was not holding his tongue. He had already let something out of the bag, and there would be more to come. Pogodin's arrest was a foregone conclusion. He himself realized this and began to try to make contact with the investigators, hoping in some way to mitigate his fate.

This was reported back to Medunov from the capital, where progress reports were being received from the investigating team on a weekly or even a daily basis. Moreover, Brezhnev's secretary, Golikov, forced Naidenov as a matter of party discipline to go to Medunov and report on the whole situation. In a sense that meant giving away his own game. No matter how much Naidenov tried to keep to himself the most important secrets of the investigation, he had to divulge some details, and Medunov clutched at these straws. Hardly had Naidenov left when Medunov summoned Pogodin to Krasnodar where they had several hours' secret conversation, then the first secretary's private jet took Pogodin back to Gelendzhik.

Insofar as this strictly documentary account is developing rather like a detective story, there should be no stopping at the most dramatic critical moment. It is unfortunate to have to hold the story back at this particular twist of its development, but I have no alternative. Unless certain details are filled in, the picture will lose important features.

It is a commonplace that real life often creates astonishing dramas beyond the creative power of a great dramatist to invent. But life fashioned this particular story for the theatre of the absurd. Two weeks before Pogodin's trip to Krasnodar, the deputy editor of *Literafurnayt Gazetaa* drew my attention to a letter that had been received, one of several hundred that arrive at the editorial offices every day. Practically every one is a story of some broken life, of dispossession and adversity, of humiliation at the hands of petty party tyrants. The letter that my boss had selected hardly differed from thousands of others, except in its defiantly uncompromising tone. A worker's family, seven in all, from the seaside town of Gelendzhik, after a ten-year ordeal had at last been given entitlement to a tiny three-roomed flat. When, that very evening, the head of this family went to his new address in order to put a new lock on the door (it is the cherished dream of millions of Soviet people, this putting in the lock – concrete evidence of the long-awaited possession), he found somebody else in unauthorized occupation. A single waiter from a local bar had taken over the flat and had no desire to leave it. All the appeals by this large family as legal owners to the mayor, the prosecutor and the courts fell on deaf ears. This was the banal story which had for some reason attracted the attention of the deputy editor and he asked me to look into it. 'How can that possibly be of interest to us?' I retorted. 'It's just another squalid little story, something for the local rag.'

'You're missing the point,' he said with a frown. 'Everybody writes about *problems*, but we are writing about individuals. We are, after all, a writers' newspaper.' Not feeling the slightest interest in this provincial story, I sent one of my colleagues, Semeon Starets, a lawyer and journalist. The day before he left, he came and said to me: 'Do you realize that summer has started down there? Where on earth am I going to get a roof over my head in the spa season? Could you ring the local party secretary – he is the only person who might sort something out. He'd hardly dare refuse you.'

Such is our life. They put me through to Pogodin. Up to that moment I had never heard of him. I introduced myself. 'How can I help?' he asked me pleasantly, hiding any agitation he might have felt. The accommodation problem was solved in a trice. A room for our correspondent was found straight away in the one hotel in Gelendzhik. I rang off and immediately forgot the conversation. It was much later that I found out what a commotion my innocent call had caused. Pogodin had immediately reported it to Medunov. The news of our correspondent's impending arrival reached Medunov more or less at the same time as the news of Pogodin's conduct under questioning and that the ring was tightening.

Iron Bella had already been arrested. A year earlier, I had slipped out of the trap that the mafia had prepared for me and now, once again, I was not going myself but sending my own man. And immediately after Naidenov's visit! These completely unconnected events appeared to the fevered imagination of these panicking criminals to be part of a causal chain. Their previous guess, that I was part of Naidenov's team and that we were working to a single plan, seemed to be confirmed anew. They were simply unable to believe that our emissary should be flying to Gelendzhik to cover such a trivial story, and that this little housing question was not merely a pretext and camouflage. The mafia headquarters tormented itself trying to guess a hidden purpose which did not exist. In this tragicomic situation, they were capable of doing anything, including the least expected.

Now let us return to the narrative. The first secretary's private jet had brought Pogodin back to Gelendzhik. Refusing any dinner, this local party secretary immediately received our correspondent. Later, Semeon Starets told me that the conversation had been calm and brief, but that he had had the impression that Pogodin was preoccupied with his own thoughts, and not really listening to what Starets was saying. In the course of saying goodbye, Pogodin followed him out of his office. Five minutes later, three of Naidenov's men from Moscow entered that office with a warrant for the arrest of 'Citizen Pogodin, N.F.' 'Where is Nikolai Fedorovich?' they asked the secretary. 'Gone to the toilet,' she answered. A half-smoked cigarette was smouldering in the ashtray in his office, and Pogodin's jacket was hung casually on the back of a chair. The three sat down to wait for him, but they waited in vain. The first secretary had disappeared without trace. They're looking for him (if they are!) to this very day.

Immediately a rumour went out, spreading rapidly not only in that district but throughout the country, that Pogodin was an agent of British and American intelligence. In order to escape detection he had fled on a Turkish submarine which had been waiting for him in neutral waters off Gelendzhik (another variant of the story is that it was a Greek freighter waiting for him in the port of Novorossisk). Despite the farcical idiocy of this rumour, many believed it. Of course it has been known for ages that the more far-fetched the story, the more eagerly it will be swallowed. An indirect confirmation of the rumours is possibly provided by the fact that the KGB itself immediately joined in the hunt for this common criminal, even if he was the first secretary of the city party.

Another version, of course, is more likely: the mafia had an escape plan for 'the Day of Reckoning'. Medunov had been tipped the wink from the very top, that the Day of Reckoning had arrived, and the time had come to put the plan into operation. It is most likely that he had passed this on to Pogodin that very morning.

However, I am going to stick my neck out and put forward my own theory, based not only on details from behind the scenes, but also on a psychological analysis of our heroes' proclivities. Since they had the power and ability to protect Pogodin from arrest, they had the same ability simply to eliminate this most dangerous witness, who, in order to save his own skin, had shown himself willing to reveal to the investigators not only the names of his accomplices but also the secrets of where their treasure was hidden. I am convinced that Pogodin has long since ceased to be among the living.

Another of Medunov's trusty lieutenants met a similarly dramatic fate. He was one the secretaries of the regional party, Anatoli Tarada. This doughty warrior for the sacred ideals of communism had long been in the sights of the special assignment investigators from Moscow. All the tracks left by the trading mafia led back to him. But each side was busy doing its own job: while the investigators were gathering evidence, the mafia was consolidating its position. With the help of leading lights on the Central Committee they managed to get Tarada into place in Moscow, where he was able to help the mafia gain advantages and 'market opportunities' outside the confines of the Krasnodar region. Tarada became a deputy to the minister in charge of meat and dairy production of the USSR. His appointment was not due to anybody's particular personal favour, but was part of a well-worked-out calculation by Medunov and his gang.

However, it turned out that the calculation was mistaken and the operation disastrously misconceived. The mafia's plan was predicated on the assumption that they were invulnerable and that, despite any setbacks, they would continue to thrive and develop. Otherwise they would never have allowed a member of their senior management out of their sight. Clearly Tarada had been better protected in

Krasnodar than he was in Moscow. Naidenov and his team were able to make use of the fact that Tarada had not been able to put down roots in the capital, and arrested him without asking anyone's permission: by that time more than enough evidence against him had been collected.

As soon as he realized that nobody was going to come to his rescue, Tarada began to fight for his life himself. He gave away names of many accomplices and identified places where money and valuables were hidden. True, it turned out later that he tried to conceal the existence of at least 200,000 roubles, hoping to get away with the revelation of the whereabouts of 750,000 roubles as well as gold and diamonds. There was one factor in all of this which told against Tarada particularly heavily: he had assiduously concealed his homosexuality, whereas the investigators were aware of his secret sexual preference and had got evidence of it using a concealed camera. The blackmail worked: when he was handed the photographs 'as a present' during questioning, he was so humiliated that he said he would like to make further sensational confessions and asked for time to collect his thoughts for the purpose.

However, he didn't manage to: that very night Tarada died mysteriously. A coroner's death certificate was never issued, and if it had been, who would guarantee its authenticity?

By removing one dangerous accomplice, the mafia saved another: the secretary of the Sochi city party committee, Alexander Myerzly. He was a member of the city and regional councils, and thereby, according to one of Brezhnev's new laws, had acquired immunity from prosecution. He could not be arrested without the agreement of both councils. Generally speaking, this legal novelty thought up by the Brezhnevites (until the end of the 1970s, only members of the supreme soviets enjoyed such immunity) was a very clever dodge. On the surface, it looked like a sign of an expanding democracy, because it appeared to strengthen the role of elected representatives at every level. In fact, it was a legalized reinforcement of the complete invulnerability of the party apparatus. This was because everybody occupying a post of any significance in the nomenklatura got council membership ex officio. And not a single council would remove immunity from one of its members except on 'recommendation' from the party leadership. This applied to Myerzly: despite insistent demands from Naidenov, who was after all the number two to the

Prosecutor General of the USSR – and he produced all the necessary supporting evidence – the regional and city councils stood shoulder-to-shoulder in defence of their respected colleague.

This offensive by the prosecution service did, however, seriously alarm the mafia. True, Medunov had saved Myerzly, his chief favourite, almost a member of his family. But on the other hand, one arrest after another was being carried out in Moscow, of the former secretary of the city party, Edward Taranovsky, and several members of his office. Highly placed informers in the Central Committee were telling Medunov that they were by no means keeping their mouths shut. The ring was closing more tightly and the mafiosi decided that they had to begin to look for ways to a compromise. A bad peace is better than a good quarrel.

The operation they embarked upon was of astonishing scope. Yuri Churbanov, the first deputy to the Minister of the Interior of the USSR and Brezhnev's son-in-law, was brought into play. At Medunov's request, he suddenly decided to hold a conference in Sochi of the top militia brass of all the spa resorts in the Union, the line being that militia work in the spa towns had its own particular features, especially at the height of the season, and therefore it would be useful to exchange notes. They invited Naidenov to the conference too, so the two mafia chieftains and the leader of the investigative team who was after them sat side by side at the same table on the conference platform. But the true purpose of the exercise was to get them together round quite another sort of table: one with abundant drinks and extravagant dishes, to have a heart-to-heart.

But Medunov was not the only one that had informers. Naidenov had his too, mainly in the KGB. Andropov had not been sitting idle. Naidenov had been given advance information about the scenario being prepared by Medunov and this is what it was: Naidenov would be invited to the bosses' table and plied with drinks. Then they would try to persuade him to see their way of thinking. If that didn't work, on the way home to his residence the traffic police would stop his car and provoke a scandal by accusing a 'drunken passenger' of insulting or even striking a militiaman in the course of carrying out his duties. Up to a dozen 'witnesses' would be on the scene 'by chance' and a medical expert to certify the prosecutor's alcohol level would be waiting by a telephone for a call from the militia. This scenario has a familiar ring: the impoverished imaginations of the

Soviet mafiosi did not stretch to anything more original than this. But Naidenov outwitted his opponents, saying that he wanted to rest after the meeting, and would turn up at supper. Instead, he set off immediately, accompanied by KGB officers, for the nearby spa town of Gagra. Although it is only forty kilometres from Sochi, it is across the border of the republic. It is not in Russia, not in the Krasnodar region, but in neighbouring Georgia, Abkhazia to be exact. There Medunov's writ did not run; as the Russian saying has it, the elbow is near but you cannot bite it.

It was summer, and Brezhnev had gone to the Crimea for his holiday. There was no way round it: it was necessary to beg for a meeting with him. Brezhnev no longer had a particular interest in getting gifts from Medunov, because he had found richer pickings elsewhere. But our leader didn't forget past kindnesses and never spoke ill of his old wartime comrade. Brezhnev greeted him at his poolside informally, wearing bathing trunks, whereas Medunov was in his best suit, complete with all his orders and medals, in the sweltering sun. The guest made his report: everything is going fine, we shall give the country a million tons of rice this year – maybe a bit more if we're lucky. Our only problem is that the prosecution service will not leave us in peace. His eyes began to fill with tears and Brezhnev himself, who was no stranger to sentimentality – he would cry like a baby at the slightest provocation, whether from happiness or grief, or for no reason at all – had a little cry, and then said comfortingly that he would get back to Moscow and Medunov should come and they would sort things out.

Brezhnev liked long, lazy holidays, and Medunov could hardly contain his impatience. Finally, the call came: the great hero of Malaya Zemlya gave permission for his battalion buddy to report to him at the Kremlin. Their conversation lasted two minutes. Brezhnev rang Chernenko, and casually said, 'Medunov needs your help,' and five minutes later Konstantin Chernenko was greeting the 'wild boar' in his office with a smacking party kiss. The Central Committee secretariat met the following day; neither Brezhnev nor Chernenko were present. They had given such full instructions that their personal presence was unnecessary. The meeting was chaired by Central Committee secretary Andrei Kirilenko, a complete nonentity and illiterate boor whose party career had got going when so many vacancies became available due to the shootings under the

Stalin terror. Kirilenko had developed a close relationship with Brezhnev in the latter's Dnepropetrovsk days, where he had slavishly fulfilled all Brezhnev's wishes, and since then had become one of his closest colleagues. Unexpectedly called to the Kremlin, Naidenov, on entering the conference chamber, spotted Medunov and immediately grasped what was going on. Nevertheless, with quiet dignity he began his report. Trying not to say any more than he had to, and not showing his most important cards, he began to enumerate incontrovertible evidence proving the existence of a widespread mafia network which was costing the state millions of roubles.

Kirilenko interrupted him. 'Perhaps you have material on us as well?' he asked, gesturing around the room, unconsciously revealing the well-springs of fear that had gripped the overlords of the country. 'Are you trying to make us relive the Terror of '37?'

'That's it – 1937 exactly!' Medunov couldn't restrain himself from saying, although he should have known to keep calm before such a tribunal.

'Are you threatening the party?' continued Kirilenko, even more shrilly. 'Our best people?'

By 'party' he meant, and with reason, those who were plundering the country; by 'best people', the thieves and extortioners, the corrupt ignoramuses that had driven the country up a blind alley. Doing everything they could to hush up and forget the truth about the far-off tragedy of 1937, they themselves had floated to the top like scum in its wake. Now that the time had come for them to save themselves, they wanted to be counted as the victims rather than the executioners of an illegal system.

Real-life drama had once again overtaken art. Naidenov tried to make his position clear, but Kirilenko continued to thunder: 'You are consciously insulting the party. We know all about your giving away state secrets to journalists and holding the party up to ridicule. "The Screen" – you were behind that as well.' ('The Screen' was the name of my article about the activities of the mayor of Sochi, Voronkov.)

Naidenov was not allowed to say anything further. Vladimir Shcherbitsky, the 'king of the Ukraine', had rushed specially to Moscow and was at the meeting although he was not a member of the secretariat. From Kiev he had already phoned our editor-in-chief, expressing his rage about the publication of 'The Screen'. Now he made a similar protest about Naidenov: 'He's humiliated us in front of the whole world', 'He's discredited the whole Soviet system.'

I have no evidence of Shcherbitsky having personal involvement with the mafia, or of his offering its members particular protection, but his very nervous reaction to the publication of 'The Screen' and to the further unmasking of Medunov does give one pause – alarm bells begin to ring. The more so because everybody who knows the situation from the inside, so to speak, denies that there was ever any friendly link between Shcherbitsky and Medunov. But rather more important motives than purely personal ones were at work here. Did Shcherbitsky not wish as a matter of principle to protect the top party hierarchy even from suspicion of corruption and any connections with the mafia?

Medunov remained silent. It was his moment of triumph. He was fit to burst with excitement, but the party code of behaviour required that he should display modesty.

'You may go now,' mumbled Kirilenko, who had a speech defect.

Naidenov stood up. Before he had reached the door, he heard Kirilenko saying behind his back words apparently addressed to those present, but in reality meant for him to hear: 'What sort of [there followed an unprintable word] put that bastard in such a job?'

To give a scoundrel the answer he deserves, even if it is a scoundrel who has clawed his way up to be a Central Committee secretary, is a suicidal act. Swallowing his feelings, and without turning round, Naidenov left the room.

A few days later the instruction for Naidenov's dismissal, bearing Brezhnev's signature, was delivered. No reason was given. Just the order to sack him – nothing else.

At the same time, Chernenko and Kirilenko, at Brezhnev's prompting, proposed to the Politburo that the investigation into corruption among party officials in the Krasnodar region should be stopped. The official motion was worded as follows: 'Concerning measures to put an end to the discrediting of individual members of the party by individual members of the prosecution service.'

It was a plenary session of the Politburo. Brezhnev's approving nod when Kirilenko read out the resolution drafted by the secretariat should automatically have meant its approval without discussion or delay. That was not to be! Andropov and Gorbachev objected strongly. They were not able to prevent Naidenov being dismissed –

Brezhnev and Chernenko had the final say in hirings and firings. Appointment to the post of Deputy Prosecutor General of the USSR was formally in the competence of the Central Committee secretariat, not of the Politburo. But they did not allow them simply to wrap it up there. Their logic was irresistible – let the investigation continue, but let it be conducted by other people capable of objectivity, who should report their results to the Central Committee. Not wishing to reveal his own major involvement and fearing a vote (he was not keen on winning it with some votes against), Brezhnev gave in to the 'rebels'.

The investigation continued. Now it was taken over by Rekunkov, who had himself now become Chief Prosecutor. Needless to say, he knew how the land lay and that it was essential to put the brakes on the process. But it was already developing under its own momentum. The normal professional enthusiasm of the individual investigators had been aroused. These were the best men in the service, top achievers who deservedly were highly thought of among their professional colleagues. The Chief Prosecutor was thus between two millstones. On top were the all-powerful masters of the country; the nether millstone was formed by the members of his taskforce. Despite constraints on them they were getting under people's skin and at the same time fearing – should their investigation end in failure – for their own fate.

Rekunkov dodged and weaved but the investigation continued to advance, if slowly. Andropov's open support and therefore that of the powerful KGB apparatus gave them strength. One should remember that above all Andropov was pursuing personal goals. With the approaching inevitable departure of Brezhnev from the scene, the situation inside the Kremlin was becoming more and more tense and nervous, and the campaign against the Medunov mafia was for Andropov an important means of eliminating rivals. Medunov himself no longer represented a challenge; it was the powerful forces behind him. Compromising the Brezhnevites would weaken them and improve Andropov's chances. Objectively speaking, however, all these political intrigues at the top helped cut the tentacles of the octopus.

A last bastion of the mafia was the indestructible secretary of the Sochi city party, Alexander Myerzly. The city and regional councils, of both of which he was a member, continued to refuse to sanction his arrest. It was not so much the councils as their chairmen, who had their instructions from Medunov. The Chief Prosecutor took a rather risky step. He secretly obtained the agreement of the then chairman of the Presidium of the Supreme Soviet of the Russian Federation, Mikhail Yasnov, to the arrest of Councillor Myerzly. As the head of a superior council he was within his rights. Yasnov had been approached more than once by Naidenov with similar requests, but now could not imagine that the Chief Prosecutor himself would dare to try to damage a powerful politician unless he had enlisted very high-level support. I think he was right and that one can say without fear of error that Andropov had advised this course of action and that Yasnov had guessed this was so. By the time Medunov asked for an explanation of what was going on, the train had left the station. Myerzly had been arrested in Moscow on one of his regular visits to the capital on mafia business.

By this time he was no longer secretary of the city party. In an effort to reduce pressure from the ranks Medunov had transferred him from Sochi to Krasnodar, appointing him deputy manager of a regional building trust. The work was less prestigious to be sure, but carried a high salary and enormous potential for mafia-type operations.

It is astonishing how confidently the tentacles operated when the mafiosi were free and how quickly they withered when not. Having lost his normal environment and the certainty of Medunov's support and help, Myerzly saw the downturn in the mafia's stock and quickly turned and began with relish to give away not only the whereabouts of the money but also his partners in crime. He also revealed the secret of the 'Sochi Belvedere'.

This was one palace in Sochi which truly deserved the name. For a long time the militant investigators from Moscow didn't feel able to go near it – nor did they try to, it seems. It is a mysterious ultra-modern building, hidden behind a high wall and surrounded by palm trees and magnolias. It was outside their remit and seemed to have no connection with the mafia. According to their enquiries it belonged to someone who had performed special services for the state. The information also indicated that the man's name, Bez-ruchko, was the pseudonym of a 'soldier on the unknown front', a top Soviet spy who had stolen secrets of American rocketry or computer technology from the Japanese. In Sochi they would talk of him with hushed awe, and if anything drew the investigators to the Belvedere it was curiosity rather than professional interest. Besides, this 'soldier from the unknown front' came under the competence of the KGB, with which the investigators and prosecutors had no quarrel. The Belvedere remained outside the sphere of suspicion until Myerzly, under questioning, advised his questioners to pay a call on Bezruchko.

The KGB had no information on this superspy. One might have put this down to simple conspiracy were it not for a discovery that absolutely stunned the best 'Pinkertons' in the land, namely that Bezruchko, far from being a pseudonym, was the real name of a former criminal, a timber worker from the far north who had come south with massive sums of money and had found his way into the company of the very top noises in the mafia. He obtained from them (not for nothing, of course) an enormous plot of land and building materials otherwise virtually unobtainable. He built himself his Belvedere, a place to lay on joys and consolations for grandees. Gold, diamonds, packets of banknotes, all these things had been stashed away for a rainy day. But the mafiosi are human after all and they wanted to snatch some pleasure then and there – a reward for their heavy labour. The 'superspy's' Belvedere provided that opportunity away from the public gaze. They would come in old, unobtrusive cars, not in the big black Chaikas and Volgas that the whole town could recognize. The big bosses would give themselves to small pleasures. They would steam in the sauna, swim in the pool, drink their whisky, gin or cognac and, best of all, rock to and fro in swing chairs with naked nymphets on their knees, watching blue films and swapping obscene jokes.

After they arrested Bezruchko, it turned out that there was no evidence against him. All the paperwork relating to the building works were genuine, legal and signed by the relevant anchorites; the materials supplied had been properly paid for with cash and nobody was able to prove that this money might have been improperly come by. Only the videocassettes disappeared – either burned or at the bottom of the Black Sea.

Under great pressure from the prosecutor's office the Committee for Party Control in the Central Committee of the Communist Party instructed a team of five of its apparatchiks to check into the accusations against Medunov. Today their report, dated 22 April 1982, is of particular interest because one of the five signatories of it is the current head of the Communist Party of the Russian Federation, Ivan Polozkov. He was at that time an instructor in the section of the Central Committee dealing with party organization, a section which came directly under Chernenko. Attached to their report there is an anonymous pencilled note, now in the party archives: 'This is the third draft. It was redrafted again and shortened. The line on Medunov was softened . . .' The conclusion was more or less critical of Medunov – it talks of his 'incorrect position in principle' and about his 'distortion of the facts', 'errors' and so on. Polozkov and his colleagues recorded their view that 'the regional party committee and Comrade Medunov in particular must bear the moral and political responsibility.' Tough talk indeed, only moral and political responsibility, when he had been facing unambiguously criminal charges! And it was with this 'moral and political' that they saved him. It is also clear that it was not Polozkov and his very junior party colleagues who decided what Medunov should be found guilty of. They were trusted executives only. And there is a particular piquancy in the fact that several years later, Ivan Polozkov took the place of Sergei Medunov as first secretary of the Krasnodar regional party committee and then mounted that step of which Medunov had secretly always dreamed.

Great changes took place in the life of the two heroes of this duel to the death. After his downfall at the hands of the Brezhnevites, Naidenov awaited a new assignment. They told him confidentially that it had been decided to let him rot in the steppe. But that great dramatist, life itself, inserted a new twist which nobody could have expected. Naidenov suddenly found himself invited socially by Yuri Churbanov. As one of the top mafiosi in the country and a powerful operator in his father-in-law Brezhnev's clique he could not but be aware of the prosecutor's downfall. Churbanov must also have assumed he was personally implicated: everybody knew how ardently Andropov 'loved' him – and would love to get him.

What was Naidenov offered by his frank and open opponent? Churbanov offered him a job under his personal patronage and protection. Enticing! Their calculation was simple: tossed aside into the gutter, the prosecutor still had lots of information on the mafiosi, the full extent of which they would not have known. He might in anger and despair blurt out a mass of damaging details. If he were to be saved by them from total and ultimate personal disaster, warmed by the kindnesses of his enemies, he might just keep quiet out of gratitude.

Naidenov asked for three days to think it over. Everybody expected the prosecutor proudly to refuse the deal. But he agreed to it. A few days later he was awarded his colonel's badges in the militia and the post of deputy rector of the Academy of the Ministry of Internal Affairs. Studying in Moscow were many militia officers from Warsaw Pact countries and new recruits from the African and Asian puppet regimes. It was Naidenov's job to keep an eye on these foreigners. This would keep him out of the way of Soviet officers and Soviet affairs.

The 'friendship' that had not gelled in Sochi might have done so in Moscow, but failed to. Naidenov quietly and carefully fulfilled his duties but avoided all contact with his enemy. The tension between them continued. The knot was pulling tighter. Sergei Medunov, godfather of the ravaged Krasnodar mafia, also moved to Moscow. However adept he had been at holding back the prosecutor's onslaught, his name was inextricably linked with the squalid scandal rumbling over the whole country.

From Krasnodar, thousands of irate letters continued to flood into Moscow. Medunov's party career was over and this was when he needed his bathhouse friends. To recall that list of guests with whom the Sochi mafia liked to steam themselves, among the names was that of Nikolai Kozlov, the party prefect for the region surrounding Moscow. Soon afterwards he had been made Minister for the Fruit and Vegetable Industry of the USSR. As his friends wisecracked, minister for apples and cucumbers. It was he who came to the rescue of the disgraced 'governor'. One good turn deserves another! They transferred Medunov to Moscow, making him deputy Minister for Fruit and Vegetables, and provided him with a good flat 'in the Kremlin gift'. He had found safe and quiet anchorage.

But no sooner had Andropov succeeded to the throne than Medunov's good fortune came to an abrupt end. Andropov had him sacked from his ministerial post and had no difficulty in fixing a decision that he should be expelled from the Central Committee. His aim was now achieved, of totally removing Medunov from the political scene. But he was not deprived of his privileges and benefits. The new leaders did not wish to establish a precedent, as they could find themselves at any moment in the same position. Medunov was given a VIP pension, kept his party membership, 'Kremlin medicare' and the 'special invalid food ration packs' at the highest grade. In a country ravaged and beggared by the party mafia, all these were vastly more valuable than any honours and awards – of which Medunov also had plenty.

Those awards have not been rescinded to this day. There is a gilded bust of Hero of Socialist Labour Medunov gracing the main street of Krasnodar. His party membership card was only finally removed under the powerful impact of glasnost (i.e. after Gorbachev came to power). In his many interviews Medunov unashamedly declares himself to be a victim of the media.*

The disgraced Naidenov awaited the coming to power of Andropov. Or, more accurately, the coming to power of Andropov and the sacking of Medunov from the Central Committee. On 24 August 1983, Naidenov sent Andropov a letter asking to be rehabilitated. For several months the party apparatchiks failed to pass the letter on. Eventually, it reached Andropov on his deathbed. He managed to issue the instruction: 'Give him an appropriate post.' Shortly afterwards, he died.

Chernenko came to power next. I have no idea whether he personally had ever benefited from Medunov's gifts, but there was no one closer to Brezhnev than Chernenko – Brezhnev kept no secrets hidden from his 'shadow'. Chernenko would, in any case, have known everything about the Naidenov–Medunov duel, as well as the interest of the Brezhnev clan in that duel. Moreover, Churbanov's stock had leaped again, so that Chernenko had no desire whatever to give a green light to the long-memoried colonel of militia. But times had changed somewhat. It would not have been in the spirit of the times to come out in favour of the already-discredited mafia. The 'companions in arms' knew very well what the dead Andropov had decreed. Gorbachev had confirmed the appointment – he thought that Naidenov had 'done a useful job'.

If Andropov had lived, it would have gone worse for the mafia: everyone was aware of his short-lived, severe steps to 'restore order

---

* In the newspaper *Soviet Culture*, 6 August 1988, a letter was published from Major General of Justice Kryuchkov, who had heard Medunov speaking at various venues. 'He heaps abuse on the authors of various articles and on the publications in which the "slanders" have appeared. Medunov is particularly exercised by an article by Arkady Vaksberg. People listen to him, but you can tell from their faces that they do not believe a word Medunov is saying.'

and discipline'. His programme to save the faltering regime was built on the Stalinist concept of the 'iron hand'. The growing strength of the mafia, the scale of which he was well aware, posed a threat, in his view, to the future of the communist system. There had evidently awaited us a series of Andropov show trials à la Stalin accompanied by uncompromisingly severe sentences. They would have had the unanimous, passionate and – most important of all – genuine support of the whole people, who were really suffering under the oppression of the mafia and could see no other way of ridding themselves of it. Gorbachev sensed the pressure from beneath no less strongly – the grumbling of millions of people suffering under the total corruption which riddled every level of the administration and every stratum of society. But he took the rise and strength of the mafia not as an isolated phenomenon with a life of its own but as the inevitable result of the collapse of all previous political and economic structures. He also perceived his main task to be the rescue of the system in which he had been born and raised – but by other means. Thus was born the idea of renewing the system, which he called 'perestroika'. Humanization, liberalization and democratization – these were perestroika's essential component parts. There was no place in perestroika for a series of exemplary, threatening, warning measures. He envisaged the elimination of the mafia by economic and political rather than repressive means. Naidenov was soon to find himself a man of the past, who had already outlived his day. However, all this was to be a year later. Meanwhile, as a person who had suffered unjustifiably at the hands of the Brezhnev mafia, he received the unreserved support of Gorbachev. The matter was resolved without any further discussion, which might have dragged on and evoked a premature confrontation.

The offer to 'give him an appropriate post' was on the table, but Naidenov stood firm: he only wanted his old job back, none other! An ingenious solution was found by those experienced in political intrigue, to reconcile the irreconcilable: Naidenov was restored to the post of deputy Chief Prosecutor, but he was not allowed back to lead the investigation – he was assigned to another division.

In those years we often met. Once in the early days of perestroika I invited him to the editorial offices of my newspaper to record a conversation for publication. It was to be about the appearance of an all-powerful mafia and ways of combatting it. An hour before we were due to meet, Naidenov rang: 'I'm afraid I won't be able to make it today. I've got a sore throat.'

I could not help myself and replied: 'It doesn't sound like a sore throat to me.'

'Well, a headache then.'

'Do you think you could make it tomorrow?'

'I don't think so ... ' he sighed. 'Best of luck ... '

The following day I paid a call on him. I couldn't wait to find out what on earth had happened. Sitting at his desk in his office, Naidenov did not let me utter a word, putting his finger to his lips and jerking his head eloquently up at the ceiling ... I would not have been surprised to see this habitual Moscow gesture anywhere – a warning not to forget the hidden microphones – but surely not in the office of the deputy Chief Prosecutor of the USSR!

Naidenov led me out into the corridor.

'It might be better if you stopped asking any more questions,' he said sadly.

I could not understand what had happened: I thought the situation had radically changed and that Naidenov was back in the saddle. He had within his grasp control over the supervision of all the criminal proceedings in every court in the country and, as well as that, so-called 'general control', that is, control over any decisions by municipalities and higher executive organs. It was an enormous field of responsibility, within which a great deal could be done if he wished.

'You'll make me a laughingstock,' said Naidenov, pulling a wry face. 'I cannot believe you are so naïve. Nothing has changed, my dear chap, they have simply become more cunning and seemingly more sophisticated. They have stitched me up completely.'

'They' referred to the mafia, of course. Not to the small fry at regional level, nor even to the big boys in the capital, but the top brass, the highest leadership level – the 'All-Union' mafia, to use a Soviet expression. His pessimism seemed unduly exaggerated, but Naidenov knew too much and his sense of foreboding proved well-founded.

Before long he was once again dismissed as deputy Chief Prosecutor, but it was done in such a respectful way that it ruled out any possibility of protest. He was appointed Chief State Arbitrator of the USSR. In the Soviet hierarchy, this post has ministerial standing. A more accurate way to describe it would be that he had finally been shunted into a siding – albeit an honourable one – with no chance of coming out again.

The arbitrator is a judge who has to resolve legal conflicts between state enterprises: late despatch of goods, mistakes in the paperwork, discovery of defects, breaches of official standards . . . penalties, fines, confiscations. These are unarguably important matters, especially in conditions of total economic and administrative collapse. But this was not Naidenov's scene, light years away from the fighting front where the life-and-death battle was being waged with the sea-dragon and octopus that were throttling the country, draining away its lifeblood drop by drop. Thus Naidenov was being destroyed, not by punishment but by 'the great trust', the enormous salary, the limousine – the whole Kremlin package.

He never really came to grips with his new job, but died two months later of a heart attack in his official car. The driver brought his still warm body to the office. Despite temporary setbacks and late in the day, the mafia had got him in the end.

It remains to relate the fate of some, at least, of the principal players in this tale.

Medunov has, at the time of writing, reached the age of seventy-eight and is thriving in his spacious Moscow apartment. He even goes out for walks, sporting his medals, including his hero's Red Star. 'If patriotism and unswerving loyalty to the people is nowadays considered to be criminal, you can call me the biggest criminal of them all,' was Medunov's boast in one of his interviews. He had lost his party membership but hundreds of thousands now 'lose' it voluntarily, losing nothing thereby, rather the reverse – at least they save their subscription. The press has frequently aired the need to investigate Medunov's misdeeds, even if 'only' his abuses of state power that are already in the public domain. I have also written on that subject. The Prosecutor's answer is always the same: 'No evidence.' 'No Naidenov' is my reaction to that answer.

Demonstrably scorning public opinion, conscience and common sense, none of Medunov's successors as First Party Secretary in Krasnodar – Vitaly Vorotnikov, Gennadi Razumovsky and Ivan Polozkov – saw fit to remove from the centre of Krasnodar the marble monument with its inscription in gold of the name of the 'distinguished fellow countryman, Hero of Socialist Labour, Sergei

Fedorovich Medunov'. If there were a formal obligation to retain such a memorial, then there would be a relevant law which they could quote in justification, but there is no such law – only clan loyalty to the party mafia and stubborn unwillingness to submit to pressure from below, even after the former party boss had been comprehensively exposed and discredited. The retention of a monument to one of the chief mafiosi has been written about in the press more than once. I wrote a stinging piece about it for *Literaturnaya Gazeta*, but the then leader of the Bolsheviks of Krasnodar, Ivan Polozkov, did not see fit to reply to the challenge and kept a proud silence. As I say, the monument continues to embellish the centre of the regional capital.

Myerzly was given fifteen years, but after only five he was seen again in Sochi. His villa and valuables – gifts from hangers-on – had all supposedly been confiscated by order of the court, but they remained intact. His faithful Valentina was waiting for him on the blissful Black Sea shore. She had been released even sooner. Voronkov was sentenced to thirteen years, but was hardly away from home for more than five. In the prison camp, he was to begin with in charge of the canteen. From accounts written by former Gulag inmates, we know what that means. Later on, he was in charge of a workshop making bicycle saddles. He returned to Sochi, to his former home, where everything remained as before, although without the singing fountain, so as not to irritate the neighbours. Voronkov is now sixty-five and has a top job in a Sochi cooperative business.

All the rest of the big shots of the old Medunov mafia have been released long since. It is virtually impossible to establish definitely who brought this about. In accordance with mafia practice established in the 1920s, there are no written records – all instructions were given verbally. But let it not be forgotten: Vitaly Vorotnikov from Krasnodar, after a short spell as Ambassador to Cuba, moved to Moscow where he became not only a member of the Politburo but also chairman of the Praesidium of the Supreme Soviet of the Russian Federation. The latter's formal functions include pardons, and it exerts informally, but in all reality, a decisive influence on the operations of all law enforcement authorities of the federation. Gennadi Razumovsky also settled in Moscow after Krasnodar and became one of Gorbachev's close colleagues. He was given the same responsibility that Chernenko had under Brezhnev – the control of party posts and personnel. This means real power.

The dismissed former regional district and party secretaries quickly adjusted to the new perestroika conditions and requalified as taxi drivers. Such proportion of the money and valuables that they had successfully hidden from the investigators, even if only a tenth of the total they had stolen or extorted, will keep them in comfort for life.

Only one person was removed immediately and for good – both from the game and from life itself. Bella Borodkina, 'Iron Bella', was sentenced to be shot and executed without delay. The press carried an exaggerated propaganda campaign in justification of the sentence. Of course, Bella had robbed millions of people. Her innumerable stores and stocks kept the whole pyramid supplied, from the dot on the map representing Gelendzhik right up to the Kremlin itself. But she thieved no more than many other embezzlers and stealers of public property. Above all, her guilt cannot be compared with the guilt of those who have destroyed millions of lives, ravished a great country, yet retained their high standing, awards, dachas and privileges.

What happened in her case? Why was it that she – a woman – was meted out the ultimate punishment? Some look for the reason in her Jewish background, but I do not think that this is the explanation. In this instance the victim's 'nationality' was only helpful in that it made it easier to enlist the support and 'understanding' of a certain proportion of the population and to divert 'the anger of the people' into a well-worn channel that offered no threat to the mafia, thereby enabling the chief culprits to remain in the shadows.

It was an irresistible temptation to portray the Jew trader as a demon seducer and the Russian party man as the victim unable to resist. Yet the fundamental and hidden reason was the same one which had necessitated the destruction of Bella's friend and accomplice, Nikolai Pogodin. She knew too much about too many and they could not be sure of how 'iron' Bella was, whether she would be able to keep her silence. It was no trouble to fix her up with the necessary sentence, nor to have it carried out; they still had their own men everywhere.

Chapter Four

The Forbidden Zone

The Krasnodar region was, of course, not a mutinous island set in a peaceful ocean of prosperity. If one were to call the local mafia excesses a mutiny, then such mutiny did not begin nor end there. It broke out simultaneously in all parts of the country. It will end (or transmute into some other form) only with the collapse of the whole system. According to official terminology it is a 'command-administrative system'. It would be more accurate just to call it 'Soviet', insofar as it is the Soviet state that has developed it over the whole seventy-odd years of its lamentable existence.

Nobody could pinpoint the exact date or place that saw the first shoots of corruption emerge and spiral towards the criminal community, and then intertwine with it in a strong and close embrace. There did exist the appropriate 'moral–political climate', that familiar expression so tediously repeated in the official propaganda. Naturally, they use it with the proper tone of ecstasy for cataloguing victories of the party and government. Nowadays, no self-respecting person would use the expression other than ironically. Actually, there *is* a moral–political climate, but the moral code is that of the criminal and the politics are those of cynicism.

The emergence of the Soviet mafia, which has attracted worldwide attention, far from being straightforward, was a process full of contradiction, one that bore witness to the decrepitude of a Stalinist-type regime which had survived, on the one hand through ideological blindness ('revolutionary romanticism') and on the other by the most cruel terror. These two elements might be considered to be irreconcilable opposites. Nevertheless, it is no accident that the first ranging shots fired by the mafia coincided with the awakening in others of independent consciousness, with the attempt to get up off one's knees and declare one's 'dissidence'. The conscious opposition to the political status quo felt by the best, most noble and honest part of society went in parallel with the unconscious opposition to the inhuman and unnatural economic set-up which was burst open from within by new Soviet businessmen who appeared seemingly from nowhere. It is curious that at this stage, economic 'dissidence' was seen by the authorities to be the greater threat to the regime, and one to which they responded with executions and long labour-camp sentences. More often than not, political dissidents were, by contrast, put into psychiatric hospitals, sent into internal exile or, more rarely, sentenced to comparatively short spells in the Gulag. Or merely to expulsion from paradise into the cesspool of accursed capitalism.

As the 'Old Bolsheviks' and 'children of the Revolution' came in time to be replaced everywhere by the next generation, the latter exploited the opportunities provided by the breakdown of the country which was then just beginning. For these people, there was no moral, idealistic or other brake on their urge to plunder anything lying around, which in that country meant and means literally everything. The only force that might have held back this pillage is fear. But by uniting together and enticing into their ranks anybody that could be a danger to them, they liberated themselves from any such fear and in the end achieved absolute security, with the occasional exception proving the rule.

A hint would come from the top, the very top. Of course, there was never an open instruction to steal, but the signal would convey reassurance and promise protection in all eventualities. One such episode remains etched in my memory.

It was late February or early March of 1981, during the Twenty-Sixth Congress of the Communist Party in Moscow. Following a tradition established in Khrushchev's time, the Union of Writers had invited some of the congress delegates – first secretaries of various regional party committees – for a meeting and discussion with a select group of literary personalities. To be more exact, the invitation came not so much from the Union as from its President, Georgi Markov, one of Brezhnev's cronies. (The name of this twice-over Hero of Socialist Labour, author of epic novels printed in editions of tens of millions, immediately vanished for good – as if the man had never been – when he lost his post in 1986.) Markov, being a native of Siberia, clung to his fellow Siberians. Thus, needless to say, the guest of honour on that occasion was his very close friend Yegor Ligachev, the 'governor' of Tomsk, who was the model for the hero of Markov's novel *Siberia*.

One of the other guests was speaking – the First Secretary of the Eastern Kazakhstan party, Alexander Protozanov. He was saying how it was that nobody wanted to work, that the harvest was rotting due to the rain, that there was no proper agricultural machinery or grain stores, that the whole region (and was it only that region?) was sinking into an epidemic of drink. And there was an occasion, continued Protozanov, when there was a telephone call from Moscow. It was Brezhnev asking what sort of harvest to expect. 'One couldn't lie to the General Secretary,' said the speaker. 'I had to tell him the whole truth – that the harvest was excellent but that more than half of it would rot and any day there would be the first frosts.' 'Never mind,' Brezhnev had replied. 'Just get on with the work – we have complete confidence in you. Try your best and do everything possible. If your efforts fail, you cannot be blamed.'

At this point, Ligachev who had remained silent broke in: 'You can't imagine, comrades, what a joy it is for all of us to be able to get on with our work quietly and how well everything is going under the leadership of dear Leonid Ilyich. What a marvellous moral–political climate has been established in the party and country with his coming to power! It is as if wings have sprouted on our backs, if you want to put it stylishly, like you writers do.'

I can't speak for the others present, but travelling up and down the country as I did I could well imagine that 'climate': a feeling of complete impunity, a sense of the most powerful protection of the apparat from the slightest upheaval from below, do whatever you like so long as you are totally loyal to dear Leonid Ilyich. Having thrown out Khrushchev, who was a threat to them, the apparatchiks put at the head of the country their own man and now demanded their dues of him – with interest. In effect, this was already the mafia – formed up, organized and all-powerful, establishing its own laws. It was by no means essential for the services rendered by one of its members to another to be paid for in the primitive form of cash. There existed a multitude of other forms, which, in the final analysis, led not only to straight enrichment but also to the acquisition of power and to the achievement of promotion up the bureaucratic ladder. The main benefit to the apparatchiks was political and occupational stability. No cataclysm could dislodge them from their perch except for betrayal of the hero of Malaya Zemlya.

In these conditions, every member of the apparat could do whatever he liked and anybody longing to enrich himself simply protected himself from downfall and sought any connection that would achieve that end, that is, with the most powerful individual representative of the apparat within reach. Thus was prepared fertile soil for the cultivation of politicians and criminals, the former quickly turned into the latter and the latter into the former. It became impossible to tell one from the other.

I shall never forget another example of omnipotent licence. It also relates to 1980 or perhaps 1981. Some friends had asked me to help an unjustly dismissed fellow railway-worker. It was a fairly insignificant story: the person in question held a modest position. It was a matter that I could have easily left to one of my assistants to take up with middle-ranking management or lower down even. But people close to me begged me to look into it myself. I decided to deal with it at a stroke by going straight to the minister, rather than going through the normal hierarchy.

On the phone the minister's assistant, without asking what the meeting was about, agreed a time for me to come that very evening. Evening, not day! Long past were the days when Stalin, always on vigil, would keep all officials hanging around his offices until dawn. Now suddenly: 'Ivan Grigorevich would like you to come if that is convenient at 10.30 pm.' It was not convenient, but intriguing, so I agreed.

The then minister was Ivan Grigorevich Pavlovsky, a colourless time-server with the reputation of being no genius but a thorough professional. When the minister came out to greet me, having as a precaution pulled down the blind over the enormous wall-map of the railway system which covered the whole wall behind him, the first thing that I noticed was that he had circles under his eyes and a mottled complexion.

'What can I do for you?' he asked mechanically. I explained my request, invoking the greatest depth of feeling that I could summon. He listened absent-mindedly, thinking his own thoughts.

'Your request is granted,' he said with an air of finality when I had finished my monologue. It remained to thank him, get up and leave. But he did not seem in a hurry to say goodbye. I was in no hurry, since I had been expecting our conversation to take longer.

'You probably noticed that I was not listening very attentively,' he confessed unexpectedly. 'Hardly surprising. I haven't been able to sleep for four days.'

The minister went to the map, pulled up the blind and reached for his pointer. 'Here, look ... ' He pointed at the virgin soil region in northern Kazakhstan. 'The grain is getting soaked here. There aren't enough railway wagons to get it away to Moscow. And here ... ' His pointer hovered over the northern Caucasus. 'Here we managed with difficulty to find some spare wagons, only thirty-four. We needed to transfer them to the virgin soil region. The whole operation was being monitored by Leonid Ilyich. We set up a military-style HQ. All the lines were choked. The schedule was overloaded to the limit. I have been on the phone round the clock. We battled to get this additional goods train through, having reports about its progress on an hourly basis. It got to the Urals but there was a blockage there and we had to change the whole timetable. Passenger trains had to wait to let our wagons through. Brezhnev's office was in regular touch, and I reported everything going all right, but at what cost! Finally, they got beyond the Urals and all the problems were sorted out – green lights all the way from there onwards. Only a matter of hours and the train should have reached the station.'

'I can see you're tired. Forgive me if I came to see you at a bad moment. But let me congratulate you on the success of this operation. As they say, all's well that ends well ... '

For a long time he didn't reply, but just kept looking at the enormous map with its little winking lights. Then he heaved a deep sigh.

'An hour ago I was informed that there are no wagons. None at all. There never were any. They were not making their way from anywhere and were not being got through to anywhere. The whole thing is a mirage, the fruit of a vivid imagination, a deception which I swallowed like an idiot. I was a general in command of an imaginary army. Funny, eh?'

He looked at me again with his exhausted eyes. 'But don't worry, the person you are seeking to help will be given his job back. At least that is still within my control.'

He begged me 'not to rush straight to my typewriter' and publicize this shattering tale. As it had turned out, the minister had been unwittingly pulling the wool over the eyes of dear Leonid Ilyich, while he was having the wool pulled over his own. In those days, would that have been an excuse?*

My colleagues and I made a joint effort to find out where the thirty-four railway wagons had disappeared, and why the minister had been led up the garden path. Couldn't they have simply said that there were no spare wagons? It is hardly likely that such news would have caused the minister to go into shock. We were all used to getting the answer 'Nyet'. The fact of the matter was that the wagons *were* there and there was the desire and intention to carry out the exceptional instruction from the minister. However, at the very last minute, when the train had already been made up, the wagons were requisitioned by local mafia, because they needed urgently to get off some fruit which was already beginning to spoil to the rich northern markets. This much-sought-after commodity, always in short supply, and the production cost of which is ten times less than its market value 'up there' where a peach or a bunch of grapes is an almost unattainable dream, brings in a profit of millions. Wheat grown in the virgin lands belongs to the state and thus to nobody, but the Caucasian fruit in the hands of the brilliantly-organized fruit and vegetable mafia, which has sunk its tentacles into all parts of the party–state machine, produces profits which feed innumerable mafia 'families', each operating quite independently of the other and probably unaware of each other's existence.

So, when the question arose of who should get priority, the answer

---

* It would not be very long before Ivan Pavlovsky's career in the railway ministry would be cruelly cut short. As the result of a letter from a 'well-wisher', the Committee for Party Control was to establish that the minister had fixed up his wife, who was a doctor, with a job at a hospital coming under the ministry for which, without actually working for a single day, she duly received a salary for several years. For her 'outstanding services' she was awarded the title 'Honoured Doctor of the Republic' which automatically entitled her to an increased early pension. The minister was fired for abuse of his position and had to repay everything that his wife had 'earned'. Misdemeanours of this kind, when they surface and cause a scandal, do not go unpunished in our country, but a whole harvest which is not got in and therefore rots, and the organizational shambles and all-round deception that go with it, are rated merely as 'inefficiency at the workplace'.

was a foregone conclusion. It was useless to invoke 'Politburo orders', 'Brezhnev is taking a personal interest', 'save the harvest' and so on. Two interests clashed and they were irreconcilable. And that was that. The false telegrams about the train's progress towards the Urals and beyond were needed in order to play for time and thus complete a simple operation. In the event, the winners were infinitely more powerful than the people whose job it was to check railway movements. Comrade Brezhnev had no direct interest in the export of wheat from the virgin lands, but some of the profits might have filtered through to him from the mafia's sale of fruit. It is thus hard to say who won and who lost.

The wagons were duly 'discovered' up north somewhere. According to the official report they had been sent in error through the inefficiency of some petty official in the railway hierarchy. A couple of dozen people were strongly reprimanded, the virgin land harvest rotted in the rain and the mafia once again pocketed several millions. And sentimental Leonid Ilyich wiped away a tear when they reported to him at what cost of heroic effort the harvest had been 'saved'. The favourable 'moral–political climate' had been victorious. The wings that had sprouted, in Yegor Ligachev's evocative and penetrating image, grew and grew.

Could anybody have imagined that Hans Christian Andersen's immortal tale 'The Emperor's New Clothes' would become the daily reality in a mighty country – on the threshhold of the twenty-first century?

Once, in January 1976, I had to call at the readers' letters department in our office. Everywhere, on the floor, on the shelves, on windowsills, there were mountains of letters. A Western reader cannot fully grasp this Soviet phenomenon of letters flooding in to the editors of newspapers and magazines, starting in the 1960s. The Khrushchev thaw set people thinking critically, but there was nowhere to express these thoughts. There was no real political life in the country. The thaw unlocked people's lips. There was no interdiction on complaining if the complaints were against particular targets and did not call into question the existing political order. But even those complaints which were allowed had not the slightest practical result. The standard replies from the bureaucracies, more often than not preprinted, became a byword. The only safety valve seemed to be the press. At least one didn't receive from newspapers those flat, cold and officious answers. Occasionally, critical letters would reach the pages of the newspaper. The flow of readers' letters grew from year to year and ours, despite being a weekly rather than a daily and regarded as largely aimed at the intelligentsia, would receive up to three thousand letters a week.

And so I was standing surrounded by this fathomless sea of paper, and the assistants in the department were hunting out for me an official answer from some government department. My attention was caught by a letter printed on challengingly bright plum-coloured paper. It was only the colour of the paper which made me pick it up, out of curiosity. I saw that it was directly addressed to me personally. 'That's not worth bothering with,' said the assistant, noticing which pile I had taken the letter from.

The fact is that the newspaper had erected a protective barrier between me and our very persistent readers, employing consultants to sift through the letters which arrived addressed to me. This letter had shared the same fate as so many others which had not been forwarded to me. If the author had not chosen to write the letter on such unusual paper, I would never have known anything about it.

But the letter was quite amusing. Amusing was the right word for it, or so it seemed to me. In the Chuvash Autonomous Republic (only an overnight train ride away from Moscow), those in charge of the local building organization had designated a part of the Volga beach a 'secret zone' together with a little wood behind it: in official documents there were shown simple shower cabins for workers, whereas in reality it was a notorious sauna for the bosses, fitted out with marble and the finest sorts of rare hardwoods. This is what the letter to me was about.

It was not that unusual a case, but the thought of announcing to everybody that I was going to take a few days' holiday in a 'restricted zone' was sufficiently amusing to send me on my way to Cheboksary (the capital of the Chuvash Republic) with the idea of writing it up for an article.

In Moscow the temperature was unusually mild for the depths of Russian winter – seven or eight degrees above freezing. I set out in a light overcoat and walking shoes. Within two days a terrible frost set in in Cheboksary: thirty degrees below freezing. When I got through to the 'restricted zone' to see the 'showers' with my own eyes, the caretaker lady suddenly announced that she had forgotten the keys. I was left waiting in the icy wind. Around me stood three enormous wolfhounds: guard dogs. My first attempt to move aroused their fury. When I tried again, one of the dogs put its front paws on my shoulders, knocked me down and pinned me to the frozen ground. Twenty, thirty, forty minutes passed. I began to understand what was going on – the caretaker lady was not coming back, and the dogs were not going to go away. The lady did return, though more than an hour later, by which time I had turned into an icicle. An ambulance had to be called. I decided not to trust the local doctors but flew to Moscow with my frostbitten feet. Meanwhile, the building in the restricted zone 'accidentally' and 'suddenly' burned to the ground. The marble disappeared. The remains were shoved into the river.

Lying on my hospital bed in Moscow I pondered this strange overreaction to my arrival. As a journalist, I had seen nothing to justify such savage measures from the managers of the construction organization. That must mean that they had something to hide. This suspicion was increased by another incident: the day before my ill-fated visit to the bathhouse, a member of the Chuvash Supreme Court with the interesting name of Engels tried to get me drunk. He appeared at my hotel and suggested we dined together. Through provincial inexperience it was he himself who got tipsy and told me in his simple way that he had been given money from 'some very big shots' to buy the vodka to ply me with: according to him, their plan was that when I had passed out drunk on the floor, a photographer waiting in the hotel lobby was to record the scene and the pictures would be sent both to my newspaper office and to the Central Committee.

To begin with, this confession had seemed to me absurd gibberish: now, after my experience with the dogs on the frozen banks of the Volga, it began to look quite different ...

I will not go into the whole saga of how I got to the bottom of this business. To cut a long story short: the notorious sauna in the 'restricted zone' served by no means only as a place of relaxation for local bureaucrats. Here in the back of beyond were set traps into which both local and Moscow bigshots were lured. They could not be lured with bribes: Cheboksary is not Sochi, the local opportunities for enrichment are not too thick on the ground. Nor could the top people in the country be ensnared from here. But reaching the top people was not absolutely necessary. To begin with, local bigwigs were lured into the trap: secretaries of area committees, ministers of the autonomous republic ... Then ministers of the Russian Federation ... Then two ministers of the Union itself, who had come to Cheboksary on business, and several of their deputies. What was the lure in the trap they fell into? Just some girls ...

The managers of the building organization who were the creators and owners of the 'restricted zone' began by hiring local champion athletes: wrestlers, boxers and footballers guarded the sauna from outsiders for big money – stolen, of course – and brought in food and drink; they prepared meals, entertained them with music, held their dressing-gowns for them. At athletics matches, all their rivals (for money, of course) would lose to these hired champions. By way of a thank you, the latter would bring girlfriends 'for a bit of fun'. Some of these girls resisted. If so, they were taken by force and photographed in indecent poses. Fearing publicity, the 'girlfriends' would give in. They were on the hook. Their duty now consisted in giving pleasure to important guests, in creating a cosy atmosphere of well-being where anything was allowed. The same hidden camera trapped the guests. In the morning they would be given the photographs as a souvenir of their night of erotic pleasure. It would have been enough to send one picture to the Central Committee for a career to be finished – without any explanation or justification. They were converted from victims to accomplices: they would grant credits, obtain unobtainable goods, sign false agreements and fictitious invoices and turn a blind eye to daylight robbery. The mafia grew strong, widened and deepened its influence.

The mechanism of seduction was obvious, but its aim was not immediately clear to me. I knew nothing at the time about the invented bills and agreements. To be honest, I never succeeded in cracking that one myself. Nevertheless, an article called 'The Bathhouse' appeared (the publication was preceded by an interdiction from the censor and a warning from the editor-in-chief: 'Hide the manuscript in your desk and do not show it to anyone, forget that you wrote it'), some third-ranking local government employees got away with a formal reprimand, some sportsmen and an engineer were jailed for rape and blackmail. But the real reasons for such a stormy reaction to my attempt to uncover the secrets of these provincial businessmen remained a mystery.

But only two or three years later my colleagues got to the bottom of the mystery. My naive assumption that in 'impoverished' Chuvashiya no mafia could develop, since there was nothing on which it could feed, was proved unfounded. The country, it would seem, is so rich, and the possibilities of obtaining 'spare' money are so widespread, that all you need is the will, ingenuity and energy to get it.

Here is just one example.

The site in Chuvashiya where an enormous tractor factory was to be built was some way from the Volga – the major transport artery for essential materials. After this construction project got the go-ahead, it was proposed to build a single-track railway line from the port to the building site. An estimate was prepared and Moscow allocated money and resources. In due course, a formal report was submitted notifying completion of this single-track line. Some commissioning authority or other signed the necessary confirmation of completion although nobody had ever actually seen this line with their own eyes. It had vanished into thin air. Or gone underground. And even then, however deep they might dig, the most talented archaeologists would not have located it. The building materials had been brought to the construction site from the port at snail's pace on lorries, while the millions of roubles 'spent' on the construction of a nonexistent railway line nestled in the pockets of the denizens of the sauna.

A railway line, even a single-track one only a few kilometres long, is not a diamond ring. You cannot hide it in a bag or a safe or a cellar. Therefore hundreds of people had to be involved in an extraordinary conspiracy of falsehood. It is an axiom that a secret known to two people is no longer a secret. But this was known to hundreds! Deception on that scale can only be undertaken by somebody absolutely certain of immunity – in that blessed moral–political climate in which Yegor Kuzmich Ligachev felt wings sprouting from his shoulders.

And, as it happens, their confidence in their immunity was not misplaced. Neither the secretaries of the area committee, nor the ministers, nor the minister's deputies (not to mention anyone higher up) – not one among those involved one way or another in this bathhouse business (was it only the 'bathhouse'?) suffered in the slightest. More than that: one of the 'bathers', a secretary of one of the party area committees, after the publication in *Literaturnaya Gazeta* of the 'Bathhouse' article sent an official reply. 'Everything in the article is correct,' he said, 'we heartily support the author, the party is horrified, the guilty will be punished.' The newspaper, which had feared most of all that an influential party boss would force his way in to see Brezhnev or Suslov moaning and groaning and see to it that the paper got a dressing-down, was so delighted to receive a formal confirmation of its allegations that it published the letter immediately in triumph. And thus the incident was closed: measures would be taken, what more was required?

This, incidentally, was a jesuitical tactic of the mafia, to avoid controversy in the press for fear of attracting heightened attention to itself. More accurately, it was a tactic employed by the more intelligent mafiosi: those out of Medunov's league. They used a meaningless confession to limit the damage caused by the article, and thereby preserved their core personnel.

A court sentenced the senior engineer of the building organization (it had been decided to make him the fall-guy, all the blame was loaded onto him) to fourteen years' imprisonment. But only two years later, I met him in Cheboksary when I was there covering another story. 'Excuse me,' I stammered, taken aback, 'but weren't you put inside for fourteen years just two years ago?'

'You're using the wrong arithmetic,' the engineer replied with dignity. He had already been reinstated as a deputy to the trust organization and gave me a cheery wave.

The web of interrelationships which developed spontaneously was the same in all republics, regions, towns and districts. They were depressingly alike, but that similarity was dictated by external conditions. It was laughably simple: the acquisition of money did not require any effort at all – only a little imagination and the guarantee of immunity. The most reliable and easily achieved guarantee was obtainable from the local party bosses – all the real power was in their hands. The task became extremely simple: to attract the 'party bosses' onto your side, get them 'in the bag', to use the underworld slang. This could be done in a great variety of ways – imagination led certain talented operators to the most unexpected conclusions – but on not a single occasion did any of the fiery fighters for the sacred ideals of communism angrily refuse the bait with which they were being tempted. I speak with conviction: not once was the bait refused – for, if there had been such an occasion, then we would certainly have heard about it in some admiring newspaper article. Who would pass up the chance of trumpeting the incorruptibility of a party functionary, firmly refusing the intrigues of the wicked mafia? But not a single such story ever appeared in print. Everybody was psychologically and morally predisposed to give in to the triumphant mafia. It was just that the mafia did not make an approach to every single person; they had not been able to establish their criminal clan system everywhere at a level requiring the necessary degree of protection, nor could they be sure of finding everywhere leaders sufficiently powerful to take risks.

Sometime at the beginning of the 1980s, towards the sunset of the Brezhnev years, fate took me on a reporting job to the old Russian town of Penza – a big regional centre boasting long cultural traditions. For example, a marble plaque commemorating the name of Vsevolod Meyerhold on a surviving old nineteenth-century town-house spoke volumes. But I was there, as usual, on quite different business: routine 'petty' (by the standards of our country) thieving, and routine 'petty' extortion.

The method employed by the director of a local poultry processing factory stood out from hundreds of thousands of similar cases because of its exceptional ingenuity and even elegance. He had not, in his search for a powerful protector, gone to the local party boss with an envelope full of banknotes. He made his approach through the man's two student sons. Even then, it was not done coarsely or primitively, but cunningly – with panache.

The director, having already succeeded in fundamentally cleaning out the factory's till, concluded an agreement to paint the administrative buildings with these two, sons of the first secretary of the regional party committee Lev Ermin, just as he had with the son of the regional council, the son of the chairman of the regional union organization and other youngsters from that circle. These young men were cyberneticists, philologists and diplomatic historians, but the brilliant director picked them out to be decorators. He ought to have paid for this according to the tariff established by law, but he exceeded it by twenty-one times. But that was only the half of it. Not one of these 'painters' did any painting himself, nor did any of them even know where the factory was. Real decorators did the work and were paid the normal pittance for it while the children of the

86

regional top dogs were sporting themselves on a Black Sea beach. But they received their 'honoraria' in full, each being paid 15,000 roubles – at that time still a great deal of money. You do not need to be a lawyer to understand that this was a barely-disguised bribe aimed openly at the most powerful people in the region. For the real recipients of this money were the fathers, not these young loungers. Who would have played with fire for their sake, and risked trouble with the law?

But even this shock-provoking article (shocking in its candour rather than its content), to which I gave the title 'A Strong Character', had no result whatever. All that happened was that I was told in the Central Committee, 'You shouldn't jeer in that gloating way at party authority.' Anywhere else in the world, a man holding high public office like Ermin and caught red-handed, if he didn't put a bullet through his head, would have fled from the town accompanied by the catcalls of the outraged citizenry. *Our* 'governor' managed to get away at an earlier stage. Mikhail Solomentsev, the prime minister of the Russian Federation and a member of the Politburo of the USSR, took Ermin under his powerful wing and made him his deputy. Solomentsev's successor, Vitaly Vorotnikov, kept him in the same post. It goes without saying that he remained for many years a member of the Central Committee and only quite recently retired without losing a single one of the privileges granted to the ruling elite.

However, my article did have one consequence. The Prosecutor of the Penza region, Viktor Zhuravlev, tried to carry out an investigation and bring the young 'decorators' to book. In law they rather than their fathers were guilty. The mafia swung into action immediately. Zhuravlev was removed from his post and sent back to Moscow to be reassigned by the Chief Prosecutor. Rekunkov tried to get him appointed to some other region, but had no success. No prosecutor can be appointed to a region without the consent of the first secretary of the relevant regional party. But which of them would approve a candidate who had already raised his hand against another first secretary? Soon Zhuravlev chose to abandon the bosom of the prosecution service, preferring to get away as far as possible from the all-seeing eyes of the mafia.

I could recount tens of similar stories. Or hundreds, even thousands. They have become the sad norm rather than the exception. In any town one visits, it is the same story. The stories are so alike that in the end they pall. Judging from readers' letters, such subjects have ceased to excite, no longer having the impact of the unexpected. So the decision was taken not to print any more such stories – we had had enough of them. And enough of writing them. And living in circumstances of complete and unbridled corruption, hadn't we had enough of that too?

It is as clear as daylight that if, say, the director of a poultry processing factory needed the protection of the 'governors' (and it did help him: his offence, according to Article IV of the Criminal Code, carries a recommended penalty of up to fifteen years in prison, whereas the director was sentenced to one year suspended, keeping his job, awards and all the benefits of the Soviet system) then it is equally clear that the 'governor' himself, in his turn, needed a protector. Otherwise he would never have dared to take the chances he did nor so shamelessly pocket bribes.

Is it possible that no one at the top knew exactly what he was up to, with whom, what bargains he was striking, what a fortune he was putting away? Also, he himself knew perfectly well he would carry no blame, whatever he did. They were all the same, all with their snouts in the trough and each of them pilfering wherever he could.

'Live and let live' was the time-honoured formula in Russia, according to which the people and their masters lived in mutual criminal conspiracy. The people had their own saying, less elegant but nearer the mark: 'A fish rots from the head down.'

Chapter Five

Friend to Thieves and Stars

Fifteen years ago, it was simultaneously and widely rumoured that the Minister of Internal Affairs was an unusually human person, a man with an open and generous soul. *Literaturnaya Gazeta* decided to try to get an interview with him – not the usual written question-and-answer format, but a live discussion and certainly not a ministerial monologue.

I was intrigued by the possibility of a face-to-face meeting with such a prominent personality in whom were being discerned those very attributes which we had all longed to see in our top leaders: cultured, courageous, innovative, broad-minded. It was widely spoken of at this time that under the aegis of the minister, Nikolai Shcholokov, a unique and unprecedented Academy of Internal Affairs had been established. Here, future police chiefs would study not Stalin or Brezhnev but Aristotle and La Rochefoucauld. There were to be departments of art and aesthetics. The best creative talents in the land would come to teach colonels and majors how to appreciate music and ballet. It all took one's breath away.

The meeting with the minister – a colleague and I went to see him together – justified our hopes. At close quarters, he was the same as he had appeared from a distance: unstuffy, approachable, relaxed, a good listener, unhurried, willing to debate issues. All this, plus a charming smile and welcoming manner. The minister's office had received a list of our questions in advance and had prepared answers; several typed pages lay on the desk in front of him. He shoved them into a drawer of the desk and said: 'Let's manage without crib sheets.' That was fine by us, and our conversation really was unscripted and candid. At one point the minister started recalling his childhood, youth and schoolfriends: 'They were a wonderful lot. There was a Ukrainian boy, a Russian, a Tatar, an Armenian and a Jew.' He remembered all their names but hesitated on the last of them. 'What was his name – oh, my memory's going. That's what comes of old age.' He heaved a deep sigh and smiled. 'Ah. I remember it. It was Abrasha Kogan. I've always been an internationalist. One must not be a traitor to one's ideals. Our generation has principles.' He fell silent, apparently lost in thought, knitting his brows. He sighed again. 'One's principles – they come before everything. Along with care for one's fellow man.' We prepared the interview for publication, sent the text for him to approve. That evening he returned a completely different text – the one that had been prepared in advance of our meeting, the 'crib sheet' which he had so dashingly discarded.

I thought his officials were up to their old tricks. In order to get the truth, I rang the minister. He was surprised at my surprise: 'Our conversation was entirely off the record. What goes into print is another matter.'

Such double standards were then the norm. There was one truth for a narrow circle, and a completely different version for everybody else. The text took up a whole page on 29 October 1975 under the title: 'Our Militia'. Shcholokov's name graced it in enormous capital letters. I declined to have my name put under this varnished rot, and so the piece appeared unattributed.

Two years passed. On the editor's instructions I went once again to see the minister, who by now was becoming more powerful. The reason for the commission was rather unusual. The Chief Justice of the United States Supreme Court Warren Burger was visiting Moscow. I do not know what lay behind this, but Brezhnev and his immediate circle were treating the visit as a very important one. Burger was received in grand style and given the kind of attention never granted before or since to any lawyer from abroad. Gromyko had told Brezhnev that Burger was one of the most influential people in the United States, so all the most powerful forces of the state, including the propaganda arm, were mobilized to accord him special honour. One of his days in Moscow was assigned entirely to Shcholokov's ministry. As a close friend of the General Secretary, he would not let the side down. Shcholokov had the idea that 'his' day could be featured in the press. An instruction came to the editorial offices from Suslov, the commander-in-chief of the entire Soviet media: to assign me for the whole day from morning until night to be at the minister's disposal and afterwards for me to produce a journalistic masterpiece on how successfully the police department had pulled the wool over the eyes of the wise US Supreme Court judge. The first deputy editor announced with a flourish the honour that had fallen upon me.

'I'm ill,' was my reply.

'All right, we'll advise the Central Committee accordingly. Only I think you are foolish to throw up a unique opportunity to see the whole thing from the inside.'

And how right he was! And glad I was that I gave in and agreed. The next morning everybody gathered at the long table in the minister's office. On one side were Burger and the US Ambassador, Malcolm Toon, and his colleagues. Facing them were Shcholokov and his whole team. I placed myself discreetly at the side with a miniature tape-recorder. And now, thirteen years later, I am listening to that tape and remembering how Shcholokov reminisced about his childhood, youth and school friends. 'They were a wonderful lot. There was a Ukrainian boy, a Russian, a Tatar, an Armenian and a Jew.' He hesitated. 'What was his name. Oh, my memory is going. That's what comes of old age.' He heaved a deep sigh, smiled and said, 'Ah, now I remember. It was Abrasha Kogan. I've always been an internationalist. One must not be a traitor to one's ideals. Our generation has principles.' He fell silent, apparently lost in thought, knitting his eyebrows. 'One's principles – they come before everything. Along with care for one's fellow man.' Burger nodded, seemingly in approval of what was being said. How could he not do so? The minister was singing a worthy song in praise of humanism, kindness and the rights of man.

Before we set off to go to a young offenders' detention centre outside Moscow, Shcholokov drew me to one side. 'Our colonels may not be able to carry it off,' he whispered to me 'But could you have a go at putting it across to the judge that he is not being taken to a special centre, but to a perfectly normal one. That all our centres are like the one we shall see. He would believe it if you were to tell him!'

The director of the Ikshinsk penal colony (60 kilometres from

Moscow), Georgi Shevchenko, had been hounded precisely because he had established a unique type of regime under which the young offenders were not subjected to cruelty and humiliation. Though not treated softly, they were treated at least decently. This had got Shevchenko into a lot of trouble, but his detention centre became a showpiece for gullible foreigners. I naturally didn't try to 'put anything across' to Burger. I don't know whether he was taken in by the charade, but all the comments he made were favourable.

We were driving at top speed in a long cavalcade of government cars through the streets of Moscow. It was the first and last time in my life that I had this experience. I noticed that we didn't get a single friendly glance from the citizens as we sped past the crowds. From the window of the black Chaika I saw their looks and their faces; an escort of roaring motorcycles was clearing the way for us, both on the way to the colony and on the way back, and later on the way to the lavish banquet in an out-of-town restaurant, as well as on the evening visit to the Bolshoi theatre.

Wherever fate took me in the company of the American Supreme Court judge, I couldn't help thinking how easy it was to mount an operation of this kind: with a well-worked-out formula, you can mount a simple and shameful deception virtually guaranteed to succeed. If it did not succeed, and the foreign guests were not entirely taken in by the proffered castle in the air, then the deceivers could easily substitute another. I decided to publish my report under a pseudonym. Earlier, I have described how I had a pseudonym forced on me. Now I chose to use one myself as the only way of protest available to me.

'One Day in the Life of Judge Burger' was the title of the article by 'A. Rozanov', which appeared in *Literaturnaya Gazeta* on 21 September 1977. I thought that I would probably never come across the name of this respected judge again. But I was wrong. Years later, in the court file on General Kalinin, one of the chief criminals in the Shcholokov clan (the file in the archive on this marked 'secret' is carefully guarded from outsiders), I read that Burger was supposed to be going to receive a gift fit for a king. Of course, he did not receive it nor did he have any idea that there was any intention of making him a present. I believe he would never have accepted it, but the most important thing is that there never was a serious likelihood of his being offered it. It was another example of what by then had become routine – a cleverly worked-out trick which killed several birds with one stone. On paper, Shcholokov should have presented his distinguished guest with a heavy judge's gavel made of white gold, beautifully engraved and set with precious stones. Brezhnev was informed that after visiting the Minister of Internal Affairs, the American lawyer would be left with a 'happy memory' of him. Being a master of such terminology, Brezhnev received this euphemism with great satisfaction. He wanted very much for his guest to go away feeling good, and the best way he knew for achieving that according to the customs of the time was an expensive gift.

Shcholokov's people knew that there were different moral standards in the US Supreme Court: money was not habitually thrown around on presents. Even so, they budgeted 20,000 roubles for the gift. I have no evidence as to whether the 'gift' to Judge Burger, when it came to rest in the hands of the mafia, was in cash or in the form of a gavel, but one can be quite sure that it did not evaporate into thin air. According to the record the golden gavel was presented, but it most certainly was not.

Interestingly enough, the success of this deft manoeuvre stood the minister and his circle in good stead. Two years later Gustav Husak came from Prague on a visit. Yuri Churbanov was hoping to be awarded a Czech decoration and induced his ministerial colleagues to agree that the President of this partner in the socialist brotherhood of nations should be given a gold watch from the State Treasury collection. Evidently Husak was rated lower than the US Supreme Court judge as they budgeted for him a mere 4500 roubles. Never mind the amount – the money was not left lying around. It was recorded as having been spent and the gift as having been presented.

Husak cannot be blamed here, any more than Burger. He had no idea that his name was involved in a web of deceit. Incidentally, the Husak story has one less element of mystery about it than that of the judge's golden gavel. The watch turned up again! It had at first been pocketed by Shcholokov. Then in a calculated gesture he had given it to his closest friend – Comrade Brezhnev. This was on the occasion which always brought joy to the whole nation – the revered General Secretary's birthday.

By comparison with that act of generosity, it was a mere prank that the minister permitted himself at a jewellery-makers' exhibition. His eye was caught by a set of chased silver wine goblets, an example of fine Dagestan craftsmanship. The minister's action is on official record in the following terms: 'wine goblets acquired for presentation to the Angolan Minister of Internal Affairs'. Whether the Angolan minister is now enjoying the use of them I cannot say.

I had further occasion to go and see Shcholokov. It was to request his cooperation in solving a crime which for some incomprehensible reason had proved too tough a nut for his people to crack. (Now I do know why the investigation had had the brakes put on it: the investigators had unexpectedly come across a connection with two leading mafiosi, both of them personally close to the minister. Having established the connection, they were alarmed by it.) Several years had passed since my newspaper interview with Shcholokov and since the Burger visit, but he had not forgotten and suddenly asked:

'Do tell me why you published that piece on me anonymously and the report on the American judge under a pseudonym. Were you being shy, or modest? Or perhaps putting yourself on a pedestal? Ministers come and go, so why risk staining your reputation with the name of Shcholokov, eh?'

He smiled but it was only too clear that he was anything but amused. 'Well you may not have been doing yourself much of a favour. You could come to regret it.' He paused. 'All right, enough of that. I don't bear you any grudge.' With a meaningful glance he added: 'Relax. I was only joking.'

He was not joking: there was clearly something serious on his mind. But this did not deter him from indulging in his usual sentimental reminiscence – about his childhood, his youth, his school friends, what a wonderful lot they were, etc. – with the same sighs, the same lapses of memory and knitting of the eyebrows. The sad smile and the familiar finale about his 'internationalism', his loyalty to principle and to his fellow man.

The rehearsed sincerity and well-honed friendliness seemed at the time like harmless posturing, a common weakness in a person in a position of power who wants people to like him and tries to appear nicer than he is. In seeking a reputation as shepherd of enlightenment, benefactor of the arts and sciences, Shcholokov liked to play on the most sensitive strings. He would fawn on writers and artists, would bestow favours on actors and musicians. They had their set phrases for it: 'creating the right conditions', 'opening the way for talent' and so forth. And let us not deceive ourselves; some of the beneficiaries, many in fact, sought those favours, thirsted after ministerial approval, ingratiated themselves without the slightest hesitation, accepting diplomas, prizes and all kinds of trinketry. The generosity with which he distributed these things did not shock them, just endeared him to them. And it was absolutely in the spirit of the times. In this, the minister showed no personal originality whatever.

Hundreds of writers, theatre directors, actors, artists and musicians earned not only financial inducements, medals and letters of thanks 'for offering your art in the service of the militia', but had access to more tangible benefits like the special passes giving the holder immunity from prosecution for any breach of traffic regulations. The top people in most mafia clans were sold these passes, especially the commercial mafia who dealt in black-market goods. People in the arts, famous nationwide, even known internationally, joined in the scramble to obtain one of these passes and thereby became hostages of the all-powerful Internal Ministry. In the reflected light of the artistes' fame and warmed by their grateful approbation, the minister and his crew were able to extort millions in exchange for these documents which cost nothing to produce, and at the same time to present themselves to the Soviet people as apostles of humanism and enlightenment.

I would not wish to portray myself here as a saint or an innocent. Although I requested no special passes or other favours of Shcholokov, with no asking from me he awarded me a trinket that cost him nothing, namely the gold badge of excellence of the Ministry of Internal Affairs of the USSR accompanied by a certificate signed by the minister himself. These are now among the prize items in my personal archive. There was one and only one occasion when I put a personal request to Shcholokov, and it was immediately granted. My daughter lived in Sofia with her Bulgarian mother. Every time she came to Moscow, I had to traipse humiliatingly round various offices and stand in queues for hours over the bureaucratic procedures. One phone call to Shcholokov solved the whole thing. My daughter was given a Soviet passport allowing unlimited visits in both directions. Thanking him, I warned the minister that this would not mean I would now write panegyric pieces about the militia. 'I would not have expected you to say otherwise,' he said with a wave and a malicious smile.

Shcholokov and Brezhnev were inseparable. As already explained, they lived in the same apartment block, one immediately above the other, which symbolized the real correlation of power between them. (One floor below was where Andropov lived, as fate – ever inventive – would have it.) In their day, they had both enjoyed wine and women, but now with advancing age they had turned to song. Often there were parties in one or other of the flats or at a dacha. Singers and musicians would be summoned for their masters' pleasure. They both had a passion for gypsy romances. On one occasion a third-rate exponent of the genre particularly appealed to them, moving them to tears. Next day he was honoured with the title 'People's Artist of the USSR' (the top such honour, of which the British equivalent would be a knighthood).

Anybody who thinks that it was only opportunists and crooks who sought to take the ministerial bait would be mistaken. Even the most respectable people fell under the spell of the minister's undoubted charm and the passion with which he delivered his interminable monologues. Mstislav Rostropovich and Galina Vishnevskaya were on good terms with him. Dmitri Shostakovich entered a competition for an anthem for the Internal Ministry – and won it. His 'March of the Soviet Militia' was awarded the highest prize of a golden sword and the composer had the privilege of being photographed with the minister. The picture appeared in all the Soviet newspapers.

Another brilliant example was Aram Khachaturian. He was happy to take the modest second prize in this unprecedented police competition, nor did his second place dampen his feelings of rapture. 'Dear Nikolai Anisimovich,' he wrote to the robber baron lounging in the minister's chair, 'I wrote that march inspired by you and by your initiative. Your interest in and love of art and music is a rare thing worthy of intense admiration. We musicians are very grateful to you. Please allow me to present to you the manuscript of my march . . . ' Very likely, out of all the wealth of acquisitions which came into the hands of the minister's family, this manuscript is the only item of genuine value which Shcholokov acquired totally aboveboard as an unsolicited gift.

He really did acquire an unbelievable quantity of valuables. Amongst them were museum pieces, including works by masters of Russian painting such as Benois, Aivazovsky, Shishkin, Savrasov, Makovsky, Falk and Konchalovsky, the grandfather of the well-known film directors Andrei Konchalovsky and Nikita Mikhalkov. Once on a visit to Yerevan, Shcholokov visited the studio of the great Armenian artist Martiros Saryan. The minister worked his charms on the old man, who gave in to persuasion and presented the minister with a large canvas for the ministry's museum, 'for the raising of the aesthetic level of militia generals'. The painting was delivered straight to the minister's personal flat.

One is struck not only by the pathological greed but by the absolute certainty of protection which such behaviour demonstrates. Obviously, while his friend Brezhnev was still alive, he could do what he liked, but it is astonishing how he continued to trust in Brezhnev's power after he was dead. How otherwise could he have gone on brazenly cramming flats and dachas – his own and his children's – full of priceless malachite tables, antique mother-of-pearl boxes, ancient Egyptian vases, works by famous sculptors, miniatures framed in gold, silver and ivory, antique furniture and no less than fifty fine old bronze and crystal candelabra?

Where did all these things come from? Not only from state collections and repositories. Very few people knew at the time what lay behind the sudden frontal attack on those innocent people who were passionately collecting and preserving all kinds of rarities in a country which had been devastated. Cases came up, dotted all over the country, in which collectors were accused of 'swindling', breaches of currency rules and other crimes. The presses were choked with denunciatory pamphlets, playing on the emotions of readers already deprived of the basic staples of life – bread, meat and milk: they were told about these high priests of beauty, frenziedly stealing the national heritage from *the people*! The violence with which these reptilian journalists used to attack antiquarians and numismatists was disproportionate to the guilt of these unfortunate people, even if one admits that some of them were to some extent guilty.

But the truth of the situation was simplicity itself. As always, in these seventy years or so, when the word 'people' was used, the accusers had themselves in mind. Hundreds of extremely valuable objects which were confiscated from the collectors did not go back into public ownership, but into the pockets, secret safes and apartments of these high-placed marauders. Some of the items came to them quasi-legally: by decree, a confiscated antique could be transferred to the museum of the Ministry of Internal Affairs –

Shcholokov's baby, destined to be a permanent memorial to his services to the country. In fact, this was the family's personal 'museum'. The public was only shown posters, diagrams and photographs of official occasions. The remaining 'exhibits' – those with real value – were not to be seen in the museum, forming as they did the private collection of the family.

Another interesting method of acquisition was developed by the mafia generals of the central militia. A network of agents would establish the real value of certain private collections. It was then a simple technical matter to fabricate an accusation against the owner. Mafia emissaries would come armed with search warrants signed by the appropriate authority, and would openly bargain with the owners. If, say, there were one hundred items to be listed on the inventory they would propose to the owner leaving off eighty of them. He was going to lose some anyway, but for twenty items 'improperly acquired', the penalty would be considerably less than for one hundred. The collector would be guaranteed decent treatment in prison or labour camp and early release. As everybody knew, both were in the mafia's gift.

Many accepted these deals and thus our art lover and friend of great composers added to his collection, in which an antique vase would stand happily alongside some Indian souvenir powder compact picked up at an airport duty-free shop, an avant-garde canvas would hang near a Bulgarian leather jacket, the latter a high-value item in the Soviet Union. Of course, it was not the minister alone who benefited. There were hundreds of generals and other officers, party apparatchiks, investigators and – even more numerous – their vassals, such as drivers, couriers, sportsmen and others, without whose biceps and street wisdom none of this would have been possible. Each of them, therefore, had to have a share in the proceeds.

For the exclusive patronage of the minister's family and their immediate circle there was even a special private shop, a branch of a large department store. It sold items otherwise in short supply, which would have cost five to ten times more on the black market. Shcholokov's household and staff could shop there for imported goods which they would buy in hundreds rather than dozens and then send to the Georgian republic for onward sale to their accomplices. These goods would be used by the mafiosi to pay off their protectors or suborn other people in authority. As was stated in court by General Kalinin, who had been on Shcholokov's staff, every autumn he would hand in 120,000–150,000 roubles in dog-eared three- and five-rouble notes in exchange for crisp new hundreds. None of this money was ever recovered and must have been carefully hidden away by the family. A rather telling illustration of this has been provided by the son of Arkady Shevchenko, well known as a former personal adviser to Gromyko and as deputy Secretary General of the United Nations. He was also working for the CIA. Later he came over to the West and his book *Break with Moscow* became a bestseller. His son Gennadi Shevchenko, a lawyer with the Institute of the State and Law of the Soviet Academy of Sciences, recalls the inventory of his father's possessions that was taken after he had been condemned in his absence to execution and expropriation of his goods and chattels.

The inventory was done by a KGB squad. Twelve icons of the school of Andrei Roublev and a silver and gold enamelled icon setting were assessed together at 500 roubles, which at the time (1978) would have been fifty or sixty times below their true value. A KGB general and acquaintance of Gennadi Shevchenko ex-plained that they gave low valuations so that the items could then be offered for 'sale' at bargain prices to people in the upper echelons of the nomenklatura.

In Europe or America no powerful mafia 'family' would chase after every last dollar or greedily acquire everything that came to hand. That was how their clan became powerful rather than petty – mafiosi rather than mere pickpockets. With the Soviet mafia it is different. I do not know a single example of a top mafia leader passing up the offer of the meanest gift – a bottle of vodka, a jar of caviar or some outmoded necktie bought in a sale. Shcholokov kept an army of personal servants, down to his own hairdresser, masseur, tailor and interior decorator. All these people were given official papers as Internal Ministry officers, likewise the whole Shcholokov house-hold, down to second cousins and great-nieces. Each of these had their own servant, also an MVD officer. On Shcholokov's instruc-tions, his ministry rented nine 'official' flats in the centre of Moscow, supposedly places for meetings with the MVD's secret informers. Such meetings actually took place elsewhere and the nine flats in question were used either to accommodate the minister's relations or, with their luxurious imported furnishings, were used as places for him and his friends to entertain their mistresses.

Every morning the minister's wife and daughters would be brought fresh flowers, paid for by the ministry and shown in the accounts under 'sundry official entertaining'. The ministry also paid for Shcholokov's father-in-law's funeral. This was charged as 'flowers for the Lenin Mausoleum'.

All this would be sadly amusing, if it concerned anyone less than the Minister for Internal Affairs of the USSR. Many knew of his greed and corruptibility. Heads of various mafia clans certainly knew. Even if he had no connection with any of them, he would have been risking his own neck if he had done his ministerial duty and deployed his forces to hound the increasingly threatening operations of the mafia. Any such effort would have led to his being mercilessly 'knocked out', and the slightest revelation of his own misdeeds would have led, if not to his downfall, then at least to a public scandal that the Brezhnevites would not have welcomed. Thus Shcholokov became a hostage to all the mafia groups and the best way for him to deal with this situation was simply to unite and combine with them. This was less risky and more profitable.

Andropov, having succeeded Brezhnev, contented himself with the removal and overthrow of a rival and left it at that: Shcholokov lost his post as minister and his membership of the Central Committee but kept his party membership, his military title of general, his hero's gold star, a large number of other orders and medals, his personal pension and staff, the Mercedes cars, the paintings and sculptures. Andropov didn't touch any of these items, remaining, as always, a loyal son of the party who would never prejudice its authority in the eyes of the people – to be more exact, the authority of its top men.

However, that may not have been his main reason. Shcholokov knew too much, including too much about Andropov's immediate circle, amongst whom were people who were necessary to the new leader for consolidating his hold on power. He therefore decided just to silence him. Having failed to make it to the top of the power pyramid, it seems that Shcholokov's assigned role was just to be grateful to the new master of the country that he was comfortably provided for in his old age. For exactly the same reasons, Yuri

Churbanov remained untouched, losing nothing materially, even though Andropov knew everything about him. This alone demonstrates the 'principles' that governed the actions of that true Leninist, Yuri Andropov. Court intrigues continued to determine the political moves on the Kremlin chessboard. The mafia, having trembled in fear of imminent unmasking, once again felt ground beneath their feet.

Nikolai Shcholokov was dismissed but his son remained in a senior position: Igor Shcholokov headed the international department of the Central Committee of the Komosomol. Thus he was still at the top of the hierarchy with access to its secrets. The 'true Leninist' decided to get rid of him. This shattered the family, particularly the disgraced boy's mother. The very next day, Svetlana Shcholokova put a bullet through her heart, using her husband's pistol. Even this did not fundamentally shake the mafia: it was seen as no more than a personal tragedy for the saddened widower. Well-informed sources told Shcholokov that no further sanctions against him were anticipated.

Andropov's long illness, which led to his death not long after he came to power, in effect kept him out of active politics, and this further raised the mafia's hopes. Raids by Andropov's men on hairdressers, shops and cafés in search of idlers and 'parasites' pursuing their own business in worktime had quickly turned into a farce and diverted the anger of the people into a channel harmless to the mafia. Harmless, because the mafia carried out its operations not in cafés but at the workplace and, as all could see, with the connivance of those in charge. If there was one thing the mafiosi could not be accused of it would be idleness or timewasting. Chernenko's coming to power meant a return to the good old Brezhnev days – a free hand for the mafia in all areas and at all levels. Every day, Shcholokov was expecting his bosom pal Kostya (Secretary General Konstantin Chernenko), with whom he had downed more than one bottle of vodka in his time, to invite him over, hug him tearfully and give him a new post of responsibility. He waited and waited, but what happened was quite different from what he expected.

Six months after Andropov's death, instead of the invitation on the telephone to a 'glass of tea', there was a ring at the door. Detectives whom he had never seen before showed their warrant and carried out a search. The reader has probably not forgotten that by this time Naidenov had once again become deputy Prosecutor General and, although he was no longer in charge of investigations, he did have a lot of kindred spirits in the prosecution service. And the very fact of his victorious return after such defeats served as an example for his colleagues, indeed a stimulus.

Chernenko preferred to leave it to the prosecution service to destroy Shcholokov. In the highest circle of cynics and pragmatists an overthrown friend was not worth a brass farthing. Those sort of people are not noted for their genuine feelings, as opposed to superficial show. They took a particularly sweet pleasure in putting the squeeze on Shcholokov, slowly and gradually. First, he was stripped of his general's rank, then he was dragged off for questioning. Then he was expelled from the party. A week later, he had all his honours and awards removed, except for those that he had won in wartime. It was perfectly obvious that this slow, purposeful torture was pushing Shcholokov towards a fateful step. Chernenko was already prostrate on his hospital bed. A court trial – even a secret one – would not be convenient to anyone. It would have been risky, of course, to depend on Shcholokov's loyalty, on a gentleman's agreement that if he kept his mouth shut he would be left in peace. A 'quiet' solution would also suit his children: according to the inventory made at the time of the search, there were still hundreds of precious objects in the family. Any court conviction of Shcholokov would result in their being confiscated.

Apart from a double-barrelled shotgun of French manufacture, everything was taken away from this figure, completely crushed by his own people and abandoned, who yesterday had been the uncrowned king of the mafia. He turned the gun on himself and the shot blew half his head off. This happened on 13 December 1984, when Shcholokov was in his seventy-fifth year. There was less than three months to go before Mikhail Gorbachev's accession to power. On the desk lay a suicide note addressed to Konstantin Chernenko. 'I beg you not to allow them to spread narrow-minded slander about me; this would inevitably be used to discredit all ranks in the leadership. We all had to suffer that in our day before the arrival of our dearly-remembered Leonid Ilyich.'

In one sentence was combined truth and falsehood. Loyalty to Brezhnev, to whom he really owed everything; and hypocrisy as far as the 'narrow-minded slander' was concerned. He couldn't restrain himself from concealing the truth even when about to meet his Maker.

This chapter will end with the words of the chief military prosecutor of the USSR, Alexander Katusev, spoken in an interview which passed completely unnoticed. His words will explain why so much attention has been devoted in this book to a squalid individual who met a squalid fate:

'He was a man of his time; no better and probably no worse than any of the others in the constellation of oligarchs of his time. The whole difference, in essence, can be boiled down to the fact that we managed to expose Shcholokov, whereas some of his contemporaries met a different fate – they died a natural death and rest in peace in the Novodevichy monastery. One or two are living out their years with squeaky false teeth, cursing both perestroika and the man who introduced it.'

An Epidemic of Suicides

Shooting oneself became a distressingly common occurrence. The sound of gunshots accompanied life in the Ogarev Street headquarters of the Interior Ministry and in the looming monster of the KGB building on Dzerzhinsky Square. In a short space of time, the following – amongst others – did away with themselves: the First Deputy Minister of Internal Affairs of the USSR, Viktor Paputin; the First Deputy Chairman of the KGB of the USSR, Semeon Tsvigun; and a member of the Board of the Ministry of Internal Affairs of the USSR and the head of its Academy, General Sergei Krylov. In each case there were, of course, specific reasons, but the epidemic of suicides which gripped these ministries – similar in their functions to the same degree that they were locked in constant warfare with each other – speaks volumes. It speaks not only of the enormous psychological pressure on their top people, but also of that endless web of intrigue in which even the most experienced can become confused, and of those permanently double and triple lives in which the slightest loss of concentration can lead to catastrophe. Insofar as every one of them was concealing crimes of his own, they were constantly haunted by the fear of exposure. The possession of a convenient weapon prompted them to seek the simplest way of extricating themselves from a tangle which was at least partly of their own making.

The fate of General Krylov strikes me as particularly dramatic. I knew him quite well, although he was not a particularly close acquaintance. Shcholokov had come across a modest major amongst the sea of green militia uniforms. One should give credit to the intuition which led him unerringly to pick this one out of all the others to take into his personal confidence. The minister was attracted by the lively mind of this officer, by his erudition, logical cast of thought and capacity for brief and clear exposition. He stood out amongst his tongue-tied, stupid colleagues like a pearl on a dung-heap, as the old fable has it

In a very short space of time, the major became a lieutenant general and he was drafting the minister's reports, toasts, speeches and lectures for congresses and conferences. Fortunately, the minister was good at reading them and the legend soon began to spread that he was reading his own text rather than something prepared for him, expressing not somebody else's thoughts but his own. The minister hardly had time to settle into this role when a series of articles (not written by him but published under his name in a small-circulation periodical in Moldavia) led to his being awarded, on Brezhnev's instruction, an honorary doctorate in economics. If only the idyllic friendship of Krylov and the minister had lasted a little longer it is possible that Shcholokov would also have wangled himself a doctorate in philosophy on the strength of the speeches written for him by the general. It was Krylov who persuaded the minister to set up that unique institution – the Academy of the MVD – and Shcholokov appointed Krylov to be its head. His first directorial order specified that every student should acquaint himself with the works of Aristotle, Plutarch, Theophrastus, Montaigne, La Bruyère and Montesquieu.

I recall Krylov coming to visit us at the Writers' Union along with his heads of department. We were expecting to see lawyers, but those who spoke one after another were sociologists, historians, art specialists and philosophers. These were the people who were to impart knowledge and wisdom to future militia generals and to try to instil in them the rudiments of culture. The audience of writers was a mixed bunch, as one might expect. A children's writer, whose works were already classics, sitting near me said loudly: 'Montaigne won't help them to catch criminals,' and a well-known dramatist asked straight out: 'Will the militia have time now to protect my flat from burglars?'

Krylov had enough sense of humour to answer this with a joke, but the next thing he announced put us into a state of shock. He said that he was going to require the students at the Academy to study the Talmud and the history of the Jewish people using a pre-revolutionary edition which he was having photocopied. 'What on earth for?' cried the audience, almost to a man. 'To teach wisdom and the knowledge of how to bring up children,' was the general's answer. One can easily imagine the reaction in anti-Semitic circles at the top and the bottom to such ideas, and the degree to which Krylov stood out – a *rara avis* – in contrast.

I was introduced to him by his friend Gregori Medynsky, an elderly writer who had devoted many years to campaigning on behalf of young offenders who had been sent to the Gulag – victims of the Stalin system and the 'model of socialism' it created. At Medynsky's eightieth birthday party, Krylov went up to him and proposed a toast 'to the union of mind' (he embraced Medynsky) 'and power' (he tapped on his own general's chest). A few days later, I was at Medynsky's place and met Krylov in a more intimate setting. He knew of me by name as a journalist. For some reason or other he immediately began to confide in me. We were sitting together, the two of us, each with a glass of brandy, and he recalled his toast at the birthday party: 'What "power" do I really have in my job? Enough, perhaps to put a bullet through my head.' It was only three years before that fateful shot, but who would then have taken his rhetorical outburst seriously?

I began to apologize for the philistine behaviour of my colleagues at the Writers' Union meeting when he was given such a shabby reception, but he disagreed: 'No, your best-selling author was absolutely right. The party, the MVD, the whole system from top to bottom reeks of corruption. And against that plague, the only weapons that I have are Rousseau and Montaigne.'

I remember him asking: 'How long will they let me carry on?' I shrugged my shoulders. He answered his own question: 'Two years.' He wasn't far out.

He was loathed by Brezhnev's son-in-law, Churbanov, the real power in the ministry and a man going from strength to strength. Churbanov was still only the first deputy but he had his sights on the minister's chair. Popular wisdom which reached the West and got into the US and European press – namely, that Shcholokov and Churbanov were in league with each other for a common purpose – was a long way from the mark. Much earlier, that might well have been the case, but very soon they found themselves in opposing mafia clans.

Owing to their criminal activities they were bound in a conspiracy of mutual protection which prevented them from denouncing each other prematurely. But Churbanov, whose star was in the ascendant, was much closer to the moribund dictator than his bosom party pal. Gradually, Shcholokov's people were pushed aside, transferred or removed, making way for Churbanov's people. One of the first victims was General Krylov.

One can only guess why Churbanov was consumed with such burning hatred of Krylov. As an ignoramus and an idiot, he probably could not bear to have a man of intelligence and erudition in his militia circle. Psychological and biological incompatibility ruled out their ever finding a common language. Knowing the kind of work that Krylov did for Shcholokov, he tried to rid the minister of his 'golden pen'. The fact that Shcholokov did not simply get rid of him but even made an attempt to protect Krylov demonstrates the underlying balance of power which existed at that time between him and Churbanov.

One mafia clan now launched into a bloody and decisive battle with the other; Churbanov disposed of Krylov with refined sadism. He accused him of minor embezzlement. The pettiness of the crime was its whole point. Churbanov had piled up millions but sent the head of the Academy a bill for a carpet runner that had disappeared from one of the classrooms – if memory serves, it was valued at twenty or thirty roubles – and a fridge which was in the general's official dacha. Krylov was dismissed from his post in disgrace. The order for his dismissal coincided by chance with Lenin's birthday, which was marked according to custom with a formal assembly at the ministry. Churbanov was there himself. Krylov asked if he could take the opportunity to say a few words of farewell to his colleagues. Churbanov refused. Krylov left the assembly hall and, in what was already his former office, put a bullet through his temple.

In October 1979, the Ministry of Internal Affairs and the Union of Writers which was cooperating with it so touchingly, organized in Tashkent one of a series of formal conferences. Guests from all the republics and all the major cities gathered for it. The subject for discussion was the representation of legal themes in contemporary literature. I was given the honour of making one of the keynote speeches.

The enormous hall was bursting at the seams. It seemed as though the whole of Tashkent was burning to find out how our writers sang the praises of our valiant militia. In actual fact, what brought them there was not so much literature but the brilliant constellation of grandees presiding on the platform. In the centre, alongside 'the father of the Uzbek people' Sharaf Rashidov, sat Yuri Churbanov. The remaining seats were occupied by members of the Politburo of the Central Committee of Uzbekistan. It would not be long before all of them, with the exception of Leonid Grekov who made a timely escape to become ambassador in Sofia, would be behind bars. During my speech, whenever I turned round towards the platform my glance inevitably met the sleepy gaze of Churbanov, who was painfully demonstrating respectful attention to the speaker. Oh, great benevolence of fate! During the break, I was asked to join Churbanov for lunch.

I went into the holy of holies backstage, with its table groaning with delicacies, but no sooner was I inside than I was stopped by a silver-haired poet who had also been invited. 'You're improperly dressed,' he said disapprovingly, tugging at my short-sleeved shirt. 'This is an official lunch with Yuri Mikhailovich himself, and you come looking like that!'

'Never mind,' said Churbanov condescendingly, overhearing this ticking-off. 'It is very hot today.'

I was placed next to Churbanov himself. 'We really ought to meet for a chat,' he whispered, downing another glass of vodka. 'When I get back from Gazli.* I cannot pretend to be looking forward to flying there, but I shall have to go. One has to do one's bit.'

He was away for one day and it was the day after that that we did in fact meet. He had the glossy look of a well-fed cat. His eyes had an oily gleam. 'I am exhausted,' he complained. 'I've been at it nonstop. The people down there are suffering and nobody gives a damn. There are a lot of incompetents in charge. If you want anything done, you have to do it yourself. I simply don't know how one can work with them.'

---

* A centre of gas production not far from Bokhara which had suffered serious damage in a recent earthquake.

I tactfully refrained from asking precisely what that work was. The answer came several years later. At the trial where Churbanov was no longer a general, nor First Deputy Minister of Internal Affairs, but the accused in the dock, the questioning turned to that day and to that 'inspection trip' to Gazli. It turned out that he had in fact come back to our literary conference in Tashkent with 10,000 roubles in his pocket, given to him for out-of-pocket expenses by the First Secretary of the Regional Committee, Karimov.

The main subject of contention between the accused and the witness (in the trial Karimov was a witness, although he was brought to court under armed guard), concerned the following detail: had they placed the packet of money under Churbanov's napkin during lunch or had they slipped it into his pocket when they were taking their distinguished guest to the gents? Churbanov insisted on the second version, but the witness stoutly insisted on the first. I did not see what difference it made, but there must have been one, and I have often wondered pointlessly: when we had that conversation immediately after his return from Gazli, did he have those 10,000 roubles in one of the pockets of his uniform, or had he hidden them under the mattress in the residence?

Our conversation was short and to the point. 'What would it take to persuade you to write a favourable article about our militia more or less straight away?' asked Churbanov unceremoniously.

'Surely somebody else already . . . '

'Yes, they are, and we are very grateful to your colleagues.' (No, I thought, they are your colleagues, not mine.) 'But it is important for us that you should write one for us.'

'Why me?'

He took some time considering his reply. 'It's important.'

'But why?'

'You'll do it better than anyone else.'

'I'm not so sure of that.'

'Well, we are. What would persuade you to do it?'

'I'd rather think about that.'

I thought my answer was evasive, but for Churbanov it had sounded like an invitation to negotiate. He sprang suddenly to life. Now he was in his element. He said: 'How about a flat?'

'I have a flat.' (I had taken the point of his question immediately,

109

but remember how astonished I was to experience the market economy in action.) 'I have everything I need.'

'That's impossible,' said Churbanov. 'What about a car? Or a dacha? Don't be shy.'

I was not being shy. I did not have a dacha, but at that moment I was ready to swear I had my own personal Palace of Versailles.

'Don't be shy,' he said again. 'Maybe a trip somewhere. To meet people. Come on now! We'll set it up for you.'

He handed me his visiting card. 'Ring me any time, and we shall be delighted to help.'

The conclusion I drew from this strange conversation was that in that period of deep political torpor, when the day-to-day affairs of the country were in the hands of well-protected despots, they were nevertheless afraid of the press. They controlled yet feared it. And the hypocritical chorus of approval of 'their noble deeds' coming from unprincipled journalists not only flattered their self-esteem but served almost as a guarantee of their importance, of stability and security. Just to pocket the mafia millions that kept them provisioned was not enough to complete their satisfaction. Thus, many were those who – by no means against their will, often the reverse – fell into the mafia's embrace: artists and sculptors who specialized in likenesses of the 'lords of creation', writers who would introduce into their novels thinly disguised portraits of the Soviet leaders, poets and composers who would combine to produce 'popular' songs about them, filmmakers who would base films on them ... Under Hitler and Stalin, the right to be recorded 'artistically' for posterity belonged exclusively to the ruling elite. Under Khrushchev, Brezhnev, Andropov and Chernenko it belonged to anybody who had the money and was not afraid to display it. It would be considered shameful for an artist of repute to accept a commission from some ordinary crook. But to respond to the call from a figure of influence was looked upon as an act of important public service. That the former and the latter might be one and the same person seemed not to be taken into account.

Thus, few knew – and, if they did, would not believe – that the richest, most widespread mafia grouping out of all those that had established themselves in the land was headed not by some super-successful director of an agricultural enterprise, or fish-retailer or manager of a fashionable café, but by the political head of a Union republic (*not* of a region or district), non-voting member of the Central Committee of the Communist Party Sharaf Rashidov.

So it was no accident that that stupid conference designed to demonstrate the comradely alliance between the militia and the writers should have taken place in Tashkent or that practically every Soviet newspaper was crammed with articles about 'successes' in Uzbekistan. Nor was it fortuitous that Georgian bazaar traders in the market halls of Moscow seemed to be driven out by hordes of Uzbeks with their eye-catching embroidered skullcaps, nor that a storm of high awards, honours and prizes rained down on Uzbek comrades of all ranks.

This was because the potential represented by Medunov's rice and fruit, by 'Iron Bella' and sleaze by the sea, etc. – all of that paled into insignificance before the vast abundance promised and provided by cotton. The little stream of gifts which trickled from the northern Caucasus was nothing compared to the wild current which suddenly gushed from the sweltering fields of Uzbekistan. Without any difficulty, Rashidov's mafia captured the commanding heights and the generously loving heart of dear Leonid Ilyich. Brezhnev now no longer needed Medunov's services and there was no tradition amongst our leaders of loyalty to those whose useful days were over. All efforts were concentrated on extracting the maximum possible from a new gold-bearing seam.

I first took the plane to Tashkent years and years ago, at the outset of my career as a journalist. There were no large jets in those days and the Moscow–Tashkent flight took, I remember, ten hours with three refuelling stops. A blizzard added another five or six hours. Shared misfortunes of this kind draw strangers together and that was how I got talking with two cheerful passengers, both ten or twelve years older than me and both on their way to Tashkent 'on editorial business'. The name of one of them, Boris Privalov, I had come across sometimes at the foot of some think-piece in the newspaper. The other one, Yuri Karasev, I had not heard of before. We seemed to have plenty in common and the company of these pleasant fellows helped me to endure an uncomfortable flight. We agreed that after landing we would share a taxi into town in order to look for a hotel.

It was almost dawn when the plane touched down at Tashkent and as soon as the gangway had been rolled into position, a convoy of smart government limousines drew up at the foot of it. A general stepped out of one car, two civilians from another. Their dress, manner and bearing all marked them out as KGB. The three of them quickly came up into the aircraft, the stewardess respectfully stood aside and the passengers, unbidden as always, (Soviet training for you!) remained in their seats, leaving the central passage clear. No sooner had the unholy trinity appeared at the entrance to the passenger cabin than my two travelling companions, without so much as saying goodbye, stood up and moved self-importantly towards them. The general saluted, and the other two chorused: 'Welcome to sunny Uzbekistan.'

Three or four years later, I discovered why two unknown men of letters had been met like visiting heads of state. Sharaf Rashidov, as a top man in the Uzbek republic – he was then still chairman of the Presidium of the Supreme Soviet and shortly to become First Secretary of the Central Committee of the party – longed for fame as a novelist even if he was only just capable of writing action instructions on letters and reports. Meanwhile his epic trilogies and tetralogies were coming off the presses in enormous editions and deluxe bindings. Critics, with the feigned rapture of the prostitute, exalted these works as 'deeply significant literary frescoes'.

The author 'Sharaf Rashidov' was no more than the collective pseudonym of the men from Moscow, Boris Privalov and Yuri Karasev. Their hurriedly written 'novels' were announced as translations from the Uzbek language, whereas it was other literary slaves that were given the task of putting this Russian job into Uzbek.★

This interest in literary fame might seem to some like the passing fancy of an all-powerful lord and master, in historical terms a mere curiosity, hardly worth a footnote. But that is not so: total deception had become so established as one of life's norms that it had even invaded the area of individual creative labour, where one might have

---

★ Whilst studying material relating to Medunov in the archives in preparation for writing this book, I suddenly came across the familiar name of Boris Privalov. Evidence from people close to Medunov showed that Privalov had been recommended to him as 'a useful chap' by Rashidov. Leaders of mafia clans, as everywhere in the world, have good mutual understanding, not only competing to the death with each other but, on occasion, rendering each other small services. But this particular service was minuscule. Privalov wanted to build himself a dacha in Sochi and Medunov instructed the mayor to give the Moscow writer a plot of land. The instruction was carried out but, alas, the project was not realized because Privalov suddenly died after a short illness.

thought such cynical fabrication would be impossible. The history of literature does show instances of the hiring of 'day labourers' for the purpose of enlarging the creative output of an author who has too many projects to cope with on his own. There are famous instances in art history of vain efforts by titled mediocrities to claim for themselves the laurels of great artists. In the case in point, it is not a question of the ambitious pretension of someone devoid of creative potential, but of the bestowing of a favourable image on the führer of a developing mafia building up to a swindle of unheard-of proportions. The complete success of this little literary experiment prompted Brezhnev, the führer of führers, years later to add to his many honours, awards and other trinketry on his chest the title of 'outstanding writer' – namely the medal of a Lenin Prize-winner for literature. Unlike his friend Rashidov, Leonid Ilyich was able to attract for the composition of his masterpieces both KGB workers and genuinely talented writers. This fact will cast a shadow over our happy memory of them.*

There was probably no mafia to compare with the Uzbek one for providing a classic, textbook example and reflection of what the Soviet political and economic system could lead to. There was an inevitability about the process which ended in losses to society running into billions and those same billions accruing to a gigantic mafia clan. The brilliance of Rashidov and his group consisted in their realizing these opportunities before anyone else, in their not wasting energy on small-scale operations but squeezing the maximum they could out of a system which by then had reached the zenith of its absurdity.

In a society where, as I have said, everything belongs to everybody – i.e. nothing belongs to anybody – a commodity is not a thing, an object, something real, visible and tangible. It is a figure printed

---

* In an interview Andrei Voznesensky once suggested that the corruption underlying the emergence of the Soviet mafia began in Khrushchev's time when his circle – son-in-law Alexei Adzhubei, personal assistant Vladimir Lebedev, court poet and boot-licker Nikolai Gribachev and other intellectual titans – got themselves awarded the Lenin Literature prize for the masterpiece entitled *Nikita Sergeyevich in America*. Most likely this was not the first corrupt act of its kind, but it was a telling sign of the development of conditions in which the mafia could form and a signal to the potentially corrupt to have no fear and to grasp the bull by the horns. But the first talk about corruption in the party and state apparatus was in the early 1920s. Thus, it would be more correct to look for the beginnings not in the time of Khrushchev's 'thaw' but in the whirlwind period under Lenin.

on paper, kept in an office in a statistical record. Since one eats bread not numbers, wears clothes not figures, it is possible and logical for the people to be destitute whilst the statistics demonstrate a country of riches and abundance. It would be more accurate to say that it used to be like that, because nowadays the 'de facto' destitution is far greater and the 'de jure' – that is, claimed – wealth has somewhat decreased. Nevertheless the essence of the point remains valid.

The public exchequer pays out on the basis of figures, not for actual goods. It surrounds the process with propaganda, and with medals and titles which carry additional benefits – all on the basis of figures. But one can put down any figure provided that the whole chain of command on which the ultimate acceptance of the figure depends and by which the payment will be authorized is drawn into the general deception, with all involved having a personal stake in it.

In this sense, Uzbekistan was a bottomless well of phantom riches.

The republic has the lion's share of the country's cotton production, and cotton is one of its most high-return agricultural products. Obedient Soviet propagandists gave it the grandiloquent nickname 'white gold'. For this 'white gold' the exchequer paid out generously with the real thing. The 'father of the nation', Sharaf Rashidov, converted the Uzbek economy exclusively to cotton production, making the country into a monoculture and depriving its population of the benefits it was used to deriving from a productive and broadly-based farming industry. It was believed that this would make the republic rich, but in reality the only ones to get rich were the class of apparatchiks who, with no effort at all – almost automatically – eased themselves into the ranks of the Rashidov mafia.

Cotton, produced almost entirely by sweated peasant labour without modern implements, brought these mafiosi officials enormous profits. And who would refuse to increase his earnings by up to ten times if it cost no effort whatever to do so? One only had to add a nought here or two or three noughts there to the records. One nought on paper was worth millions of roubles – the possibilities were enough to make the head swim. The most astonishing aspect of the situation was that central government, in the person of dear Comrade Brezhnev, also had an interest in the success of this grand deception. He would probably have welcomed an enormous real, as opposed to paper, crop of 'white gold', but insofar as hoping for that would have been sheer wishful thinking, central government had to be content with the propaganda illusion. Tankerloads of ink and tons of paper were expended on trumpeting across the land the mighty successes of the wonderful Soviet cotton-growers.

On the other hand, the real cotton pickers had to be paid at least something for the real cotton they did produce, even if it was carefully selected others who were paid for the pseudo-tonnages. Yet it has to be acknowledged that there were even too many of those within the republic. That was Sharaf Rashidov's great inspiration – to involve such a significant proportion of the whole rural population in the great collective fraud. Practically everybody got a share of this giant pie, which in reality did not exist. When, years later, this crime was uncovered (a crime on a scale hard to grasp for people with no personal knowledge of Soviet reality), our lawyers had to face a task no less hard to carry out: to put in the dock practically the whole population of the republic. This was a task which, needless to say, nobody dared to undertake.

But all this was in the future. At that time, the fictitious noughts were increasing year on year, and correspondingly the by no means fictitious roubles paid out for these noughts. A large proportion of these roubles went on bribing officials in various central ministries.

Brezhnev's circle – both friends and family – naturally had first priority. Leonid Ilyich personally was pushing Rashidov for further 'pripiski'.* Listening to Rashidov's successive reports very much in the style of Baron Munchausen, and 'socialist obligations' promising the country fairytale cotton crops, Brezhnev would fondly advise, 'Round the figures up, Sharafchik. Add on a little millionchik.' And Sharafchik would be pleased to add a noughtchik to his socialist obligation, the bank would pay him wagonloads of crisp new banknotes and the Supreme Soviet – that is, its chairman, the same dear Ilyich – would pin another gold star or an order named after that other favourite Ilyich, Comrade Lenin, on Sharaf's chest. In response, Sharaf would present Ilyich (Leonid, not Vladimir) with a carved solid gold bust four metres high. In response to that,

---

* A Soviet technical term, untranslatable into any language. It is the indication in an official document sent in for accounting and audit purposes of nonexistent 'production achievements' which attract material rewards or honours.

Ilyich would lash out with another medal for Sharaf and Sharaf with a generous motion of the hand would add another nought in the appropriate statistical column.

Sharaf beat all national records in our country. He wangled himself ten Orders of Lenin (leaving aside a host of others). Such a stream of highest awards was not experienced by a single military leader in World War II nor by any other Brezhnev favourite nor even by that champion in the medal stakes, Comrade Brezhnev himself. Thus they bamboozled and plundered the long-suffering country.

Years later, Telman Gdlyan and Nikolai Ivanov became widely known as the investigators heading the team that began to look into this 'crime of the century'. They were confronted by a situation which astonished the imagination even of professionals that had seen a thing or two. Bound up in the general criminal conspiracy were not nearly all but absolutely all the party, state, Komsomol, trade union and economic managers of the republic and of its regions, cities and districts. Being professional lawyers, these investigators immediately realized that all these people could not be found guilty a priori; it would be necessary to prove the guilt of each one of them in separate proceedings, not en masse. But, being possessed of common sense and knowledge of Soviet reality, they could not conceive even hypothetically that there would be a single person who would have passed up the attractions of becoming a fully-fledged member of the all-embracing mafia structure. The general claim that they were all tarred with the same brush (that is, they could all be reckoned in advance to be criminals) was as unacceptable from a forensic point of view as it was accurate in fact, alas.

I do not wish to touch on every aspect of the Gdlyan/Ivanov investigation: doubtless in some respects they broke the laws of procedure, although with the blessing, even the formal approval of their immediate superiors, the Chief Prosecutor in particular. Both of them were themselves products of that system of 'socialist legality' (to be more exact, illegality), under which people were none too fussy about exact observation of the procedures which they disparagingly referred to as 'legal formalism'. I am deeply averse to the concept that it can be expedient to disregard the due processes of law, even in exceptional cases, and to the idea that the end justifies the means, but psychologically I am capable of understanding their attitude: it was appalling for them to see the heights of cynical licence which the pillars of 'communist morality' could reach whilst claiming the interest of society as their highest goal. They did what they liked with the country, herding millions of people into slavery – and this at the end of the second millennium and under the eyes of the whole world.

It didn't matter which personality came to the attention of the investigators or what fact they tried to check out; they only needed to scratch about a bit to find that the threads led higher and higher. One level would give way to another, everywhere there would be deception and bribes, bribes and deception – nothing but deception and bribes. And all roads led to the Kremlin.

And it would be strange, whichever way you look at it, if the investigators had not wished to get to the bottom of these shameful, dirty, Kremlin secrets. And, whichever way you look at it, it would have been strange if those involved in those secrets – even tangentially – had not tried to cover them up by putting blockages and obstructions in the way of excessively nosy investigators who dared to take too many liberties. Thus arose a famous conflict in which those in power were victorious, albeit temporarily.

After sacking Shcholokov from his post as Minister for Internal Affairs, Andropov set about cracking a tougher nut, namely Sharaf Rashidov. He was a tougher nut because, unlike Shcholokov, Rashidov was a candidate member of the Politburo and first secretary of the party central committee of a republic. Thus in Moscow, and especially in Uzbekistan, he was backed by powerful forces who would defend him fiercely with all means at their disposal, since they were all either tied up together through their common 'business' or belonged to other mafia clans. Their criminal solidarity reflected in essence their instinctive fear of exposure. Andropov was guided, of course, not only by high principles but by awareness of the strength of the mafiosi who (just like decent honest people) feared the all-seeing eye and the secretive power of the KGB which, needless to say, could activate powerful levers in order to push aside or at least weaken the mafia. The KGB knew too much and was capable of too much, which is always dangerous.

Andropov issued an instruction to the chairman of the Uzbekistan KGB, General Melkumov, to do whatever was necessary to find at all costs a material basis on which to open an attack on the Uzbek mafia, of whose existence he was well aware. The local KGB people

117

who had been completely idle up to that point (they were supposed to be on the lookout for dissidents but didn't dare go near the mafia) took only a few days to catch the first victim at the scene of his crime red-handed, since he had not the slightest suspicion that he might be in danger of apprehension. He turned out to be the head of the anti-corruption squad in the Department of Internal Affairs for the Bokhara region, Akhat Muzaffarov. The fact that it was him they got was of course a coincidence. It might just as well have been anyone else. They caught him at the very moment when some local shop manager was slipping him his monthly 1000-rouble protection money.

That was in April 1983. The tangled skein began to unwind itself with almost cosmic speed. The search of Muzaffarov's home produced results which even the KGB could not have foreseen: in money alone more than one million roubles and in costly fabric such as gold brocade, one and a half kilometres, not to mention diamonds, rubies or Japanese and Swiss watches of which there were thousands. And jeans, jeans and more jeans, so prized in the Soviet Union.

Literally a few days were all that was necessary to set off a chain reaction of disclosure. But Rashidov was still in power. He understood where it would all lead and raised the alarm. He demanded that the investigation should be conducted by the Ministry of Internal Affairs. Secondly, to have Muzaffarov murdered, and thus cut all the threads, would have been a most simple task, easily accomplished. That was his plan.

But Andropov did not agree to Rashidov's request. In a matter of weeks they had arrested eight of the top Bokhara people, including the head of the Department of Internal Affairs (the very person that Rashidov had wanted to be in charge of the investigation). Things were moving quickly. Then came an unexpected development: Andropov went into hospital. The final stage of his fatal illness was now upon him. From his hospital bed he continued to make some decisions and sign the most important documents, but lesser matters did not reach him. They were handled by Chernenko. Into the category of 'lesser' matters came certain changes in appointments which Rashidov managed to push through. Melkumov, the head of the KGB in Uzbekistan, was suddenly transferred, becoming Minister-Counsellor at the Soviet embassy in Prague. This was regarded as a considerable promotion, leaving behind the problems of the Uzbek mafia to take on Vaclav Havel and his friends. Mel-kumov's deputy General Lagunov, was also transferred, from Uzbek-istan to Russia. And the head of the investigation department of the Uzbek KGB who had been in charge of this case was summarily pensioned off.

This was the moment when the investigation should have been taken over by the Ministry of Internal Affairs. But the prosecution service now seized the initiative – at Union, not republic level. That is how the group under Telman Gdlyan came to be formed, which later gained worldwide repute. His group energetically set about its task when suddenly there was a divine intervention: Rashidov died. Up to the present day, there is no certain proof of one version of events which immediately gained currency, namely that Rashidov had taken his own life. But the epidemic of suicides in Uzbekistan following Rashidov's death does lead one to wonder whether the mafia godfather might have been responsible for setting a trend.

The official medical report speaks of 'death arising from a chronic heart ailment'. This is a fairly vague formula and one which carries no conviction whatever. It is known that, before he died, Rashidov was summoned to the Central Committee and had a one-to-one meeting behind closed doors with Chernenko. One can only surmise what they discussed, but indirect evidence suggests that Rashidov knew where he stood: both Andropov and Chernenko were prepared to sacrifice him in order to breach the solid mafia wall and thus divert the attention of a society that was becoming restive onto those whom they could declare responsible for the people's woes. Thus one can say with certainty that if Rashidov himself did not put a bullet through his head, he did die as a result of the pressure to bring him under control which was gathering inexorable force.

Nevertheless, however paradoxical it might seem, the death of Rashidov strengthened the position of the mafia because the brakes were applied to the investigation, even if not for long. They accorded Rashidov an extravagant funeral in the Oriental tradition, in a clear attempt to establish an exploitable cult of the dead führer. They buried the godfather of the Uzbek mafia on the central square of Tashkent, within the so-called Lenin Memorial, not far from the Lenin Museum and the local KGB buildings. On this square stands the highest Lenin statue in the world and alongside was the resting place they chose for his faithful disciple. Here also is the rostrum upon which Rashidov and his comrades stood so many times on Soviet festive occasions to salute triumphant demonstrators. When their legs and arms ached from the standing and waving, they would go down into the underground chambers where they and their guests would find tables piled with festive fare and delightful young ladies ready to put the spring back into their step. It was next to this subterranean place of ill-repute, known to have provided him off and on with the usual services, that Rashidov got laid for the last time.

The last time? No, it was only three years later that the great mafioso's remains had to be removed to an ordinary cemetery and his memorial bust destroyed. By that time, the truth had come out about Rashidov's real life, as distinct from the façade. But all that was still to come.

Those who came to power after him were the most ardent Rashidovites. They could feel how unstable their position was and how little time they had left to save their own skins. This they proceeded to do with all the skill of professional criminals. Rashidov's successor as First Secretary of the party, Inamzhon Usmankhodzhaev, also took over from him 'ex officio' as the head of the mafia clan, in a vain attempt to rescue it. But it was too late.

Arrest followed arrest, undeterred by some terrible killings organized by the mafia with the assistance of hired assassins. The price of a life in whose owner the mafia showed an interest rose to 200,000 roubles – for this sum, daredevils were prepared to risk eliminating those who knew too much and were prepared to give evidence against their accomplices. Not that long ago, there had been hit-men in Uzbekistan willing to commit a murder for only 10,000 roubles.

The astonishing thing is that the value put on a life has continued to fall sharply. In the wild inflation of recent years literally everything has gone up, except for the price of human life. The number of murders has increased so much and with it the number of people wishing to bump people off that by the second half of 1990 no hired assassin was paid more than 7,000 roubles per job.

Prices for services rendered by the mafia rose more sharply than those in the general marketplace. Everything and anything could be bought or sold, but one commodity which suddenly appeared in this free-for-all was particularly dramatic and terrible. The majority of mothers and fathers threw themselves into saving their children from being sent to Afghanistan to fulfil 'their international duty'. The military occupation contingents were formed in Tashkent and this brought the mafia more and more thousands of roubles.

I remember how one of our female colleagues suddenly took a few days' leave and flew straight down to Tashkent. Unabashedly, she had told everyone that it would cost her 4,000 roubles to buy her son out of being sent to Afghanistan. Our colleague flew back after only one day: in her naïveté she had taken exactly 4,000 roubles with her, but meanwhile the price had jumped to 6,000 ... We advised her to take the precaution of taking 8,000 with her – and we were proved correct: the price had risen to 8,000 in the few days that it took her to gather the additional funds. In defence of the mafia's 'honour' I will say that it did fulfil its side of the bargain: the son of the hapless lady was recruited into another division and completed his national service within the Russian republic.

That mouldering old living corpse, Konstantin Chernenko, could no longer withstand the gathering momentum of the investigation. Up till then, no government prosecutor, even the most senior, had felt able to sanction the arrest of a powerful party member or minister without first obtaining the permission of the Central Committee. In the filing cabinets of the Kremlin lay becalmed various similarly well-supported dossiers justifying the arrest of mafia leaders whose guilt was beyond question and confirmed two, three or even four times over. Chernenko and his team had been playing for time – but eventually made a decision: they delivered two people up to justice. They were the first secretary of the Bokhara regional committee, Abduvakhid Karimov, popularly known as 'the Emir of Bokhara', and the Minister for Internal Affairs of the Republic, Kudrat Ergashev.

By the way, Karimov at that time had already lost his job as first secretary: in an attempt to save the 'Emir', Usmankhodzhaev transferred him to work in Tashkent – as the deputy to the Minister of Water Management and Improvement. Karimov decided to celebrate his appointment at a government dacha – in the mountains by a lake, 400 kilometres from the capital. He took with him a double set of security men – his personal bodyguard and a government squad to protect him against any eventuality. A delicious pilaf, expensive brandy and the caresses of professional beauties – the traditional accessories of pleasure – lasted until 3 o'clock in the morning. The group of investigators led by Nikolai Ivanov lay waiting in ambush. The time came to go into action.

Showing the guard a false identity document, one of the detectives brusquely announced: 'Personal delivery from Tashkent,' and went on through the park up to the house. The other waited with the guard complaining about the unhappy lot of an official courier, never left in peace even at night. The indoor guard was in a drunken sleep – a character straight out of *Treasure Island*, but exemplifying the squalid present-day reality on the opposite side of the planet to Stevenson's creation. Roused with difficulty, the guard said to Karimov through the bedroom door: 'Comrade Deputy Minister, a personal delivery has come for you from Tashkent.' The door opened a crack, a naked arm was stretched through it; 'Hand it over then,' said a voice from within. Instantly the handcuffs were fastened to his wrist. They managed to get the prisoner out through the gates of the property in the dark and bundled him into the car. The stupid guard at the gate, belatedly aware that something was going on, remembered the number of the car and raised the alarm. But the investigators had thought of that and changed the number-plates at the first turn in the road. And they did not head for the airport, but turned in the opposite direction, to a clearing where a helicopter was waiting for them.

Five days later, hearing of Karimov's arrest and not even knowing that the order had been signed for his own arrest, Kudrat Ergashev, the Minister for Internal Affairs, committed suicide. Whereupon one after the other, the erstwhile masters of the republic who had exercised untrammelled power over the fates of millions began to pay for this with their lives. The corpse of Ergashev's First Deputy, Colonel Gennadi Davydov, was found in a hospital bed with three bullet wounds in his head: this was described as suicide. A few seconds before his arrest, the first secretary of one of the regional party committees, Rais Gaipov, plunged a kitchen knife into his heart. Immediately afterwards, his son, pilot commander of the Tashkent division of Aeroflot, brought to the Prosecutor's office half a million roubles and a chest full of gold rings and bracelets. Incidentally, this did not save him from being arrested himself.

The valuables discovered in the caches of the party and state bosses far exceeded the standard hitherto known in the annals of Soviet criminology. Taken alone, the 'Emir of Bokhara' was discovered to have more than 100 kilos of gold, more than 5,000 gold coins of Imperial mint, about 12,000 items of diamond-encrusted jewellery, five cars, eleven television sets, twenty stereo systems, hundreds of expensive furs, tableware and tea-sets, chandeliers, coats, leather jackets, not to mention such minor items as a million roubles in cash. Even the fairy-tale estimate by the court of the bribes which must have been received by Karimov – almost two million roubles – barely covered what was actually discovered in his possession, although it was undoubtedly the case that he must have had to pass on by far the greatest part of what he received in turn in the form of bribes to more powerful and important people both in Tashkent and in Moscow. It is equally beyond dispute that not all of their hoard was recovered from any of the high-ranking mafia executives: a large part remained untouched, guaranteeing not only a prosperous life for members of their families but also leniency from the court, amnesty, early release from prison and special conditions during whatever sentence they actually served.

It would take a whole book merely to list those arrested in Uzbekistan and give a short description of their exploits. They were nearly all members of the party hierarchy, who gave evidence one after another against their colleagues. The whole of the staff of various cabinets of the council of ministers of the republic were transferred to prison and labour camps. In his funeral oration in memory of Rashidov, prime minister Narmakhonmad Khudaiberdyev, following the style of Stalin in his famous eulogy over Lenin's grave, pronounced with a flourish: 'We promise you, Sharaf Rashidov, that we will fulfil your command – we will report to Moscow that we have grown six million tons of cotton.'

They sent in their report, of course, which is available for scrutiny. In return for their report they received cash in full. Not for the cotton, let it be understood, but for the reported cotton. Soon afterwards, Khudaiberdyev was arrested. He and others at the same level of power confessed everything to the investigators, but at his trial he denied everything. The legal consequences of these switches of behaviour were considerable – the moral and social consequences were nil. For the public, the picture was laid out for all to see; however much they denied it at the trial and whatever the fate of any particular accused, the truth was incontrovertible: a cancerous mafia growth permeated the whole republic from top to bottom, spreading incurable paralysis through the whole body and reaching its very heart and head – the Kremlin.

The uncovering of the Uzbek mafia evoked a great reaction in the country, but at the top everything was done to stifle it. They were frightened by the penetration of the rot which had been revealed. The extent of that rot was suddenly grasped and – more important – the connections with the very top names in the party who, at least up till then, had remained uncompromised and untainted.

The first sign of Kremlin displeasure – displeasure, that is, at the extent of the investigation into the Uzbek mafia – was a year and a half's delay, a breathing-space granted to Yuri Churbanov – and this at a time of 'glasnost' and 'perestroika'! There was already plentiful evidence of his personal and, moreover, active participation in the doings of the Uzbek mafia, his direct link with Rashidov and everyone else at the top of the Uzbek hierarchy. Brezhnev, Chernenko and Shcholokov were already dead, his closest friends, drinking cronies and fellow patrons of massage parlours had already been deprived of all real power. Already rumours had spread widely about his arrest – whereas he was still at his desk as a deputy to the Minister of Internal Affairs. True, not the first deputy, but one of seven. Nonetheless, he was a deputy. True, they took away from him the command of internal troops, and all his concrete responsibilities, whatever they were. He became deputy minister for God knows what questions. And so he hung on . . . and on . . .

The fact is that to this day, *to this very day*, just as under Stalin and all his successors, not a single important person can be subject to any legal sanctions without the agreement of Old Square (where the Central Committee of the party is situated), still less a candidate member of the Central Committee, which Churbanov still remained. Still less a near relative of the late General Secretary. This rule was not written down anywhere, but it is followed without fail. The investigators and prosecutors awaited the agreement of the Politburo to Churbanov's arrest for nearly eighteen months! It is easy to imagine how much money and valuables he managed to salt away in that time. Even easier – how witnesses were prepared, how accomplices were persuaded about their forthcoming evidence to the investigators and at the trial. The most important question is: who precisely did save Churbanov and why? He was of no use to anyone any more. Perhaps up there at the top, they wanted him to follow the example of Shcholokov and put the double barrel to his own skull! But they knew he would never do that: he was a mummy's boy, as the old saying has it. They had to save him.

Why? First, they did not want to create a precedent: no Soviet bureaucrat of that level had ever been in court before, for criminal as opposed to political charges. To the extent that practically everyone remaining in power was involved to a greater or lesser extent in illegal activities, they wanted to avoid that particular finale. Maybe it wouldn't be right away, but at some future point they knew that the same fate awaited them. And that kind of future is not a pretty thing for anyone to contemplate.

Secondly, and I think this is the most important, those at the top had a pretty clear idea of how much Churbanov and the others involved with him knew in general about party corruption. The investigation and any subsequent trial, however it might be staged, however it might be prepared, was to a certain extent out of their control. One stone moved drags another behind it and no one could really predict the consequences. While this arm-wrestling was going on in the great offices of state, Churbanov was meekly awaiting the outcome of the investigation, certain that he would not be allowed to fall. Once during this period I spoke to him on the telephone. Someone had come to me with a complaint about the disorganization in the Saratov fire brigade, a discontented lieutenant in the MVD, and I, for a laugh, decided to refer him to Churbanov. It is easy to imagine what this effrontery would have cost me in other – quite recent – times, but on this occasion the minister, bored by having nothing to do, agreed to a meeting of unthinkable lavishness for a Soviet functionary. With tea, cakes, sweets – it went on for three hours! I do not know what on earth they talked about, but I immediately received a rapturous letter from the lieutenant: this 'heart-to-heart', he wrote to say, he would never forget 'to his dying day'.

Churbanov also reacted: he rang me himself to thank me for his 'interesting visitor' and asked me to send him any more people who needed help, saying I was not to stand on ceremony, as if nothing had ever taken place between us ... I had had occasion to call on him in the past, whether 'on ceremony' or not! I asked him how things were, how he was feeling. He replied that things were not bad, but that he was soon to be transferred to another management job. This could be interpreted as black humour, except that he had absolutely no sense of humour whatever. He spoke in a bleak, dry businesslike way and then I thought that his call was no accident: evidently, he wanted the word to go round Moscow that everything was okay with him, he was as strong as ever, his friends were not going to allow him to be disgraced, so people were not to bury him prematurely and those who were trying to do so should hold their tongues. This seemed to me the reason for his call. I had nothing in common with him and was certainly not wont to gossip on the phone with him.

Some time afterwards, however, he was arrested and an announcement of the charges against him was printed in the newspapers. The sum he was accused of taking in bribes melted away before one's very eyes. Each fresh newspaper announcement mentioned a smaller sum than the last. Running ahead of my story, I will say that towards the end of the court case the amount had become absolutely trivial – 90,000 roubles instead of the 600,000 announced four months earlier; the rest could not be *proved*. It would be wrong to imagine that the purpose of this reduction in the sum was to save Churbanov himself: the real measure of punishment (he was sentenced to twelve years) could not be affected one year more or less – either way could not have had great significance. No, the purpose was quite different: to narrow down as far as possible the circle of people involved in his doings, to confirm beyond doubt the seriousness of purpose of those who had been negotiating with him all those months, promising not to extend the affair and to minimize his sentence in exchange for a promise of silence. That such trading went on with some result is beyond doubt.

Towards late August–early September 1988 I was spending a short holiday in a little Bulgarian seaside village not far from the Turkish border. It seemed to me that I had succeeded in cutting myself off from the everyday treadmill of newspaper worries: it was nearly a kilometre to the nearest telephone. But no, they managed to track me down even there! The deputy chief editor asked me to return to Moscow as quickly as possible: it was Friday evening and at 9 o'clock on the Monday morning the long-awaited trial was to begin, at which the list of charges would be announced. In the dock were Yuri Churbanov and the previous Minister of Internal Affairs of Uzbekistan, Shcholokov's appointee Khaidar Yakhyaev, whom

Rashidov had managed to replace with his own man, Kudrat Erga-shev.

'It's a unique opportunity,' the distant voice of the deputy chief editor sounded down the telephone, 'and we've got hold of a pass for you to attend the trial. It opens at nine and at noon your first copy should be on my desk. We are going to run a piece on it in every issue until the end of the trial. Do everything possible or impossible – fly back at once.'

I had no 'possible' alternatives to hand: all the tickets on the only plane were sold up to the end of September. I did the 'impossible': the pilots took me on board, putting me in an air-hostess's seat. 'This chap is going to write up the Churbanov trial in the new-spaper' – these words were my entrée to the plane. The whole country was awaiting the trial with impatience. On Monday morning I was at the Supreme Court. At midday, as agreed, my copy about the opening of the trial was on the editor's desk. But the editor did not even bother to read it. He passed me a paper which had just come over the wire – the 'Tassovka', as the Tass teletape is called in Soviet slang. To begin with, it listed the papers and magazines to which it was circulated: there was no need, in my view, for this list since every central and regional newspaper in the USSR was included in it. The notice itself, though, was quite short: the afore-mentioned organs were categorically forbidden to publish so much as a line about the Churbanov affair except the official information over which Tass had monopoly rights. There was no signature under this order – unique even before the era of glasnost. There was no signature, but its tone did not leave any room for doubt: it was impossible to disobey, the order came from the very top. To disobey would have been unthinkable even for a daring editor, if such a one could have been found: the censor would simply have blocked any report.

One editor alone, I must add in parenthesis, decided on a sur-prisingly bold step. Yegor Yakovlev, the editor-in-chief of *Moscow News*, made use of a mistake in the Tassovka. Because his newspaper was not named in it, he published an article by Viktor Loshak accompanied by three photographs. An unbelievable scandal erupted: Yakovlev lived for many days in fear and trembling, await-ing his enforced retirement. On Old Square, Yakovlev was blamed for 'bad faith' and wilful disobedience because the Tassovka had only mentioned 'Novosti' (which publishes *Moscow News*, which of course meant that the ban extended to all the papers published under the auspices of that agency. But the conflict did not arise because of niggling legalities – all the more, since in the published article there was not a single word going beyond the bounds of the official Tass communiqué. The issue was one of principle: would the reports in the papers be a carefully doctored, anodyne, selected version of the facts or, giving the newspapers their heads, could any surprises be anticipated from them? Yegor Yakovlev, supported by Alexander Yakovlev, stood his ground and insisted, the conflict was resolved but there was nothing more about the trial in *Moscow News* or in any of the other papers except the identical Tass communiqué which appeared throughout the Soviet press.

I went back to the Supreme Court for the start of the afternoon sitting: my pass which I had obtained that morning was valid for me to get back in. But things had changed! My long-time friend and colleague, an employee of the Supreme Court, was waiting for me out on the street. He begged me: 'For God's sake, don't drop me in it, don't go in! We've had our orders not to let any journalists in.' 'Can a mere observer go in?' 'A mere observer can. By special permission.' 'Will you let me in then?' 'You've taken leave of your senses! Everyone knows you by sight. Do you want to get me into trouble?'

Of course I did not want to get him into trouble. But I did want very much to find out what sort of madness had suddenly seized the Kremlin.

Who had panicked in there? Why these hysterics? What – and who – were they afraid of? The secret was not to be discovered that day or the next. It was Yegor Ligachev who had given the orders to clamp down on glasnost. He was then the second-in-command in the party and in the country. The head of state was in the Crimea: Gorbachev was spending his holidays there. If he had been in Moscow, he would hardly have been likely to pick a quarrel with his second-in-command. He did not act, as we know, in even more serious cases.

Simple logic yields a simple and more obvious explanation of this scandalous act: Ligachev himself had a direct connection with that all-embracing net of corrupt officials in the higher ranks and, making use of his still unshaken position at the top of the party, was trying to save himself rather than his accomplices. He was afraid: something would suddenly be said, suddenly his name would ring out unexpectedly in the courtroom and then anything could happen . . .

There were well-known grounds for this explanation of the sudden clampdown on reporting the case, which I heard more than once in various Moscow salons. For example, one of the 'secrets' of the ongoing investigation into the other bosses of the Uzbek mafia had come out and was spreading: the man who had taken over Rashidov's top post as First Secretary of the Central Committee of the Communist Party of Uzbekistan, but who had moved straight from his luxurious party office to a prison cell – Inamzhon Usmankhodzhaev – had given evidence that he personally had given Ligachev 60,000 roubles in the form of a bribe.*

Meanwhile, as often happens with rumours arising from an absence of reliable information, the reason here was confused with the consequence, the chronology was destroyed. Usmankhodzhaev did indeed give such evidence. Not to the investigation, but to the prosecutor, to the deputy Chief Prosecutor of the USSR, Vasiliev. And not before, but *after* Ligachev had, with rough lack of ceremony, and abusing his power, attempted to muzzle the press and the journalists.

Usmankhodzhaev gave this evidence on 26 October 1988, nearly two months after the Supreme Court had begun to hear the Churbanov case. It was precisely then that Usmankhodzhaev named the names of highly-placed bribe-takers, a bouquet that would make any lawyer's head reel if he were leading the investigation, and take his breath away: Ligachev, Romanov†, Solomontsev‡, Kapitonov§,

---

* I must confess that I do not place much credence in this accusation. To begin with, Usmankhodzhaev revealed that, since he hoped to take Rashidov's place after his death and counted on Ligachev's help, he had given the latter a valuable 500-year-old carpet. These confessions were recorded in the protocol. But then it became clear that such a unique museum piece must have a history. Where did this carpet come from? Where was it kept previously? How did it fall into Usmankhodzhaev's hands? Without giving the matter further thought, the inquiry changed the carpet into 60,000 roubles, as if given in two instalments – that was more understandable, normal and simple.

† Grigóri Romanov: until 1985 a member of the Politburo, for many years First Secretary of the Leningrad regional committee, then secretary of the Central Committee, in league with Viktor Grishin leader of the 'hawks' who opposed the election of Gorbachev to the post of General Secretary after Brezhnev's death.

‡ Mikhail Solomontsev: member of the Politburo, chairman of the Committee for Party Control.

§ Ivan Kapitonov: secretary of the Central Committee, then chairman of the Central Inspectorate of the Central Committee.

Rekunkov, Soroka*, Terebilov† – in all, seventeen figures of the very highest party rank.

To what extent these accusations were well-founded and what really lay behind them I will come to later. Now, it is necessary to understand that it was not these accusations which led Ligachev to do what he did. However, his undoubted personal interest in the maximum stifling of glasnost arose from a different concern. At any price, it was necessary to limit the circle of 'victims' of justice. Any extension of that circle could affect those who were numbered among 'his' men. Some had been promoted to managerial status by Ligachev himself, either as head of appointments at the Central Committee or using his position as number two in the hierarchy. Others, having obtained important posts even without Ligachev's direct intervention, were kindred spirits, making up that powerful clan of apparatchiks who were clinging to their posts for dear life, sensing that perestroika was beginning to dislodge them. It would have been sufficient for their names to be mentioned once in the course of the trial – they would immediately have appeared in the press and the future fate of those 'touched' in this way would have drifted out of strict control from Ligachev's point of view. The protection of 'his' men in the naked confrontation between reactionary and democratic forces in the increased struggle for power – that was what was behind it all.

And of course there was another reason why Ligachev was obstructing the increasingly inquisitive press. In official language, this was an attempt to protect the party from being compromised by slander of its leading cadres. In this connection, I am reminded of an anecdote which enjoyed currency in those years. The secretary of the area committee rings the chairman of a collective farm:

'Listen, Ivan. Some American journalists will soon be arriving at your place. I hope you won't even think of showing them everything.'

'They've already been and gone about an hour ago.'

The area secretary says, horrified: 'You mean you showed them the cattle shed where the cows are dying from hunger?'

---

* Oleg Soroka: at that time deputy to the Chief Prosecutor of the USSR, an official of the investigation division.
† Vladimir Terebilov: at that time chairman of the Supreme Court of the USSR.

'Yes.'

'And the hospital where the roof is leaking and the walls are falling down?'

'Yes.'

'And the school where there are rats running everywhere?'

'Yes.'

'You must be out of your mind – they'll write it all up in their newspapers.'

'Yes, isn't it a shame,' replies Ivan. 'They'll be telling their malicious lies again!'

But in fact there was an agreement: in return for silence and 'sensible' behaviour in court, sentences would be lighter or maybe commuted to a discharge. Having very publicly sealed the journalists' mouths, the powers behind the scenes had convincingly demonstrated: 'Our promises are not empty words, the "other side" is keeping its promises . . . '

When the trial came to an end on the threshold of the New Year, and the judge, Major General Mikhail Marov, pronounced the sentence, people even slightly in the know – on the inside track of the legal 'kitchen' – glanced knowingly at each other. The former deputy Minister of Internal Affairs of Uzbekistan, Petr Begelman, who had not entered into a secret agreement behind the scenes and had confirmed his evidence in court about a dacha and bribe-taking, was sentenced to a harsher punishment than those who behaved 'sensibly' at the trial and denied everything. But most surprising of all was that the second most important defendant at the trial, Khaidar Yakhyaev, was allowed home from prison to see in the New Year among his family and friends. The press, which for four months had not had the right to report on the progress of the trial except for the unconvincing Tass bulletins, now had to explain this mysterious happening to many millions of readers. But can the inexplicable be explained?

I said that Yakhyaev was the second in importance among the accused at this trial, but I am not sure that he deserves this position. Or, more accurately, I am sure that he was not the second most important.

Of course Churbanov was a striking figure, even if only because he was the scandalously notorious son-in-law of Brezhnev. He was a man with an almost music-hall career: for instance, his being

awarded – albeit secretly! – the State Prize for 'exemplary organization of public order in Moscow during the Olympic Games'. But
in reality, judging by the place which he occupied and the role which
he played in the mafia network, Churbanov was a small-time, even
insignificant figure. His position – not as a deputy to a minister but
as a member of the first family – allowed him to bluff, creating the
illusion that he was really capable of doing something: appointing
people, promoting people, helping people. And they brought him
gifts which hardly dented the mafia's budget. Even if they didn't
look to him for particular help, they could rely on him not to interfere
with their activity. Nor did he.

But a genuinely powerful figure in this trial was the man apparently
overshadowed by the 'brilliant' Churbanov, Lieutenant General
Khaidar Yakhyaev.*

Vladimir Oleinik† one of the best Soviet investigators, knows the
real power structure in the mafia hierarchy and confirms that it was
precisely Yakhyaev who helped establish the 'Rashidovshchina',
creating in Uzbekistan a system of hounding and ruthless punishment of all who got in the way of mafia business. At the end of
the day, he turned out to be as powerful as he had become dangerous
to those who had relied on him to work for them and protect them.
And Rashidov had replaced him with someone who was absolutely
'his' man, namely Ergashev.

But these intrigues common to mafia groups everywhere are of no
interest to us. Their outcome is. Churbanov, whose charges had been
reduced both in scale and number, was nevertheless sent down for
twelve years. But Yakhyaev, who had received no diminution and
had been blamed, stigmatized and come under the fire of many a
procuratorial phillipic, was allowed home happily under the pretext
of a series of procedural errors in the course of the investigation.
Thus we found out who occupied what effective position in the mafia
hierarchy, to whom the mafia were indebted and whom the mafia,

---

* A curious detail which might amuse the reader: this general, not wishing to lag behind the
'successful prose writer' Rashidov, decided to become an 'outstanding poet' and published
six collections of 'his' poems. At his trial he boasted that a copy of one of these collections
was in the library of the University of Illinois, USA.
† Because he was the best and because he knew too much too well, Oleinik was removed from
the procuracy 'at his own request' and taken off investigative work. In the capacity of a 'retired
examining judge' he was elected a people's deputy of the Russian Federation for one of the
Moscow constituencies.

dutifully fulfilling their obligations, were protecting.

This leads to the thought that the secret disposition of forces within the Soviet mafia has not yet been revealed. We are possibly nowhere near disclosing these secrets. In *Pravda* there was a down-the-page mention that in those infamous October days when Churbanov was gracing Tashkent with his presence, and while I was peacefully dining with him in the 'special room', he and Rashidov were discussing a most important question: how to help a certain small-time pub-keeper who had fallen into the hands of the militia. In *Pravda* this fact was recorded as if it were an unimportant detail, evidence perhaps of the depths to which such important figures had fallen.

But in fact, this piece of information tells us something quite different: that the arrested bar-owner was someone special, whereas Rashidov and Churbanov were small fry who, in underworld slang, were at best 'holding the ladder'.

The following comment by a Soviet academic lawyer may not be far from the paradoxical truth:

'It is not impossible that this pub-owner was a minister in an illegal cabinet, whereas Churbanov and Rashidov were effectively just his security men.' That is, they belonged to those whose official position in society enabled them (and that was their main responsibility within the mafia system) to protect and guarantee the inviolability of the real bosses whose positions and names and functions are unknown to us. It wasn't the 'Rashidovites' or the 'Churbanovites' who appointed the pub-owners to real ministerial posts (i.e. those carrying real power) but the pub-owners who elevated and demoted the party–state bosses.

I do not think this is a paradox, a fantasy or even an exaggeration. If according to official data alone, the so-called black economy is worth 150–200 billion roubles (in the opinion of the most competent Soviet economists this sum should really be 400 billion), I ask again, which economy, measured in real terms, is the 'shadow' and which the 'real' one? Whoever has the real money has the real power.

An incidental proof of this hypothesis is provided not so much by these logical deductions but by obvious facts which are available to everyone. Is it any accident that the very worst and, in everyone's opinion, absolutely most powerful figure in this clan, known to everyone in Uzbekistan as 'Godfather' – Akhmadzhan Adylov – has been awaiting trial for over six years in a prison cell and the end of his custody is still nowhere in sight? Even if he were brought to trial at the moment this book appears (which is extremely unlikely) a fact remains a fact: under the noses of the whole country the mafia has done everything it could to save its 'prime minister' (even a minor part of Adylov's crimes accepted as proven by the court would normally carry only one possible sentence – the death penalty) and not allow the leakage of undesired information about the members of the 'shadow cabinet' remaining at liberty, which would be perfectly possible in the circumstances of a public trial.

Although he was director general of an agricultural production combine in the Namagansky district, deputy of the Supreme Soviet of the USSR, a member of the Central Committee of the Uzbek Communist Party and a Hero of Socialist Labour – despite all this, Akhmadzhan Adylov still wielded no administrative or political power de jure. But, de facto, he possessed more power than anyone else in Uzbekistan. Anyone Rashidov might consider appointing to any significant position had to appear in person before Adylov and obtain his consent. Most often, Rashidov did not even get to seek Adylov's consent: Adylov himself simply 'recommended' his own candidate to Rashidov. A 'recommendation' meant a command.

One of Adylov's 'nomenklatura' – the president of a district committee of people's control – once dared to disobey Adylov and was instantly (instantly!) brutally murdered, not in any figurative sense but literally: with staves and knives by Adylov himself and his colleague, the first secretary of the area committee of the party, Sitdikov. But the mafia, as is well known, are not keen on witnesses. For his convenience brother Adylov gave Sitdikov a gun: a pretty transparent hint which Sitdikov did not understand. Several days later, he was found with a bullet hole in his brain. Beside him lay the gun . . .

Another party worker – Buriev – called in comrades from Moscow to help him against Adylov: from the MVD and the KGB. The comrades immediately notified Adylov. That night the 'traitor' was taken away into the desert and brutally murdered. A member of the Supreme Court was present at the execution, appointed so to be by the mafia. The same judge several months earlier had sentenced Buriev on a trumped-up charge: well aware with whom he was dealing, Buriev preferred to accept his sentence silently than be smothered in his prison cell.

In order to become the chairman of the Presidium of the Supreme Soviet and therefore also the First Secretary of the party of Uzbekistan, Usmankhodzhaev had to obtain Adylov's backing. For this, they gave him a 'qualifying test' – to deal out summary justice to one of the 'turncoats'. But Usmankhodzhaev could not face the prospect. He begged for forgiveness on his knees, licking Adylov's boots ('licking Adylov's boots' in this case not being a metaphor but a precise description of his actions).

He had begged forgiveness, and Adylov believed that in so doing he had become his bondsman and creature: but anybody being appointed to such a post depended (and depends) on many people. Not only and not so much in the capital of the republic, but primarily in Moscow. As Usmankhodzhaev and Adylov themselves admitted, this cost them millions of roubles. Where did this money go? Brezhnev and Suslov (at a minimum) must have been involved, and Chernenko, Andropov and others would have had to sign under the word 'agreed'. One of them must have been acting not purely in good faith: why pay millions to those lower down the pecking order if all the people at the top had agreed to everything on a disinterested basis?

Of course in many of Adylov's actions it is all too easy to see traces of pure Oriental sadism and despotism. The same sort of thing happens in Russia without the licking of boots or the smashing of skulls. The Medunov mafia, although no less cruel in itself, would probably never have dreamed of creating, as Adylov did, an underground prison for insubordinate minions and other offenders. Nor would they have organized methods of torture which Adylov himself called 'the Karbyshev treatment', whereby people would be tied naked and half-dead with cold to a stake and sprayed with icy water in sub-zero temperatures. This was the punishment meted out in a World War II German prison camp to the captured Soviet General Professor Dmitri Karbyshev, who froze to death as a result. Here it is not the individual striking details which are important – they can hardly shock readers who have had their fill of the bestialities committed in Cambodia, Afghanistan or Uganda. Rather, it is those hidden mechanisms which are used by the mafia at the highest levels of the party hierarchy to gain power and to establish its members in key positions. Boris Svidersky, who was in charge of the investigation into the Adylov affair, stated in one of his interviews: 'Adylov and his group had been placing their people in key posts for more than twenty years. The majority of them continue today to occupy leading positions in various branches of the state apparatus. It is in their interests to frustrate the investigation.'

It is obvious from these few laconic words that such influential people are interfering with the uncovering of crimes and that even now the investigators dare not say their names aloud. Moreover, it is known without a shadow of doubt that among such people there are prominent journalists holding high posts in the media. Adylov had links not only to Moscow but also to the Baltic states and Siberia. His close personal acquaintance with Brezhnev and Suslov is well known. There is direct as well as circumstantial proof that Adylov's wealth comprises several tens of millions of roubles both in valuables and in banknotes. All they found was a few hundred thousand. The remainder continues to be in use, providing support and security for the unsinkable mafia. Therefore who is it actually running the country, not on stage but behind the scenes? This question is by no means rhetorical. It requires an answer. But whether we shall get one I rather doubt. Meanwhile (guided by worthy and unassailable concepts such as the presumption of innocence, the inadmissibility of a priori deductions or prejudice and that the benefit of the doubt should always be given to the accused – what wonderful concepts, who could quarrel with them?), one after another the leading figures of Uzbekistan are being released from detention and removed from investigation. These people are Rashidov's closest circle of friends and colleagues, such as the former Central Committee secretaries Timofei Osetrov, Rano Abdulaeva (whose case reached court, but a verdict of not guilty was returned by the Supreme Court), the chairman of the Presidium of the Supreme Soviet of Uzbekistan, Yagdar Nasriddinova, and many others.

What have we here? The triumph of justice or the workings of a mafia? Time alone will tell.

Chapter Seven

Royal Hunts

It was 1986. Gorbachev's perestroika was just beginning to get under way. In Uzbekistan the investigation into the cotton affair was in full swing. The KGB had handed over to the prosecution service all the information in its possession about the extraordinary fiddling of inflated statistics and more and more confirmation of this information was being turned up by the team of investigators sent from Moscow, headed by the Senior Examining Judge in the Chief Prosecutor's department, Vladimir Kalinichenko. The whole exercise was expanding and drawing the topmost officials into its web.

At the height of the investigation, which looked like running for many years, came a phone call from the Chief Prosecutor himself. Alexander Rekunkov was recalling Kalinichenko urgently to Moscow. There he was given a new assignment of extreme state importance, namely to go to the Kazakhstan republic, Uzbekistan's neighbour, in order to help its leaders unmask corruption in high places.

An experienced investigator like Kalinichenko should have immediately sensed that there was something strange and dubious about this unexpected and superficially attractive offer. He did confess to me later that he had not immediately felt this. He was long accustomed to his superiors' impulsive and illogical decisions. The illogicality of the assignment was the only thing that struck him at the time. Why on earth take someone off an incomplete case and throw him onto another, even if equally important, case?

But it soon became clear, on the contrary, that the decision was entirely logical and carefully thought-out. It was evidence of the fact that the mafia was being advised by experienced, intelligent professionals capable of calculating cause and effect. It is well known that breaking the rhythm always leads to a slowdown. Thus, even if not starting from scratch, a new investigative team would need to work its way into a case in unfamiliar surroundings. The Uzbek mafia had gained a breathing space. Kalinichenko had been seen by them as the most experienced, indefatigable and incorruptible Moscow investigator – Moscow would be hard put to come up with another like him. At that stage, his replacement in Tashkent, Telman Gdlyan, was an unknown quantity. Who could have foreseen that the new Uzbek bosses who came after Rashidov would soon be weeping bitter tears having ended up, contrary to their predictions, with someone cruelly determined to exact the 'people's vengeance'?

Kalinichenko's transfer had been engineered by Brezhnev's friend and favourite, Dinmukhamed Kunaev, a member of the Politburo of the Central Committee and first secretary of the party in Kazakhstan. Kunaev could reckon that the operation had been a success and that he had outwitted his enemies. He had realized in good time that it was no good waiting passively for his gigantic republic to come under the attentions of the Moscow Pinkertons, so he had seized the initiative and started to lead the campaign against corruption in his republic. Attack is the best form of defence!

So he had asked the Chief Prosecutor to help him deal with the mafia by sending for this purpose 'his best investigator, Comrade Kalinichenko'. What Chief Prosecutor could refuse such a request, coming as it did from a member of the Politburo? If the Communist Party, even now after all the changes the world knows about, should remain a real leading force, then we should not forget what it was like in 1986. Not only had Kunaev not yet been overthrown, but he remained at the top, an all-powerful and unsinkable member of the leadership. That was the situation when Kalinichenko arrived in Alma-Ata, the Kazakhstan capital, in order to carry out his 'personal assignment' from the Politburo member and first secretary of the Central Committee of the Communist Party of the republic.

Kalinichenko very quickly began to rumble the Kazakh führer's crafty designs. Kunaev himself would determine which groups of people might be involved in corruption, and those regions where corruption was flourishing. His attention focussed constantly on the town of Karaganda and on the Karaganda district. Even if there were people in the republic's capital, Alma-Ata, who were suspected of corruption, they all somehow turned out to be natives of Karaganda and neighbouring districts.

It is hard to grasp the reality of these interregional conflicts if one is a stranger to the local Kazakh customs and to what life is really like in those immense spaces unknown to the outside world (Kazakhstan covers almost the same land area as does Europe – excluding European Russia). The fact is that the top leadership, behind its firm façade of monolithic unity, is torn apart by power struggles. In Kazakhstan there is practically a state of war between two groups of 'fellow-countrymen'. By birth Kunaev himself comes from the district around the capital, Alma-Ata, as do all those in the topmost jobs, consisting of absolutely reliable people. Additionally, the members of the ruling class are bound by family ties, ranging from the very close to the more distant; these are not simple for an outsider to unravel. In this respect, no problem is presented by Kunaev's younger brother, Askar, whom Kunaev had appointed academician twice over – at Union and republic level – and President of the Kazakhstan Academy of Sciences, which enabled him to exercise total sway over every scientist in the republic. The whole Kazakh intelligentsia despised this alcoholic dullard. Nor is any research needed to point to Askarov, the first secretary of the Chimkent district, since his child married Kunaev's. Such connections are the obvious ones. But there were also unseen ties, such as school, university and neighbourhood connections, and the whole republic was entangled in them.

When, as Gorbachev came to power, Kunaev's throne was rocked, if only slightly to begin with, a Kazakh 'opposition' materialized which in name alone stood against the Kunaev clan on the basis of some unspecified points of principle. In reality, however, this was a group simply fighting to take power. This challenge to the Kunaevites came from the Karaganda group headed by Nursultan Nazarbaev, formerly a secretary of the Karaganda district party committee, who had already in Brezhnev's day managed, as a result of inter-clan discussions, to have himself appointed a secretary of the central committee of the Kazakhstan Communist Party. Brezhnev was giving his whole-hearted support to Kunaev, but completely to cut the others out would have meant sharpening internal conflict and Moscow was not ready for this.

Being twenty-eight years Kunaev's junior, Nazarbaev on grounds of age at least had a big advantage over the decrepit 'father of the nation'. The ambitions of Nazarbaev's associates to get appointments which would open the way for them to acquire unlimited power pushed him into taking active and decisive steps. For him it must have seemed now or never, because he took the bold step, almost unthinkable in those early stages of perestroika, of openly criticizing Comrade Kunaev himself at the republic's Communist Party Congress.

Comrade Kunaev, being no fool, realized that Gorbachev was behind Nazarbaev and that the gauntlet had been thrown down. The 'opposition' would now have no other aim than to overthrow him as speedily as possible. How would he counter Nazarbaev and his friends? 'Ideological' struggle? Argumentation? Parliamentary debate? Even if he had been in possession of some concrete facts he was absolutely sure of one thing: the Karagandaites were just as involved in mafia crimes as the representatives of any other region of Kazakhstan. Everybody knew pretty well everything about each other, but in accordance with unwritten mafia rules one gives no sign of this until somebody first puts down a challenge.

As the Karagandaites had now done this, it was possible for the Kunaevites to deliver a counterblow. It was all the more palpable because Kunaev had reliable if not detailed knowledge of one of the Karaganda mafia's most cynical and audacious operations. It was in order to deliver this counterblow that he had called for the services of Kalinichenko. It was a brilliant plan and, as will be demonstrated, it can be said to have succeeded.

Anatoly Karavaev, the Minister of Road Transport of Kazakhstan, was a native of Karaganda. Moreover, he was a Russian, not a Kazakh. That was enough to make him something of an outsider, or at least someone whose fate need not be the cause of the slightest concern to Kunaev, when pointing the newly-arrived Kalinichenko in the direction of Karavaev's mafia clan. Of its existence there is no doubt whatever; the only uncertainty is whether it was Karavaev or somebody else who was head of it. In betraying a by-no-means innocent but still key participant in it, Kunaev had diverted the investigation away from the main personalities. And at the same time, they had struck a blow at their most dangerous rivals.

There was an absurd simplicity about the main source of the

Karanganda mafia's income. In such an enormous territory the towns and settlements are separated by great distances and there are practically no means of transport between them. There are light aviation facilities in one or two areas and the railway network is antiquated by Western standards. In practice, the only means of communication are the intercity buses, and they are the monopoly of a single passenger organization.

Passengers would be willing to pay anything for a ticket but that way of profiteering would carry the risk of exposure: some stickler for the regulations would be bound to inform about it. The mafiosi knew better. Rather than taking a single extra kopek from the passengers, 75 or 80 per cent of them after paying their fare on the bus would simply not be given a ticket. All the ticket inspectors and accountants were in on the swindle, so it was practically impossible to expose this deception. Added to that, all the drivers were in on it. It would not be inappropriate to call this outfit a shareholders' company, Soviet style.

Each 'shareholder' received income in proportion to his input and the more senior people naturally enjoyed larger dividends. Part of the money went on 'presents' to party and administrative bosses in both Karaganda and Alma-Ata. But this modest-sized mafia had no need to do likewise with the Moscow bosses – they were well looked after by bigger fish handling much greater sums. It was precisely to protect the latter that with all party zeal Kunaev deflected the investigators from Alma-Ata at the centre onto the 'disgraceful crooks of Karaganda'.

The team of investigators from Moscow, under instruction and guidance from Kunaev, the Politburo member, pounced with total success on the local drivers and their insignificant managers. The minister, Karavaev, was only needed by Kunaev in order to distract attention and so that the whole affair did not look like taking a sledgehammer to crack a nut.

Nobody could accuse the investigators of pouncing on innocent people. Indeed, the prosecution service was faced with a moral rather than a legal problem. If they had strictly followed the dictates of the law, it would have been necessary to bring several hundred to court – other estimates suggest a figure of up to two thousand – all of whom had demonstrably committed offences, whether minor or major. Apart from purely humanitarian considerations, and an evident fear of an almost inevitable outbreak of mass protest, there were pragmatic aspects to consider: it would be necessary to arrest each and every bus driver in the region. Obviously that was not a course the prosecution could follow. This in turn gave the Kunaev clan the opportunity to accuse the investigators of being 'in the pocket of the mafia'.

Kunaev tried to keep a personal hand on the investigation, channelling it where he wanted and carefully protecting key postholders from exposure. In so far as he was then still a Politburo member and sovereign master of the republic, no matter how honest or impartial the investigators were or however much they wished to be true to their professional calling, they could not in the real conditions of 1986 actually go against Kunaev. Consequently, the mafiosi gained at least six months in which they were able to hide their loot and cover their tracks. The loss of impetus, as explained already, put the prosecution at a disadvantage. Thus Kunaev fulfilled his principal task, which was to protect the central mafia group and their 'winnings' and to deny the investigators the possibility of attacking on a broad front. In Kazakhstan it proved impossible to organize anything on the scale of the 'Uzbek affair'.

Moreover, it had proved possible for the Uzbek mafia to save the greater part of its money and valuables. When they realized in Tashkent that there was a real danger of their being routed, sackfuls of money, gold, jewellery and antiques had been sent over the border into Kazakhstan, where the all-powerful Kunaev was not yet under suspicion and his associates were able to put these countless riches into safe hiding places. Only a small part was later located.

Nevertheless, Kunaev was politically doomed and he could not have been unaware of the fact. Nowadays neither Gorbachev nor the Politburo acting together as one can on their own initiative remove or appoint leaders of republics. However great their powers might previously have been, the final word no longer rests with the Kremlin, nor can Moscow conceivably send down a 'governor'. But in 1986 all that was still possible. Thus Kunaev's elimination by imperial decree from Moscow and the appointment in his place of the Muscovite Gennady Kolbin can be regarded as the final instance of its kind in the history of the Soviet colonial system.

Kolbin was brought to Alma-Ata by Central Committee Secretary Gennady Razumovsky and introduced by him on behalf of Gorbachev to the Kazakh leadership. (Three years earlier when Kolbin was appointed 'governor' of the Ulyanovsk Oblast he was taken there by Yegor Ligachev – these are significant, even if minor, details.)

Kunaev's rout was essential for Gorbachev. This Brezhnevite satrap was openly hostile to Gorbachev and to the policy of perestroika. Wielding enormous power in the republic and having extensive contacts within the party apparatus and beyond, Kunaev was capable of putting a brake on progress and the planned transformations. The central KGB was also well aware of the local mafia structures and of the active participation in them of people close to Kunaev. He in his time as the true 'godfather' enjoyed the fruits of their bountiful generosity.

But Gorbachev failed to take two very important factors into consideration, which, even if they didn't save Kunaev politically, restrained Gorbachev from undertaking a thoroughgoing clear-out, from weeding out some of the top hierarchs in the republic and in its many regions, and from attacking the Kazakh mafia on a broad front without fear or favour. The first of those two factors is common knowledge: the appointment not of a Kazakh but of a Russian to the top position in the republic made it possible for Kunaev and his followers to play on national feeling, to incite it as a principal weapon of opposition to perestroika. There was no other effective weapon immediately to hand. Gorbachev did not realize what genie would be released from the bottle by his blindly following the old-established methods. For the Kunaevites this short-sightedness came as a gift and 17 December 1986 saw the beginning of the disturbances following Kunaev's downfall and his replacement on Moscow's orders by Gorbachev's man, Kolbin. In fact one could say that this day marked the birth of a new political phenomenon – the nationalities problem now shaking the walls of the Soviet empire.

The second factor is closely connected to the first. However, it needs to be examined separately because it applies not just to Kazakhstan but to other Soviet republics. It also helps one to understand the contradictions and complexity of those processes that had been going on for years and years under Brezhnev, leading to the emergence of a host of separate mafias and to the collapse of the Soviet colonial system. A full exposure of this unique Soviet phenomenon (i.e. 'Brezhnevism') must demolish any a priori stereotypically simplistic understanding and disapproval of developments such as the birth and gathering strength of a national mafia network. Enormous sums, unearned and unrelated to any actual trading transactions, were pumped from the central treasury into the treasuries of separate republics. There were not only imaginary crops of Uzbek cotton; there were similar phenomena everywhere – grain, fruit and industrial goods, for example. These money transfers led to the personal enrichment of numbers of smaller mafia groups who would, as has been seen, use much of it for bribery or for presents to people in the central mafia. The process led at the same time to the enrichment of the republics themselves.

It was due to this alone, for example, that Alma-Ata, the Kazakh capital, was transformed under Kunaev from a provincial village into a fine, well-planned city. Whenever I walk along its modern avenues, admiring the architecture of its spacious squares, or the hotels, theatres and art galleries – with a snow-capped mountain panorama as backdrop – I cannot help thinking that virtually the whole thing was done with funds acquired through criminal deception on a grand scale to which both the deceived and the deceivers turned a blind eye. Such was the paradoxical and contradictory situation resulting from the rapid swelling of the mafia abscesses on the body of the state. Taking Kazakhstan alone, this applies not only to the capital city but to many regional centres. Attractive towns were springing up all over the place. Tens and hundreds of thousands of people were getting rich at the expense of the central USSR budget. That is why a significant proportion of the population of Kazakhstan regarded Kunaev as the father of the nation and the people's benefactor.

This process doubtless contributed to centrifugal tendencies and to the rapid growth of nationalist feelings. Total corruption in the republics became a very significant political factor, reinforcing the alienation of the periphery from the centre. Any attempt by the central prosecution service to get to grips with national mafias would run up against the powerful forces in the republics as they expanded politically and economically.

The showering of money, valuables and other gifts on the top people in the state led to these top people pursuing and punishing not the criminals but those who were fighting against criminality. In this Kunaev and his circle were more successful than most.

There was thus the paradoxical situation that the vassals were in fact buying from their imperial masters relative independence and freedom to get rich in return for their guarantee of political loyalty. Then suddenly this arrangement came under threat when the 'father of the nation' was replaced by an 'agent of Moscow'. The powder keg was already charged to the brim. The mafia (both the political and the economic – they had long since merged into a united front) realized that to go along quietly with the decision dictated from the Kremlin would be tantamount to suicide, the more so since the assault on the mafia in neighbouring Uzbekistan was simultaneously in full swing.

There was a third factor which Gorbachev underestimated. One cannot blame him for this. There had, after all, been no precedent in Soviet history, but the very substantial goings-on upon various rungs of the social ladder under Brezhnev, particularly in the union republics, generally remained unknown. Information on this was not supplied to the ruling elite, the phenomenon was not subjected to proper analysis, so no scientifically based forecasts were being made which would provide essential information for any serious politician.

Young people and students are usually the most sensitive and easily roused stratum in society and will easily react to any 'detonator'. In Kazakhstan, particularly in Alma-Ata, the student body consisted almost entirely of mafia protégés – children of apparatchiks and other functionaries, youngsters from families who had managed to get their offspring into institutes of higher education using mafia connections or by massive bribes. A student place, especially one whose final diploma would lead to employment abroad, jumped in price first to 40,000 and soon to 60,000 roubles. Although only a third of the 15-million strong population of the republic is Kazakh, they in fact take up the overwhelming majority of student places. Officially this used to be explained as necessary for the development of skills and ability amongst the indigenous population and for the creation of a Kazakh intelligentsia. The reality behind this decorous smokescreen was the making of an easy path for representatives of influential mafia forces, drawn largely from fellow Kazakhs from outlying regions. The loss of political support for this social stratum deprived them of their career prospects and – worse still – deprived them of their very attendance (which was void from a strictly legal point of view because of their unsuitability) at universities or other institutes of further education. There was every reason for them to fear this. Some time later an academic selection committee established that not a single one of a control group of students, including students of languages, made less than twenty mistakes in the simplest dictation exercise, and that their essays on a theme of their own choosing demonstrated a level of illiteracy and inadequacy in terms of knowledge or learning that one might expect of savages. But these were the people who were destined shortly to become 'top managers'. And one can readily understand how simple it was to get them to rise in defence of the 'father of the nation' on that unusually frosty December day.

If it had been, say, 1989 rather than 1986, the major demonstration that began on Brezhnev (*sic!*) Square in Alma-Ata would have been repeated in all towns in the republic and the 'father of the nation', as the 'godfather', would have been defended by the mafia, which would have risen under the flag of nationalist rebirth against the Russian colonizers' attempt to get at its riches. But in 1986 it was still possible to use military means to put down 'nationalist' outbursts. I put the word in quotation marks because this was in effect a mafia uprising, disguised as nationalism.

This does not mean that those who protested against national humiliation and Moscow's imperial diktat were exclusively members of mafia clans. The great majority of those participating in this genuinely popular uprising were people who were infuriated by the witless, sickening behaviour of those successors of Stalinism and Brezhnevism who cared not a jot for the feelings and interests of a whole people. But in my opinion it is clear that the mafia clans acted as initiators and detonators of the explosion, having immediately sensed that their end was nigh. They set passions raging that had long been waiting to surface.

Four years after the event the Kazakh supreme soviet acknowledged that it had been mistaken in assessing the events of 17 December 1986 as 'nationalist'. It is curious that this reappraisal was carried out under the chairmanship of the president of the republic, Nazarbaev, who in that unforgettable December so stoutly defended Moscow's point of view. So be it – *tempora mutantur et nos mutamos in illes*. The uprising in Alma-Ata was, of course, not a nationalistic one in the Moscow interpretation of the word; it was, I repeat, turned into a noble national cause by those forces who had felt and foreseen the signs of their own impending doom. Thus the author's assessment and that given in 1990 by the Kazakh parliament do not contradict each other.

The crowd's shout of 'Give us a Kazakh, not a Russian!' represented a demand to leave the mafia in peace. The mafia was unable to save Kunaev but, as an organization, came through almost entirely intact. Moscow immediately feared spontaneous nationalist outbreaks and preferred not to stir up a dangerous hornet's nest. For the Kremlin's prestige and the achievement of its immediate purposes it was quite enough to insist on replacing Kunaev with Kolbin.★

Rescuing the mafia may have been Kunaev's greatest achievement. If the anti-mafia campaign had not even begun in other republics such as Armenia, in Kazakhstan it had begun but had come off the rails at the first bend. The defence system, which has yet to be penetrated, worked perfectly.

In 1989, three years after the events on Brezhnev Square, a minor incident took place, which speaks volumes despite its banal simplicity. It needs no interpretation – it can speak for itself.

A local militia criminal investigator, driving his own car, ran over and killed a pedestrian – a perfectly straightforward criminal case. The prosecution service investigator who by law has to deal with such cases suspected that the driver had not only run over the pedestrian on a deserted highway but had also robbed him. This suspicion prompted him to carry out a search of the suspect's home with the possibility of finding there missing items belonging to the victim.

But what they discovered were not his things at all, but more than a hundred hidden files on criminal cases raised against the local mafia both before and after Kunaev's downfall. The local prosecutor

★ Gennady Kolbin, the 'governor general' sent from Moscow, straight away introduced a series of openly populist measures designed to get the population on his side. He started learning the Kazakh language and was soon capable of saying a few sentences to an audience. He had dozens of former Kunaev palaces, residences and hunting lodges transferred to trade unions or converted into medical facilities. But this did not win popularity for Kolbin. He simply could not shake off old party habits. For example, he decided to have a special plane laid on to transfer his family and their personal baggage to Alma-Ata, the cost being charged to party funds. This soon became common knowledge in Alma-Ata and everywhere else in the republic. This might seem a trivial matter, but the decision, apart from being typical, was, in the heated atmosphere then prevailing in Kazakhstan, a stupid one. Kolbin's rule over a foreign land lasted three years.

reported this to the prosecution service headquarters in the republic, and this was duly passed on to Moscow. An investigation was started. In various hiding places they found another ninety or so files tucked away. This led to similar searches all over Kazakhstan. Altogether proceedings had been instituted (and then mysteriously dropped) in more than five thousand cases. Some experts believe this is still an underestimate.

All those involved in criminal abuse of their positions were encouraged in it by the Kunaevites, and as well as being well paid were often rewarded with decorations. Moreover any of their colleagues who tried conscientiously to look into these matters were driven out of the service under any excuse, or were themselves made victims of perverted justice.

The most interesting aspect of this little-talked-about case is its outcome. The revelations should have been sensational enough to lead to the exposure of major figures. However, all that happened was that a few second-rank office-holders were disciplined and that the cases on ten to fifteen minor mafia dealers were reopened. The mafia itself survived, its full strength unimpaired. The invisible conductor of the orchestra was in total control.

All of this does not mean that the Kazakhstan mafia suffered no losses whatever. Things followed the Uzbek model but on a small scale. In order to weaken the Kunaev clan the KGB handed over to the prosecution service part of the information in its files on the activities of the members of the inner circle around the 'leader of the Kazakh nation'. Thus after a few months his assistant, Dyusetai Bekezhanov, was arrested. This man had been the effective ruler of the country, since Kunaev had permitted him to operate on the basis of his own judgement, but using the formula both written and spoken, 'Comrade Kunaev requests your help'. As a result of such requests thousands of people in return for backhanders on an ever-increasing scale jumped the queue for flats (getting one in two to three weeks instead of the usual wait of fifteen to twenty years), jobs, passports for foreign travel, imported video equipment, furniture, clothes, the right to buy a car, plots of land for dachas ... Apart from Bekezhanov, several other close associates of Kunaev were involved in these operations, but Kunaev himself seemed to keep apart from it. His personal signature was never found on any incriminating document. One of the characters in Gogol's timeless

Government Inspector preferred to take bribes in the form of borzoi puppies rather than money, reckoning that a puppy was a harmless present rather than a bribe. No accurate, firm evidence was uncovered as to whether Kunaev received any actual monies, but as for 'borzoi puppies', these came to him in the form of guns. Kunaev was a keen sportsman and an even keener collector of sporting guns. Needless to say he wanted no truck with primitive Soviet-made pieces, but to get expensive foreign makes required foreign exchange. It was quite out of the question to satisfy the 'father's' whim by legal means, but the graft system worked perfectly instead. With the help of bribery one can obtain foreign currency, indeed any heart's desire. Dozens of guns, encrusted with precious stones and metals, were bought for Kunaev in England, Belgium and West Germany, making up a collection of several hundred barrels. At the same time they 'looked after' another keen sportsman – Brezhnev, and thus behind his powerful back the whole operation was well protected. The retinue were not left out of things either: thanks to the principle that it is always cheaper to buy at wholesale rates, valuable guns found their way to Bekezhanov himself and to Kunaev's true and faithful servant, Baiken Ashimov, who served under him as prime minister of the republic.

And the gifts were not only sporting guns. Kunaev's collecting passion applied to anything that was really valuable, even if this half-educated 'academic' (he was supposed to be a mining engineer) had the most vulgar artistic taste. Knowing this, his toadies got him for his birthday a Swiss watch covered in diamonds, buying it in Paris for a sum equal to US $50,000. A Western reader might consider that a paltry sum in relation to somebody of Kunaev's high position, but in the Soviet context totally different parameters apply. To obtain such a sum in foreign currency illegally, one would need an utterly fabulous amount of roubles. To do it legally would cost a fairy-tale fortune in bribes. Apart from that the real value in the USSR of such an item, probably the only one in the country, increases tenfold, if not a hundredfold. Plenty of members of mafia clans are ready, without any ado, to pay any sum for an object so easy to keep safe and guaranteed to retain its value. Thus to relate an object's value to the sale price is to disregard Soviet reality.

The investigators were unable to establish by whom and where the money was procured and the purchase made. But hang on!

Whatever one's respect for those investigating this episode, who can possibly credit such incompetence on their part? The simple explanation is that there was an instruction from Moscow: don't push this one too far, try to keep things cool. But a concrete act of criminality having been documented, guilty parties should have been brought to book, including Kunaev himself. The trail would certainly lead to Moscow, and finally onto whose desk? Moreover, there was then a desperate fear in the Soviet Union of churning over the past, a need to avoid stirring up feelings of vengeance amongst the population.

These, then, were the high-principled concepts that forced the Moscow leadership to shield this personal pensioner of Union status.* An unspoken agreement was reached: Kunaev could continue to live quietly and modestly in his personal palace, away from inquisitive eyes in its densely planted private grounds in the middle of which rises the statue of the occupant. In return this Hero of Socialist Labour (twice over) would keep his mouth shut when the sword of vengeance fell on his closest colleagues. They would act as lightning conductors – or, rather, as sacrificial lambs.

Once during a routine party gathering in Moscow the first lady of Kazakhstan, Mrs Kunaev, was strolling with the first lady of the Magadan district, the wife of the party first secretary. They were discussing a burning topic for both ladies: who had acquired what since they had last seen each other. Lady Magadan taunted Lady Alma-Ata with the news that their district had been supplied from nearby Japan with some amazingly pretty tea services. Lady A was desperate to have one of these. I used to think that at such levels this kind of request would be handled on a simple basis of putting in an order and receiving it through a special delivery service. But no, party etiquette would regard such a straightforward approach as

---

* The caste-ridden 'socialist' society cannot avoid placing people on various rungs of the social ladder, even when they go into 'deserved retirement'. Apart from the ordinary state pensioners there are the so-called 'personal pensioners' who are favoured by the state for past services to it. These in turn are broken down into three classes – respectively personal pensioners of the state, of the republic or of the district. On this latter classification depends not only the amount of pension paid but a whole range of other benefits on offer. The privilege system goes on after death, even now in the age of perestroika. Depending on services to the state or party, a person's body will be buried in a normal or in a special cemetery. In Moscow, for example, one has the highest category (the Novodevichy cemetery), the first class (the Novokuntsevy), the second class (the Vaganovskoye) and so on ad infinitum.

Two 'heroes' – Leonid Brezhnev and Sergei Medunov.

Behind the scenes of a meeting held in Sochi. Front row, first on left, Yuri Churbanov; second from left, Sergei Medunov; second row, second from right, Viktor Naidenov, second from left Razumovsky. Within a few minutes of this picture being taken, Naidenov escaped from his smiling 'friends' in order to avoid falling into their trap.

Left: The city fathers of Sochi at play. Seated centre, Mayor Vyacheslav Voronkov.

Right: Militia pictures of Voronkov after his arrest.

Gold jewellery – bribes taken by the mayor of Sochi, Vyacheslav Voronkov.

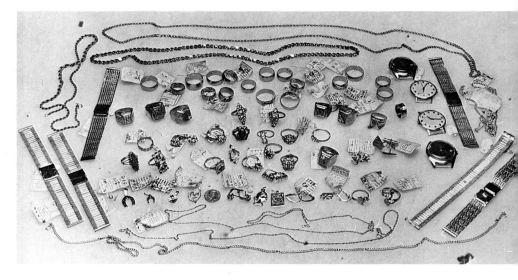

The Sochi–Krasnodar party mafia on a picnic. Third from right: Tarada.

Money, valuables and bank account books confiscated from party mafiosi in Krasnodar and Sochi. Also shown, the 'packaging' in which they were hidden.

Arkady Vaksberg and Yevgeny Bogat of *Literaturnaya Gazeta* interviewing Nikolai Shcholoko

The Minister of Internal Affairs of the USSR, Nikolai Shcholokov (second right) greets the Chi Justice of the US Supreme Court (second left). First left: Ambassador Malcolm Toon. At the far end on the left: the author.

ief Justice of the US Supreme Court Burger (second from right) at a meeting with the Soviet
litia. On the left in glasses is the present Chief Justice of the USSR, Yevgeny Smolentsev.
st left is the author of this book.

ief Justice of the US Supreme Court Burger (first left) in a children's prison camp near
oscow. Under the star (centre): the author.

Sharaf Rashidov, Yuri Churbanov and one of the leading officials of the Union of Writers of the USSR, Yuri Verchenko; Tashkent, 1978.

The rebellious investigators: Telman Gdlyan and Nikolai Ivanov.

Yuri Andropov, who fought against corruption as head of the KGB, and cracked down when he succeeded Brezhnev as General Secretary.

Yuri Churbanov under a portrait of his father-in-law.

The top party team. Kunaev making a speech of thanks for yet another gold star. First on the left, his assistant, Bekezhanov; on the right, Leonid Brezhnev, behind Brezhnev (right), Chernenko.

Kunaev (centre) with his hunting staff and bag.

Kunaev (left) with his wife and the
present president of Kazakhstan,
Nursultan Nazarbaev.

Investigator Vladimir Kalinichenko
(front centre) and his colleagues
with money and bank account books
seized from party mafiosi from the
Krasnodar region.

Part of the mafia's capital was found hidden in the basement of this hut.

Anatoly Churganov, one of those who opposed the Medunov mafia.

Investigator Vladimir Kalinichenko.

eidar Aliev (third from left with medal) at a meeting with Moscow writers.

odoly Averbukh, one of those who opposed
e Aliev mafia.

The former Prosecutor of Azerbaijan, Gombai
Mamedov: campaigner against and victim of
the mafia.

Nakhichevan, 1990: Geidar Aliev's return to the political stage.

On the platform at the Supreme Soviet of the USSR: Mikhail Gorbachev, on his left Anatoly Lukyanov, the Prosecutor General of the USSR Alexander Sukharev and Telman Gdlyan.

blatant and unacceptable. Thus, the Kazakh lady had to enlist the help of her husband's military staff and work out with them a plan for capturing the china of her dreams.

Even the simple solution of sending a man to Magadan* was considered unseemly. A way had to be found, of course. And such was its originality and refinement that it deserves its own little page in the history of the Soviet mafia.

Until very recently every single member of the Politburo had his own personal plane. At the top it would be an Ilyushin 62 or Tupolev 154; those lower in the ranking would have a Tupolev 134, which is what Kunaev had, and he had total and unrestricted use of it. So that was the way to solve the problem, just take the plane. But that would not be as simple as ordinary mortals might think, because it was laid down that the plane must always be on standby in case of a sudden summons to the Kremlin for a Politburo meeting. Even given all his power and authority, Kunaev could not have said he would not be able to set off until his wife had returned from an outing to the Soviet Far East. And for him to fly from Alma-Ata to Moscow on any other plane was out of the question since the precious life of a Politburo member is always protected by a special body-guard.

And then the Kazakh führer's brain hit upon a truly brilliant solution to this highly complex and important problem. They drew up an official report that one of the aircraft engines was giving cause for concern and that, rather than put a VIP's life at risk, it should be replaced immediately. For the same reason of guaranteed safety the Kremlin rulers also laid down that Politburo members should not fly on aircraft after an engine refit until it had been tested with

---

* The Soviet Far East has been for a long time an oasis sui generis in the USSR, thanks to the privileged position it has acquired for itself over imports from Japan. With infallible reason it is considered a pointless waste of money to transport imported household goods into the depths of the interior when there is a limitless market for them on the spot. So these goods remain at the disposal of local powers that be or, more simply, mostly if not entirely in the hands of the local mafia. With such high-value goods at their disposal and through their contacts with mafia groups in other parts of the country, these 'independent representatives' of officialdom controlled a whole system of benefit distribution and quickly multiplied their fortunes. Incidentally, I should not be writing this in the past tense. Even today the Soviet Far East has a monopoly on the purchase and subsequent import of secondhand cars from Japan. The mafiosi in the local ruling elite purchase at the 'state' price of approximately 15,000 roubles per vehicle, then sell to inhabitants of the Soviet 'continent' for 50,000. Sold to Central Asia and Transcaucasia these cars can fetch 100,000 or 150,000 roubles.

engineers on board over a distance of 20,000 kilometres.

The point of this brilliant move is clear. Some of Kunaev's closest associates were happy to take on the 'kamikaze' role. They worked out a route that, there and back, would clock up the required distance of 20,000 kilometres. There would be stopovers in Krasnoyarsk, Irkutsk and Khabarovsk. They would return via Petropavlovsk–Kamchatsky, for it would have been unthinkable to visit the Soviet Far East and not go and gawp at geysers and an active volcano. Everywhere they were received at the highest level – after all, they were emissaries from Kunaev himself. Those that have clawed their way to power have an astonishing passion for recording their pleasure on film. Thanks to this hobby we can today see with our own eyes how their trip went. Lavish picnics everywhere with the traditional shashlik and variety of vodkas, saunas and royal hunting of boar, elk and deer especially put up in front of them for easy shots.

The first lady herself did not take the trip, needless to say. Like her husband, she was not allowed to take chances with her life. However, the jolly kamikazes came back with the passenger cabin and baggage hold crammed with gifts from the Soviet Far East and Siberia. They brought not only dozens of Japanese tea-sets but also Japanese sound and video equipment, furs, carvings on rare deer horn – the finest art of the indigenous craftsmen – thousands of jars of Pacific crab and other fruits of the ocean. All these things were brought back to Alma-Ata like trophies.

According to the documentation, all the goods came from special stores and were paid for at the official state price. This probably was the case. For the Soviet mafiosi roubles present no problem; they are just printed paper, available to them by the sackful for loading into the aircraft. The goods they bought could be resold by the Kunaev clan at ten times the official price. Many were those who would do battle to get onto the list of those permitted to make purchases. Such permits constituted one of the rewards for faithful service to the mafia.

That funny but disreputable air trip was regarded as one of the principal criminal episodes during the investigation into the cases against Bekezhanov, Kunaev's deputy, against Andrei Statenin, a top official in the central committee of the Kazakh Communist Party, and against the prime minister of the republic, Baiken Ashimov. The latter, among other things, was party to purloining items from a visiting exhibition of Yugoslav furniture – a fact which bears eloquent witness to the paltry taste of these highly-placed pygmies. Despite everything it was impossible to have the flight classified as criminal because the rules stipulate a compulsory 20,000-kilometre test flight – and the rules were silent on questions of destination and passengers. It proved impossible to establish where the goods went to; they just disappeared into thin air. Thus one more successful mafia operation was complete.*

True, the trip to Magadan and back, with all its echoes of operetta, was silly rather than sinister. Also it gives an idea of the massive scale of the illegal activity of the powerful and widespread mafiosi organizations and of their hold on massive capital resources and on power itself. The episode does tell one more of the morals, tastes and habits of yesterday's (and even today's) men than of their criminal abuse of power. And the picture would be incomplete without such thought-provoking insights into facets of Soviet life and reality.

One could write a separate book about their ways. There is an over-supply of relevant material. But such a book would soon become tedious, so pathetically similar are the individual episodes, in whatever region of the USSR they occur.

Anyone who makes a study of the Soviet mafia, a phenomenon which has only recently become talked about – and even then rather sotto voce, will examine it from a social, economic or political point of view. That is to be expected. However, there is also the so-called human factor. In the final analysis all of them from top to bottom are human beings with the normal human qualities. All their dangerous and convoluted schemes to expand their power and increase their wealth are not the end but the means. The end they serve is

* Aerial high-jinks amongst the nomenklatura became a regular feature not only in Kazakhstan and not only in the Brezhnev–Kunaev period. The following episode dates from late 1990. A hush-hush flight was due to depart the Siberian city of Omsk, the plane being a Tupolev 134 belonging to a military aircraft factory. Anonymous 'well-wishers' reported over the phone that on board were weapons destined for the Armenian resistance fighters. In breach of military security, armed militia stormed the plane immediately before takeoff. What they found, far from weaponry, was a dozen or so young Communist League officials and a similar number of their leggy girlfriends, plus cases of alcohol and baskets of unobtainable delicacies. Under the guise of a secret military mission this flight was laid on to take some of the ruling elite to a resort in the Caucasus and thus stretch the summer out a little more for them. It is curious that no one had the right to intervene, although it cost the taxpayer tens of thousands. Nor was there anybody that could be held responsible.

the guaranteeing of a life of ease and maximum self-gratification, a life with nothing denied and every whim satisfied. To this end everything else is subordinated: operations, decisions, every move, no matter how these are 'dressed up' ideologically as being for the common good. To bring this about millions of worker-slaves have to toil and suffer, the very people who are proclaimed to be the 'true masters in their own land'. Thus, in order to comprehend the morals of rulers, who in turn prove to be leaders of mafia clans, one must understand the ends to which the means are applied by them.

An acquaintance suggested that he and I should spend a few days in a 'corner of heaven' on the borders of Kazakhstan and Uzbekistan. The man held no government post but did (and still does) have entree to the topmost elite; he knew then (as he does today!) how to adjust to the leadership.

In truth I felt like a break and was happy to accept the man's invitation, the more so as the 'Council of Ministers' Vacation House', as he called it, was built among orchards in the picturesque foothills of the Tien Shan range.

Before setting off for the vacation house I received some instructions from my acquaintance which at first I took as a joke. In smooth and fairly transparent phrases he gave notice that, immediately on my arrival at the vacation house, as a matter of custom (I remember particularly the phrase 'matter of custom') I would have presented to me various ladies on the staff: doctors, nursing sisters, chambermaids, 'duty officers' (this vague indefinition could hide a multitude of sinners). Then followed the assurance that whichever of these I found most to my liking would be appointed my 'personal carer'. Listening with amusement to all this, I simply didn't realize my acquaintance was serious.

And so it was. Almost immediately after my arrival there began the strange and very prolonged ceremony of introductions of the staff. It was conducted by 'matron', rather a stout lady, already enjoying her second youth. She showed traces of earlier beauty and was dressed expensively, if without taste. In fact, there was no ceremony as such, simply a number of appearances at five-minute intervals. There would be a knock at the door followed immediately by the noiseless entry of a representative of the fair sex, a succession of them, each one very different: brunettes, blondes, slim ones, chubbier ones, some plastered in make-up, others angelically cleancomplexioned like high-school girls before the Revolution. Thus every taste was catered for. One of them checked out the contents of the refrigerator, another brought in a few extra bottles of mineral water, yet another for whatever reason rearranged the flowers in the vase, and yet another enquired how I would like my breakfast egg cooked.

I answered this and other questions and expressed my thanks for their kind service. At one point I thought that the 'ceremony' was over. Oh no! After half an hour the whole thing was repeated from the beginning. When it ended, the 'matron' with the traces of earlier beauty came in and asked guardedly whether everything was satisfactory and whether I had requests of any kind. 'Yes,' I said, and noticed her face light up for an instant. 'I should like to be left in peace in order to have a lie-down.'

Her face fell again and she went away with her lips pursed. Several days later, nevertheless, I did have a chat with one of the 'maids'. She proved to be not only a lively conversationalist and a well-educated young woman, but also one of my readers: to prove it, she brought me one of my own books, dog-eared from being passed from hand to hand, which I signed for her with pleasure. We struck up a good relationship as a result of which she told me her life story which I recorded on tape. I will set down some excerpts from her tale which I kept for my files, but I will keep my word in accordance with a custom no doubt familiar to my readers – her name must remain anonymous for the time being at least.

'I live not far from here. I am one of seven children in our family: three daughters and four sons. My father died nine years ago. He was an alcoholic. His liver failed and as a result he died. My mother worked as a cook in a government sanatorium in the days before there were automatic dishwashers. Mum supported the whole family on her own, and one of the boys was given compassionate exemption from the call-up to national service. He also worked to help Mum bring us up and get us younger ones on our feet. Then my older sister started to work here at the vacation house as a cleaner. I don't know quite how she came to get the job, but it was probably through Mum because the sanatorium where she worked and this place belong to the same system, which we call the "Kazakh Kremlyovka". When my sister came home from time to time she would shut herself up in a room with Mum and I could hear her crying her heart out. Mum would comfort her, saying over and over again: "Things are as they are, they are as they are." My sister told me: "If they try and get you to work at the vacation house, you should run away. Don't get mixed up with it."

I was only eleven years old at the time. I didn't understand anything, so I just said: "Yes, I'll run away." Then as time went on, my sister changed a lot. She did not seem upset any more, and when I asked her how her work was going, she said: "Well, a job's a job," and stopped telling me not to get involved. Then she got married to one of the managers of a vegetable farm. He got divorced so that he could marry her. They live in another town, and they have a little boy. But then they got onto me to come and work at this place – as if I was a replacement for her, except I was a maid not a cleaner. Mum said: "Go on, take the job. Your life will be sorted out." I had only just got to the tenth grade at school, but they told me: "Don't worry about all that. You can go to evening classes. You don't need to go to school any longer, you won't have to sit for any exams but you'll get your school leavers' certificate all the same."

Nobody warned me what my "work" was to be. I thought a maid was a maid. But ten days later, when I was looking in to see if one of the guests had everything he needed, he said: "Stay with me." I refused. There was a row and the matron – the same one that you've met – gave me a talking-to. She was a "maid" herself once, then she was promoted to manageress. She persuaded me not to refuse. She said they would force me to do what they wanted anyway, and if I refused or started to complain I would be in trouble – and so would the rest of my family. Because they had total power, including the police and the prosecution service on their side. Even if I ran away to Moscow or somewhere, they would still find me and shut me up for good so that I didn't create trouble. But if I behaved myself well or "correctly" – as she put it – then my life would be protected, I would always have money, a job, they would give me a flat and find me a husband like they did for my elder sister. And only then did I understand what sort of "cleaner" she had been and what my sister would have been talking about behind closed doors when I was little ...

And they explained to me as well that my "work" was important government work. Of course, that must seem funny, but they said this in all seriousness. The people who come here to relax have very important jobs. They don't even have time to relax, they have such important and exhausting jobs to do. So they are chosen to come here for a few days to this vacation house so that they can throw away their cares and relax from all that stress they are under. After all, they are like everyone else – they need a woman's caress. They cannot go to a discothèque or anywhere like that to find a girlfriend. Everything has to be set up for them ... To begin with, I found it repulsive, but I got used to it ... They did everything they said they would: I got my school leavers' certificate, and money in an envelope every month in addition to my salary. I will soon have a flat and I can get married if I find a husband, but if I don't, they will choose one who is at their beck and call, like me – but in a different line of business.

I have a younger sister who is nearly grown up. They will try to get her to come here too, but I'm going to outwit them. I'm not going to allow her to come here under any circumstances. I'm not as stupid as I was before ... '

This was the story she told into my tape-recorder. I asked her three last questions – and got no answer to two of them. The first was – who were 'they' who organized everything and whom my 'maid' feared so terribly? And the second – how much money did she receive in the envelope? Fear of being eliminated by those who were still as powerful as ever prevented her from giving me their names, and as far as the money in the envelope was concerned she said – with a smile – that was a 'government secret'.

But as far as my third question went – why had she risked confessing to me? – I did get a reply. This is exactly what she said into my tape-recorder: 'I have stopped thinking of myself as a slave and I wanted to get it off my conscience so that I don't despise myself to the end of my life. Who could I talk to here about it? They would just go and grass on me ... For some reason, though, I trust you ... I don't need help, I can manage on my own.'

I would have refrained from making any sort of commentary on this monologue – it is eloquent enough to speak for itself. I quote it practically in full rather than boiling it down to a single sentence. I do so for the reason that all the problems arising from the existence of the Soviet mafia tend to be assessed in socio-political or in economic terms, whereas the oligarchy in power, now transformed into a criminal conspiracy, breaks and tears human life to shreds, blind to moral scruple and deaf to the cracking of the heaps of broken bones on which they dance.*

The whole range of pleasures in which the Soviet mafiosi like to indulge has been known long since. It is the same at all levels, from Politburo members down to the local district chieftains. The only difference is in scope and scale, not in essence, since somebody on his own cannot at one sitting eat ten dinners, drink a barrel of vodka or make love to a whole harem. Though not everyone in our country can have a Mercedes, even if he has millions of roubles tucked away. These cleaners and waitresses doing 'work of state importance' are only one more item added to the basic list of pleasures enjoyed by the mafia at public expense.

But neither the odalisques, nor the saunas and swimming pools essential to every mafia residence cost as dear as the countless hunting establishments spread over our whole country. The hunting craze began to spread in Khrushchev's time. He would from time to time like to relive his younger days and exercise his trigger finger, hitting the live targets presented to him with amazing accuracy. But the real outbreak of the hunting epidemic came under Brezhnev, who was a fanatic for this ancient sport and found ready and grateful shooting partners amongst his bored and idle marshals and generals. The epidemic spread rapidly and soon there was no republic, no region, no Godforsaken district that did not have its hunting place reserved to cater for the whims of local officialdom, all their mafiosi connections and visiting guests.

In 1972 a special reserve, Zavidovo, was set aside for Brezhnev and his cronies. It was situated near Moscow on the border with the Tver region. A reserve is a reserve to protect flora and fauna from destruction by man. But the imaginative mafiosi came up with a definition consisting of two mutually contradictory words – a

---

* A fellow journalist, Valery Agranovsky, told me of a similar set-up in neighbouring Uzbekistan. In the spa town of Shakhimandan, near Fergana (made world-famous by the bloody events there in 1989), the local mafia turned a government rest-home into a brothel for the use of the local top officials and guests from the 'organs of control'. Female employees at the nearby textile works provided the welcoming hostesses, waitresses and chambermaids. They were simply forcibly transferred to this other 'work' and kept there under lock and key. Their only way of protest was suicide.

'hunting reserve'. Over an area of 125,000 hectares they raised elk, wild boar, roe deer and many bird species: black-cock, capercaillie and others. They introduced Siberian stags and spotted deer. Millions of roubles went on keeping this place going – it had several hundred employees – and it served only one purpose. This was to pamper Leonid Ilyich and his marshal cronies and to give them a chance to rest from their exhausting burdens of office.

The Tadzhik nature reserve Tiger Gorge was very popular with top people. A hunting lodge was built here for the King of Afghanistan, who was popular at the time with the Kremlin. And it was here that he killed the last Turan tiger in the USSR. Other honoured guests at this 'reserve' who killed irreplaceable fauna had been not only Brezhnev, Podgorny and Shcherbitsky, but also Ceaucescu, Husak, Fidel Castro and other flaming warriors for the happiness of the world proletariat.

The total cost to the state of these nationwide 'hunting reserves' has to be counted in billions. There was the Crimean reserve, the Azovo-Sivashski, the Telekhanski and the Redenski, the unique Bear Lake on the Kazakhstan – Kurgan border, the famous Belorezhskaya Forest in the west of Belorussia on the Polish border. It is impossible to give a complete tally of the gigantic territory made over to the nomenklatura for the pursuit of its hunting pleasure. The word 'reserve' seemed to legalize the ban on access to these places by unwanted outsiders, whereas there was ready access and no entrance charge for people offering their services to the ruling elite like the 'cleaning ladies' or 'waitresses'.

Being invited on one of their hunting trips was a sign of having joined the elite. The huntsman's or gamekeeper's job became no less prestigious than that of a diplomat or foreign-currency tart. In the provinces the cars used by top- and middle-ranking officials are frequently seen, widely recognized and their normal routes known to the public. To get over this, spare number-plates are put on the cars when they go hunting. These are not stolen from other cars but issued by the traffic police, which thus joins the corrupt circle of mutual protection. As these are not private but duty cars, the drivers according to the Soviet rules have to mark each journey on the so-called route-recorder: where to, why, time of departure and arrival and so on. But throughout the land a simpler formulation has been adopted for cars on hunting trips and bearing spare number-plates.

159

One just has to write 'special journey'. The Soviet ear is accustomed to vague, mysterious phrases; the word 'special' works like magic and excludes any possibility of being checked out. Anyway, who would bother to make a check? All checkers of every kind are automatically embroiled in the mafia network and if one of them gets awkward his obstinacy can always be rewarded, by transfer to other work if he is lucky or otherwise by sacking him and even putting the law onto him.

In recent years when this mafia hobby and burden on state finances became too well known, an attempt was made to camouflage the damage. This was done in the usual way in current Soviet conditions. The 'hunting reserves' were redesignated as tourist zones for the purpose of attracting foreign currency. It was as if they existed only for the benefit of wealthy foreign visitors longing to divest themselves of their millions in the game-rich Russian forests, the Kazakh steppe or in the mountains of Georgia. To reinforce the deception, Intourist published publicity brochures ('come and enjoy a hunting holiday in Russia') and naïve souls – of whom there were then still plenty – swallowed it. And it would have been difficult to investigate it: then as now anything to do with 'abroad' is hemmed about with strict secrecy.

However, some braves did manage to infiltrate these holy of holies and they came across a pretty picture. For example, the Intourist hunting lodge season in the Rostov district lasts eight months, from August to March. Two ecologists (forerunners of the Soviet 'greens') contrived to get into the management records and established how much foreign currency had been earned in all the reserves of the region over one season in return for the continuing ecological destruction. It turned out that over eight months no more than thirty foreigners had come to shoot. The staff employed to look after them totalled sixty-six huntsmen, eight keepers and 108 other workers. Also employed were seventeen lorries, sixteen light trucks, six minibuses, twenty-three motorcycles, thirty-eight motorboats, five ships and launches, forty-seven horses, several field radio systems and various tractors and other heavy equipment.

'To look after them'? Of course not. These reserves, as before, remained vacation places for the high authorities and their staff where they could enjoy pleasures denied to the millions of their fellow citizens and at the same time fill their food stores to the rafters. The files would have one believe that thirty foreign tourists consumed several tons of delicatessen, meat, fish, butter, drank thousands of bottles of vodka, champagne, fine wines, and got through a hundred kilograms of coffee. In fact all this went to the parasitic mafia. And one should remember that we are talking of the hunting grounds in just one district which seldom if ever was favoured by a visit from a Kremlin sportsman.

Now there is a new craze bringing in a fortune for the mafia which, as it ploughs back all its profits into the business, will grow and grow. One could say this business was a child of perestroika because in the Brezhnev–Andropov–Chernenko era it would have earned you not money but several years in prison. This business is in pornographic and erotic videos plus thrillers and other films, which are now being shown in expensive video halls all over the country.

Needless to say, high officials and their families and hangers-on had for some time been able to get these materials, but on the quiet, and they were not making money out of them. Such private screenings have lost the allure of forbidden fruit now that they are shown openly. The money is flooding in. In a country where there used to be little entertainment provided even in cities, let alone towns and villages, the video hall has come to the rescue. And people are prepared to pay any price to go into them and see what they will not find in the shops or in the cinemas or on television.

Yet it should not be forgotten that the commercial showing of films obtained God knows how is strictly against the law – moreover, the video halls by and large evade paying any taxes. Video piracy is a known phenomenon in the West. In the USSR it has assumed the gigantic proportions of gluttony after prolonged hunger. In fact one phone call would suffice to have the video pirates arrested. But no such calls are made because of the vast income the business brings to the mafia network. Here at work once again there is the combination of the party bosses and of the organs of 'law and order' – the prosecution service, the militia and the courts.

Yet another of the indulgences of the mafia elite was turned into a profitable business, likewise thanks to the perestroika that had swept away previous prohibitions, certainly the open ones and some of the secret ones too. It was realized that without any effort at all good money could be made out of the 'cleaners' and 'waitresses'. Prostitution is so long known in the West that its discovery in the

USSR may not seem newsworthy. But in the Soviet Union when this business came on stream it was a fundamentally new phenomenon and one which offered enormous new prospects for the mafia. A trade that had been carried on by unqualified lone operators became a flourishing industry, which from this point on was taken over by the mafia, particularly in view of the potential for easy foreign-currency earnings both in the principal cities and in the ports.

It is probably the only mafia operation in the USSR that does not differ by some Soviet quirk from its counterpart in other countries. It is organized along the same lines as in the West: the strictly defined territories, the pyramidal structure of control by the pimps, the punitive commissions the prostitutes have to pay to their protectors and to those on whom the ongoing existence of the oldest profession depends, namely hotel doormen, the police and local KGB men who, if not induced to turn a blind eye, might nab you.

An assessment carried out in Moscow, Leningrad, Odessa, Sochi and Alma-Ata established that on average about 40 per cent of the prostitutes' earnings – whether in foreign currency or roubles – is spirited away into anonymous hands, that the prostitutes keep no more than 20 per cent for themselves* and that of the remaining 40 per cent the small change goes to the police, KGB men and hotel doormen whereas the big money goes to the racketeers, whose growing power has recently become a cause of serious alarm for the party/state mafia, because the racketeers are threatening to encroach on the mafia's rightful share! It is not difficult to guess at the identity of those 'anonymous hands' and thus where the money earned by prostitutes ends up, especially the foreign-currency element. It is of course the party/state mafia, which has quickly adapted to the new situation in the country. Without giving up the traditional sources of income and enrichment (i.e. principally the exploitation of their monopoly of goods in short supply), the mafiosi were quick to seize the new opportunities for further advance which were offered by the

---

* In the middle of 1980 the net foreign-currency income of a prostitute working in the centre of Moscow was about 1500 dollars a month, whilst the net income of those working for 'wooden money' was 4000 roubles. In the provinces the sums were obviously lower. Thus each foreign-currency prostitute would be producing for the mafia about 3000 dollars a month. One should remember that the real purchasing power of these dollars is far greater in the Soviet Union than in the West.

weakening of the powers of prohibition, even if the potential of the organs of repression were preserved intact.

More recently there was an attempt to legalize prostitution, to set up licensed brothels under proper official and medical control. The first instances of this were in Latvia, but other republics soon followed suit. As was to be expected, this was given a hostile reception by the central authorities who used their control of the media to whip up public disapproval. One can easily imagine the 'high moral arguments' that lay behind this. Meanwhile everywhere there were attempts at legislation. Freely elected democratic politicians appeared who wanted to take control away from the mafia and to release the prostitutes from dependence on the underground and from the fear of mistreatment. These people understood perfectly well that high moral principle would never bring the oldest profession to extinction. What happened, as expected, was that the all-powerful mafia, supported by 'public opinion', assumed the role of guardian of human morality and national tradition and blocked the legislation whilst continuing (for the time being!) to monopolize the income from this flourishing trade.

Anyone who assumes that this income accrued to the governing elite is quite mistaken. Such a conclusion would be unsophisticated, even absurd and easily disproved, though there is doubtless deep down a connection.

In complicated ways, using a multitude of intermediaries, none of whom has any idea of the identity of any of the others, a single mafia 'bank' feeds the enormous army represented by the official state apparatus, the nomenklatura, taking especial care to look after its generals and marshals. It is in the strength of the nomenklatura (which is currently trying to change its name) that the guarantee of the mafia's continued stable existence lies.

The question remains as to how Kunaev and almost his entire clan managed to hold out, despite all the revelations and the impassioned speeches of denunciation, including those delivered to the Congress of People's Deputies of the USSR itself. Why were there practically no consequences? The mafia got away with quite minor losses – a few prosecutions, and those found guilty were provided in the prison camp with maximum benefits (by Soviet standards) and given early release. The more senior mafiosi in some cases changed posts or indeed lost their posts, but remained inside the underground mafia structures, either controlling the processes at work in the republic or acting in parallel with or independently of them.

Narsultan Nazarbaev won the intended victory over Kunaev; he became first secretary of the party central committee of Kazakhstan, president of its parliament and later president of the republic. He was by no means just a figurehead, but worked energetically not so much to please Moscow as to further Kazakhstan's interests. Before long Gorbachev will have to reckon with this powerful and ambitious character who enjoys the support of a significant proportion of the population of his republic. But Kunaev is not giving up. He has recovered from the blow that was dealt him. He realizes that he is not in danger of imprisonment and, knowing that the mafia has hardly suffered any losses, he decided on the eve of his eightieth birthday, if not to return to the political stage, then at least to remind people that he has not given up nor has he the intention of doing so. He toured all the regions where his 'old guard' remain loyal to him and was greeted with ovations and assurances of support. No matter what the outcome might be there has been a show of strength. The mafia is not going under.

Nazarbaev was practically unknown outside his republic, but he had won local popularity, before becoming Kazakhstan's top person, by public criticism of continuing denunciations of a deceased fore-runner of economic reform in the USSR, Ivan Khudenko. He was an economist and agronomist who obtained from Kunaev a large parcel of agricultural land in order to carry out a unique experiment – unique, that is, as far as the Soviet Union is concerned. He was authorized to take on as few or as many farm workers as he thought necessary, to decide on their pay himself – and to settle with the state purely on his results. In one year productivity on his state farm rose fourfold, the workers' earnings eightfold and the income of the farm and its production for the state even more. The whole party/state mafia, which provided for itself by submitting false statistics and made money from soap-bubbles, felt under threat. Kunaev and the second secretary of the Central Committee, Valentin Mesyats (who later became Minister of Agriculture of the USSR and until 1990 was head of the Moscow district committee of the Communist Party) set about the merciless destruction of Khudenko.

Their vengeance seems unjustifiably cruel, but this was the normal fate for somebody who had exposed for all to see the army of parasites living off the long-suffering Soviet people. A fabricated case was brought against Khudenko, he was found guilty, sentenced and later perished in a prison camp. The best economists, writers and journalists campaigned unsuccessfully first for his release and then, after his death, for his rehabilitation. At the final stage, Nazarbaev joined in. It was not until 1989 that Khudenko's innocence was declared by the Supreme Court of the USSR. Nothing, however, happened to Kunaev or Mesyats despite their personal participation in the destruction of an innocent man.

Gradually changes did take place in various parts of the power apparatus of Kazakhstan. Nazarbaev's people achieved major if not total success in pushing the Kunaevites out of office. Gorbachev's obvious mistake in appointing a Russian emissary – Kolbin – to head the republic was corrected quickly and quietly. But this did not lead in any way to the rout of the Kunaevites or to the public revelation and denunciation of their misdeeds. All the old mafia had to do was to share out its spoils with the new one, and to renounce further territorial expansion and live off its accumulated wealth. That was, naturally, by no means what they would have chosen for themselves having yesterday, so to speak, been the all-powerful ones, but it was a long way from the very worst option – prison or labour camp or confiscation of property. Kunaev himself lost virtually nothing, and his bust even continued to grace the centre of Alma-Ata.

What is the explanation for all this? There is one apparent explanation which should not be passed over, even if it is far from satisfactory. It suggests that the Kazakh mafia was well prepared for the approaching clash and worked out in advance its tactics for fighting the investigators and the courts. These tactics were perfectly simple and rather cunning.

Kunaev's mafia decided it would be counterproductive simply to deny the corruption charges. The investigators would count on eventually wearing anybody down under investigation, would find circuitous ways of securing a conviction against him and would pile up circumstantial evidence to set him apart from others involved. (In parenthesis one notes that this is what happened in Uzbekistan with Adylov, as has already been related.) The Kunaevites chose a different route. As soon as anybody from their clan fell into the investigators' hands he began by admitting everything and witnesses gave damning evidence against him. They avoided confrontation with the inquiry – in fact, they willingly cooperated with it. Their confessions were accompanied by a wealth of detail which made them more convincing: the accused did not just say vaguely: 'I gave a bribe', 'I took a bribe' – no, they specified more or less precisely the date and the place, and this according to Soviet legal terminology is called 'corroboration of evidence given'. The inquiry was beside itself with delight. The touching cooperation of the accused very quickly allowed the case to be brought to court.

And then in court the case fell apart: for all to see and ignominiously. It turned out that the accused had simply been fooling the inquiry. The details so highly prized by the lawyers were time-bombs which exploded in the courtroom. Not only could no single detail be corroborated – on the contrary, they could be decisively disproved. For instance, Akhmetov, the head of the science and further education department of the Central Committee of the party, gave evidence against Bekezhanov. He accused him of having given him a bribe – in one of those notorious vacation houses. He specified when Bekezhanov had given the bribe and for what services. But at the trial the lawyer presented evidence that that particular vacation house had not been built until years later and that the circumstances he had described as grounds for the bribe were likewise impossible.

Another of the accused – in another case – told how he flew with Kunaev's entourage to such-and-such a town on a scheduled flight, went to dine at the airport restaurant; during the meal he was given a bribe and then they all went off together to sunbathe by a lake and three hours later they flew back. During the trial the lawyer easily showed that the scheduled flight arrived that day at about 11pm, the airport restaurant had already been closed for repairs for six months, and so on.

I happened to be there for one such courtroom collapse. The trial was of one of the former high-ranking Kazakh party apparatchiks who even in prison had not parted company with his great fat belly, and his face was still glossy from feeding off the fat of the land. His evidence was read, and the investigation report: how on 9 May, Victory Day, he was having a party with some friends in the government residence near Alma-Ata and how on his way back to town another reveller – an apparatchik slightly lower down the scale – had left for him on the seat of his car a case containing 25,000 roubles.

The accused lazily, with a condescending smile, listened to this evidence which the judge was reading out. Having read it out, the judge asked him: 'You are quite sure that you said it was 9 May – you could not have muddled up the date, could you?'

'Of course. I remember the date exactly,' the accused replied with satisfaction. And gave a nod to his lawyer. His lawyer quickly laid out on the judge's table some previously prepared documents. They showed without any doubt that on 9 May the accused was having treatment for his liver at the Czech spa of Karlovy Vary and therefore the whole of the confession which he had given to the investigation was not worth a brass farthing.

'Why did you make these admissions?' wondered the judge.

'The investigator blackmailed me and forced me with threats to indict myself,' was the reply.

Absolutely all the admissions of guilt by various people were designed more or less along the same lines, which showed convincingly that the pattern must have been thought up by some unknown person at the centre, conveyed from there to the attention of all ruling members of the mafia core and applied by them obediently. The model justified itself to the full: the investigation was discredited, all the evidence collected was cast into doubt and rejected by the court. This tactical victory led to the investigation losing impetus. It did not find the strength to start again from scratch.

Whilst paying due respect to the foresight and skill of the highly-qualified lawyers who were employed as expert advisers in the mafia headquarters, it has to be admitted that the biggest guarantee of escape was not the virtuoso tactics of behaviour during the investigation of the already-ruined mafiosi. The greatest guarantee was the tortuously slow manoeuvring battle in the Kremlin at the top, and in this battle for power whose outcome no one could predict with accuracy, none of the players wished to create a dangerous precedent. A trial of a former member of the Politburo could become like a mountain pebble that causes an avalanche – that kind of thing wouldn't suit anybody. It became known, although not from the officials but from totally authoritative and well-informed sources, that anonymous (again anonymous – it seems that this regime cannot get along without that!) experts predicted 'the sparking-off of illegal and unpredictable mass movements' should even one of the top leadership appear in the dock. This was because, as it was phrased in the document, 'the people's desire for vengeance is still very great'. In the final analysis, the spectre of 'ethnic disturbances' on nationality grounds was too ominous, as events in recent years have confirmed, including what happened on 17 December 1986 on Brezhnev Square in Alma-Ata.

Public criticism of Kunaev, however ruthless, was permitted. It served as a means of letting off pent-up steam. He himself was not threatened by anyone or anything. Even all the trinkets which adorned his chest were left where they were. In contrast, it was enough for a retired general of the KGB Oleg Kalugin to lift the corner of the curtain just a tiny bit to reveal the secrets of his former duties, and instantly there followed a powerful reaction from the Gorbachev–Ryzhkov–Kryuchkov axis, one of the components of which was to strip the 'traitor' of all his medals. But the whole pectoral iconostasis of Kunaev, Medunov and the other mafia leaders, awarded for false accounting, sham triumphs, non-achievements – all stayed put, however much protest there was in the press on behalf of the outraged citizenry. It made and will make not the slightest difference.

No difference! Of that even the leader of the sacked investigation team, Vladimir Kalinichenko, is convinced, having been prevented not only from concluding his investigation into the Uzbek mafia and then the Kazakh mafia, but having been time and again transferred from one bush fire to another. This is what he told me in conversation:

'Don't think I am trying to defend Kunaev, but on the basis of all the material I gathered during my investigation I have one hypothesis and I think it is the correct one. Kunaev could hardly have known each chain in the criminal network. Even he of course did not suppose that I would find under his protection underground millionaires who were maintaining not only him but also his political enemies. For this reason, political bosses at various levels in turn being put in positions of power are far more closely allied with one another than they themselves realized. They could be sacked, moved to other posts, new people could be appointed in their place but their career and fate were bound up in the same tangled knot which it is impossible to penetrate. It is impossible because it is in nobody's interest to do so. The real leaders of the mafia are not at all those who are in the public eye. We know nothing whatever yet about the real leaders.'

I think that this conclusion, arrived at by a competent lawyer, explains the reason for the unsinkability of many mafia leaders – both visible and invisible – in various regions of the Soviet Union. Existing in the same social conditions, the mafia acts according to its own general internal laws, however great the particular 'national characteristics' might be in a given locality. And does the mafia have particular 'national characteristics'? My rich experience of the multinational Soviet Union gives me leave to doubt it.

Chapter Eight

And God Came Down
from Heaven

About six years ago I had a phone call from a very old friend, a man of consistently honourable record and a person never to bother one over trifles. He wanted me to meet a visitor who had arrived from Baku. I suggested we put it off for a few days but my friend showed – for him – an untypical determination and insisted it must be 'no later than tomorrow'. Evidently to soften his insistence, he added intriguingly: 'If the first sentence the man utters does not excite your interest, you can throw him out straight away!'

The following day my friend's nominee was with me in my office at the newspaper. He was a powerfully-built man of about sixty. His large face showed signs of extreme exhaustion with dark bags beneath his inflamed and bloodshot eyes. Pinned to his jacket were three medal ribbons which I immediately recognized as not being the junk workers' awards handed out in Brezhnev's day to millions of liars and swindlers. They were proper campaign medals. On his right lapel was a guardsman's badge, faded with age, something awarded in the war to soldiers and officers only in the most prestigious units.

I was waiting for that intriguing first sentence. Here it is: 'Sitting before you is a dangerous criminal wanted throughout the land. You can phone the police, hand me over and get a reward of 10,000 roubles.'

So that I should not think he was either joking or crazy, he reached into his briefcase and took out a poster, folded in four, from which stared out at me the face of my visitor. 'All-Union Search' it said.

'Potentially dangerous criminal – Reward for information' and in great fat figures, '10,000 ROUBLES'.

As he had clearly anticipated, I did not make any move to phone the police and so he went on with his story.

Godoly Averbukh was from Baku, an economist by training who worked at middle-management level in the accounting department of various trading organizations. He was frequently called upon by local prosecution services as an expert investigator of fraud cases. To plough through the sham financial documents of Soviet undertakings with all their deliberate obfuscations – perfect for the fiddler's purposes – was a soul-destroying and thankless task. There are few who are prepared to carry out this difficult, risky (since people's livelihoods are at stake they are inclined in Eastern style to wreak their revenge) and badly-paid work. But Averbukh found satisfaction in it, to the extent that it allowed him, through the exercise of his professional skill, to take on to some extent at least the local robbers and swindlers. So long as the case concerned 'small fry' and did not involve the mighty of this earth, this was fine by the Baku investigators who did not exactly dote on him, although he was a superb specialist who worked very thoroughly and conscientiously. But one day in the course of investigating an apparently trifling affair, he was misguided enough to stray on his own initiative beyond the bounds of his initial brief. The case was against a woman worker in one of Baku's petrol stations, accused by a certain 'finger-pointer' (as vulgar parlance calls the over-keen citizen who cannot just 'turn a blind eye') of selling petrol reserved for government cars to a 'private' driver. Such actions, illegal under Soviet law, happen thousands of times an hour everywhere. Everyone has long since got used to it and only those who have lost all sense of self-preservation and are looting the state without shame in full view of the public get caught.

This was the case which had been brought against the woman petrol-station attendant: it should have begun and ended with her. But our vigilant expert Averbukh had no sooner started work on the documents when he realized that there were threads leading elsewhere and there were many more people involved in the crime. Not wishing to tire my readers' patience, I will merely state that the preliminary conclusion he drew – naïvely and carelessly enough – he passed on to those who had asked him to take on the case. Every day thousands of litres of petrol from one town petrol pump alone were being sold for cash not recorded in any financial document and so finding its way into the pockets of the mafia network; all the petrol pumps in the town (and maybe not only in the town) were linked to each other and were up to the same game. It is impossible to estimate their combined revenues accurately, but in a year it must have run into at least tens of millions of roubles. Not conventional, depersonalized book entries, but real live banknotes. Ready cash ...

He requested an immediate audit. This sudden extension of the case was not just against an ordinary worker – a tiny cog in a great illegal machine to which people of far more powerful rank belong.

Averbukh awaited a torrent of praise, but was greeted with a guarded scepticism. Even among lawyers that he approached, who were honourable, incorrupt people, they understood what awaited them all in any attempt to stir up the antheap. The die, however, had been cast: the prosecutor had signed an order to seize all the financial documents of the town's petrol pumps for the previous three years. When the prosecutor's staff tried to carry out this order, a good half of the documents simply disappeared. Only two or three weeks before, Averbukh had held them in his hands and had made notes from them, but now they had vanished into thin air. The lawyers hastened to get their hands at least on what remained, but without success. The first witnesses who were questioned (they were bus and truck drivers belonging to state organizations) and who had begun by telling the truth, immediately began to experience severe consequences of their actions: one of them had his flat set on fire, the son of another fell under a car, the brother of a third was sacked without any reason from his job. The 'hint' was taken: the next witnesses refused to give evidence, excusing themselves on the grounds of poor memory.

But the main quarry against whom the mafia launched their manhunt was, of course, Averbukh himself. By the simplest, most primitive methods a false charge was fabricated against him. Powerful forces in the wings had no difficulty in obtaining statements that he had taken bribes from people who, thanks to the efforts of this expert, had been found guilty and served time in prison. The figures mentioned were enormous – anything can be claimed on paper.

Thanks to his long-standing militia and prosecutor's office contacts, Averbukh came to know in advance – by sheer coincidence –

that an order had been signed for his preliminary arrest. That was on the eve of his arrest. The order was signed in the evening and the militia were empowered to enter the bribe-taker's house and arrest him at dawn. That was their fatal error: by dawn, Averbukh was already far from Baku, hiding in the village home of an old wartime comrade.

There is always a good supply of criminals not in a hurry to go to prison. But it is only in rare cases when one is dealing with murderers, members of an armed gang, terrorists and gangsters that an All-Union alert is sounded. Even more rarely, an enormous reward is offered. Even then, it is not done immediately but only in a case where the usual methods of search have given no result. But in this case the All-Union alert was sounded immediately and they were not stingy about a reward: this is evidence of what powers had been brought into play and how frightened they were. It was clear that Averbukh perhaps accidentally had stumbled not just on a group of fiddlers, however numerous and working on however great a scale, but on a group which had access to a very high level. Otherwise such energetic and urgent measures would not have been taken – the obtaining of an official signature alone usually takes a month.

Up to the time that Averbukh appeared in my office he had managed to switch hiding place no less than four times in various towns in the country. With great caution, trying not to reveal his whereabouts, he had been sending letters and telegrams to the Kremlin, to the KGB, to the Chief Prosecutor – asking them to intervene or help. He could not give a return address, and for that reason he did not expect a reply. But he did get a reply: his flat in Baku was ransacked and there were attacks on people close to him.

I had never encountered a case like it in my professional life. I asked Averbukh to ring me in a few days, and went myself to see Naidenov – not long before he had come back to the prosecution service after a three-year enforced 'leave of absence'. I simply told him that a letter had arrived in the newspaper office from some bloke called Averbukh – why was no notice being taken of his appeals?

After listening to me, Naidenov smiled cunningly. 'Don't try pulling the wool over my eyes. I can tell you that Averbukh was in the newspaper office' – he glanced at the calendar – 'the day before yesterday from 5.30 pm to 6.40 pm and then went to the flat where he is hiding.' At this point, Naidenov mentioned the address. I was amazed at the extent to which he was informed. Naidenov was no longer involved in investigative work – therefore his interest must have sprung from some other cause. (It transpired later that he had started to interest himself in the Azerbaijan mafia before his overthrow and now that he was back in the prosecution service he was following the progress of the struggle against them. Alas, it was apparently getting nowhere ...)

A terrible fear seized me: now Averbukh would be arrested, I thought, and I would never be able to prove that I had absolutely nothing to do with betraying him. But Naidenov read my thoughts. 'Tell Averbukh that he is absolutely safe for the time being. Only, tell him not to walk about in the street. If the situation gets dangerous for him I will let you know.'

I had expected to hear anything from the deputy Chief Prosecutor, but not this! He once again anticipated my question: 'You cannot imagine how accurately your protégé hit the bullseye. The petrol mafia is one of the most powerful in Azerbaijan. Even more powerful than the cotton or fishing mafia. It has contacts at the highest level and now they have protection not only in Baku but also in Moscow.' (It was not difficult to guess the identity of the figure in question. Not long beforehand Geidar Aliev, the absolute monarch of Azerbaijan, had become a full member of the Soviet Politburo, had transferred to Moscow and moreover been given the post of First Deputy Prime Minister.)

'Anyway, until and unless rescinded, an All-Union search warrant for a state criminal remains in force and must be respected by all, even the deputy Chief Prosecutor. How, then, could he offer a state criminal in hiding his care and protection?'

Naidenov was then briefly silent as if he was loath to touch on the closest operational secrets. Then briefly and without any embroidery he said: 'Averbukh will be put into a cell with criminals. One of them will pick a quarrel with him and in the ensuing brawl will simply kill him. There'll be no investigation, no court case. It is expensive but the mafia is happy to spend money on such things.'

Expensive? In those days in Baku a hired killer would have cost them 6,000 to 8,000 roubles. Later, as explained already, this increased tenfold. Now it has decreased again.

The Prosecutor for Azerbaijan, Gamboi Mamedov, was by this

time no longer in office. He had been dismissed 'for unsatisfactory work' and likewise thrown out of the Communist Party. Until very recently this was the most severe punishment for an apparatchik and meant the complete end of his career. One could suppose that there might somewhere be someone – even if only one such person exists – whose work is totally satisfactory. Anyway, this is the established Soviet formula, used when it is essential to get rid of some official, far better than any specific accusation which might provoke an open rebuttal. Gamboi Mamedov was not a fervent or resolute campaigner against the mafia. He just carried out orders from above con-scientiously and to the best of his ability (but no more than that) and would bring to book the occasional thief or embezzler. But he did not join the mafia and avoided having any contact with it whatever. This alone made him, due to his key position, not only of no use to the mafia but simply a danger to it.

On top of this he was well, perhaps too well acquainted with Aliev. This meant that he had information on Aliev which the Azerbaijan leader would prefer kept quiet. For this reason sooner or later Mamedov would have to meet his fate. Much has already been written about Aliev, but a résumé of some of the traits of this prominent personality is necessary particularly since, unlike his disgraced Politburo colleagues, his name once again flashed across the political firmament.

It has long been noted that many top-flight Soviet politicians started in the KGB and began their career ascent aided by the support of that all-powerful institution. One thinks of Andropov, Shevardnadze or Chebrikov. In these ranks Aliev is something of an odd man out, being the only one who had no past experience other than in the KGB. At the outbreak of war the eighteen-year-old Aliev was not to be seen at the army recruiting station but in the NKVD (a forerunner of the KGB) of an autonomous republic with the exceptionally high rank for his years of Lieutenant of State Security (equivalent to an army major) and with the post of supervisor of the secret NKVD archive of the said autonomous republic.

This had been preceded by the presentation of a false medical certificate detailing the grave tuberculosis from which this youth in his prime was supposed to be suffering. The young man was from a poor family and all that he had done to attract notice was to par-ticipate in school theatrical productions – playing Hamlet, no less!

So to get himself appointed to such a responsible post – especially in Stalin's time – meant that he must have had a very powerful backer. This version is confirmed by the following stages in the extraordinary career of the young Chekist. At nineteen he was head of a secret department of the sovnarkom (i.e. the government) of the Nakhichevan Autonomous Republic, and at twenty-one of the operations department of the NKVD in Azerbaijan.

Only once was there an unfortunate setback in this rapidly developing NKVD career. Being in charge of the 'work' of all the informers in Azerbaijan, he had at his disposal countless secret flats where professional Chekists could privately meet their unofficial colleagues, the so-called volunteer helpers. Among these volunteers there were women and the organization's property holdings solved the problem of secret rendezvous for them and their men friends. This was perhaps the key sense in which these flats were 'secret'. Using his official position, Geidar Aliev would encourage his 'volunteer' helpers to make love to him. One of them went along with it, but then changed her mind and kicked up a fuss. (This was after Stalin's death and the terror of what had been Beria's outfit eased for a while.) Unseen protectors saved the lover-hero; all that happened to him was that he was given a slightly less senior post and his rank reduced a notch – not for long, of course. He soon recovered and resumed his upward career path.

But there was an annoying fly in the ointment. A member of the investigation committee to whom the victim of Aliev's amorous attentions sent her complaint was the very official of the Azerbaijan state security investigative department, Gamboi Mamedov, who nine years later was to become the republic's prosecutor. It was he who had demanded that the case should not be hushed up but that Aliev the 'violator of moral principles' should be fully reduced to ranks and sent before a tribunal as a deserter – the commission set up to investigate the original complaint had also brought this fact to light.

So it was that an unusually complicated scenario developed in the mid-1960s: on one hand the 'sworn friend', the prosecutor of the republic Mamedov – on the other the chairman of the republic's KGB, Aliev. And several years later this duo combined in even more complicated and dramatic ways. Our first 'friend' was, as before, prosecutor of the republic, while the other had become indubitably and absolutely his boss: Aliev had become head of the Central Committee!

Without these background details the situation which developed a little later cannot be fully understood. Having seized and consolidated his position as top dog in the republic, Aliev began weeding the ranks in an effort to get rid of those who had been put in positions of power by his predecessors and to replace them throughout with his own men. His highest priority was to get rid of Mamedov. He not only knew more than he should, but also had revealed himself as an enemy of Aliev. Moreover, the post of prosecutor of the republic was an absolutely key position because by use of the legal system the prosecutor could appeal against any dismissal and bring a case to court or, alternatively, not allow someone to be arrested. But it was most difficult of all to get rid of the prosecutor. Since Lenin's time the appointment and dismissal of prosecutors – even at the lowest level – has been the absolute prerogative of Moscow. No prosecutor, of course, can be nominated without the consent of the local party bosses. But Mamedov was already in the job before Aliev's time. Now to get him dismissed required long and careful 'preparation of the ground', to find a pretext. Aliev did not yet have the kind of powerful allies in Moscow which would allow him simply to pick up the telephone and without explanation announce to the 'relevant authority': 'Please get rid of that useless son-of-a-bitch.' He could not. Even Andropov, although he was already the chairman of the KGB and had provided the post of top dog in the republic for Aliev – even he could not get rid of a prosecutor without any reason. To do that required either a weighty reason or an order from Brezhnev. But Brezhnev was still beyond his reach.

Meanwhile, the mafia was gathering strength: the 1970s had begun. The mafia needed the prosecutor to be 'one of them'. A brutal struggle began to develop.

Among Brezhnev's Soviet party nominees both at the centre and in the provinces, Aliev stood out for one very important reason: he was a complete exception to the usual run of the new Soviet elite. Neither the 'royal hunts' nor noble fishing expeditions during which it would sometimes happen that underwater sportsmen would skilfully attach a bream or a pike to the high-ranking angler's hook, nor baths with masseuses, waitresses or 'cleaners' – all of this passed Aliev by. Not because he was in principle opposed to the dolce vita

177

(he did not advertise his amorous liaisons, but they were no secret to anybody), but because the sweetness in his life lay in completely another direction. It could be said that he was a direct descendant of the Stalin type of ascetic lifestyle. Not in the literal sense, of course. He made full use of all the benefits which came with the job: a large flat with a private swimming pool, a government dacha by the seaside. But no movie-star-style luxury, no idiotic excess. And again – not from principle but because of his personal leaning towards other pleasures, namely absolute and unfettered power over people. And ambition to get to the top! The very, very top ...

Other bosses also aspired to power – as a means of ensuring heaven on earth for themselves. For Aliev, though, power itself was heaven. It was not the means but the end. And for that reason his external way of life – comparatively speaking, of course – appeared modest. It disarmed any potential criticism of him.

I do not think that he was a complete stranger to the 'golden calf', but his relations with those who henceforth ran the republic were not based on that principle. It was a very simple system. In the towns, areas, ministries, institutes, large and small offices – everywhere he put people in power who idolized him, who had thrown in their lot with his. And if their commitment was complete and unconditional, if they had never once given grounds for suspicion of hypocrisy, lying or cunning, then they could feel themselves to be like kings of their own little patch, free to do what they wished and to pursue their own ends. Taking from life what they – not someone else – but they really desired. For the mafia this created an unprecedentedly propitious environment and all the necessary conditions to flourish. Nobody dared touch a single member of the mafia, if they had a 'business' or personal contact with a local party (municipal, militia or KGB) official. Nobody dared touch such an official if he was under the protection of Aliev or one of his inner circle. At the same time there was no need for Aliev to have any personal interest in these mafiosi games. His personal interest was to ensure that he enjoyed total and unswerving support, not in theory but in daily practice, and that nobody should hold anything on him.

Most of these people, as one might have expected, were from his native Nakhichevan. This was a repeat of the set-up described in the previous chapter. The Kunaev brotherhood in Kazakhstan was similar to the Aliev one in Azerbaijan. It worked as follows: wherever the boss came from, his team would come from the same place. This gave rise to absurdities: anyone who came from any other region of Azerbaijan, but wanted to get ahead, had to move to Nakhichevan for a year or even for six months. A Nakhichevan stamp in your passport bestowed 'most favoured nation' status on a candidate for any kind of government service. Of course, such a manoeuvre could be seen through without too much difficulty, but nobody was trying to see through it – it was too obvious. What was obvious and important was that anyone who decided to employ this manoeuvre was giving a sign that he understood the rules of the game and would serve honestly and truly.

Meanwhile, a parallel battle against corruption was continuing. And it was a real battle against real corruption. There is no disagreement about that, and no paradox. Targets of Aliev's attack on corruption were without doubt members of a mafia – the mafia which had operated under the sphere of influence of the previous regime. In a way, it was a battle for 'market share' – commercial competition. According to the traditional Soviet model, several birds were killed with one stone. Not only were competitors eliminated, but also henchmen of the deposed high-level party apparatchiks, namely, those who would always pose a threat to the new holders of power. They were eliminated not just at the whim of the boss, but for real offences of which it was very easy to find them guilty, since Aliev himself knew that corruption pervaded every echelon of the whole system from top to bottom. He could pick off anyone and find a case against him. But there was a third 'bird' which was the most important of all for Aliev's future career. With feed-in from Aliev, the press embarked on a no-holds-barred clean-up campaign which was to be carried out in Azerbaijan under his leadership. He became the embodiment of the morally clean Marxist-Leninist personifying honour, incorruptibility and modesty. He was nicknamed 'hammer of the mafia', ardent warrior against corruption. And he really was these things. There was only one flaw in his furious attack on bribe-taking, forgery and embezzlement: it was selective and tendentious. Those who had to suffer did so as a result of the merciless logic of the struggle for power. Others were left unscathed by his attack.

On one flank he was fighting against deception and thievery – on the other, deception and thievery were flourishing. Little Azerbaijan decided not to fall behind vast Uzbekistan in the cotton-growing stakes. Fruit orchards – the true wealth of the republic – were grubbed up and vegetable plantations uprooted, pastures, everything was put down to cotton. It was conveyed to Moscow that the increase in the cotton harvest was thanks to an increase in the productivity of the old cotton plantations, rather than taking account of the new land devoted to growing it. As a reward, Moscow sent enormous bonus funds and awarded a 'hero's star' to Aliev. When all the new land had been turned over to cotton production, but Aliev's 'socialist obligation' to his friends continued to grow, he had to resort to a well-tried device – the falsification of figures. For these false returns there followed a new cascade of stars, orders and medals, new armoured railway trains bringing to Azerbaijan millions of newly-minted roubles by order of Brezhnev: the Uzbek model was followed step by step. Hundreds of thousands of people were drawn into the mafia – to begin with in little ways and then on a bigger scale.

During this time Aliev was already establishing and fortifying some solid and very promising positions in Moscow. The important moving force, clearing a path for him and preparing the way upwards, was Semen Tsvigun, who was inextricably connected to Brezhnev. When Andropov talked Brezhnev into making Aliev the leader in Azerbaijan, Brezhnev appointed the chairman of the republic's KGB, Semen Tsvigun, to fill the post left vacant by Aliev. Brezhnev had established friendly working relations with Tsvigun in Moldavia. Aliev and Tsvigun quickly found a common language and became friends. When several years later Tsvigun became Andropov's first deputy at the KGB, he did not forget his dear friend in Azerbaijan. The name of Aliev was mentioned with respect in the offices and corridors of the great party buildings on Old Square as the name of the 'closest and truest companion-in-arms of Ilyich' – a man with a great (very great!) future who would soon outgrow the confines of a rather small republic: a big ship needs a bigger sea.

Who can follow the business and personal meetings of a 'servant of the people' in their town and country residences, in the spas of the south, during large or small receptions or on their foreign travels? I do not know precisely how or when, but at some point a personal friendship developed between Aliev and those nearest to Brezhnev: his assistant Andrei Alexandrov-Agentov, prime minister Vladimir Tikhonov, Minister of Civil Aviation Boris Bugaev. In conjunction with Andropov and Tsvigun they represented for Aliev not only a powerful shield from any conceivable attacks, but a no less powerful battering-ram with whose help he could break down any obstruction which stood in his way. However, he needed neither shield nor battering-ram. Fortune smiled on him. He only had to stand on his own two feet and enemies great and small melted away.

I say again, virtually no one with whom he settled accounts (by imprisonment, expulsion from the party, or sacking), all those secretaries of area party committees and town party committees, chairmen of executive committees, militia commanders, judges, prosecutors, inspectors, inspector generals – I cannot say I am sorry for any of them. They were simply bribers, thieves, demagogues, swindlers sitting on the people's back, and they only lost out because a new mafia had taken the place of the old. They had lost out whereas their conquerors under Aliev's wing got richer every day, extracting for themselves by every possible method that wealth so liberally possessed by Azerbaijan. The petrol kings did business in stolen oil, cotton barons dealt in fictitious figures, fruit and vegetables stolen or bought in at low state prices were sent to Siberia and the north of the Soviet Union where in otherwise empty town markets they were worth ten, fifteen or twenty times more. The railway and airline mafia got rich using aircraft and railway wagons which, against all laws and regulations, were put at the disposal of their brothers in the associated mafias. The fishing mafia poached tons of costly sturgeon; in state factories there existed totally unrecorded underground plants for packing caviar. In association with them worked the export mafia, in league with colleagues in the West. Across the Iranian and Turkish borders enormous quantities of caviar were sent in standard factory packs – purchasers in many towns in Europe and Asia could hardly have guessed what a complicated route this exotic and costly product had taken before arriving on the shop shelf. But could such an operation have taken place without the cooperation of a customs mafia? Without the participation of a mafia with a base in the midst of the government (or, in Soviet parlance, 'people's') control? Without a militia mafia – for in the Ministry of Internal Affairs there is a special service with the initials OBKhSS (the Division for Fighting Violators of Socialist Property and Speculation)?

These 'underground workshops' consisted in fact of production teams working at normal state factories, drawing their normal wages there, putting out the same products as other workers in factories belonging to the same group. The difference was that they did not supply the products to the state but passed them to their own masters for them to profiteer from. This kind of sharp practice occurred more or less throughout the country but it was particularly prevalent in Transcaucasia. In essence all this was a reaction to the suppression of individual initiative, to the ban on private property, to a deformed system of industrial relations and to the absence of a free market. This reaction was the equivalent of the living plant that pushes its way up through asphalt. As would be expected from a proprietor who feels his income threatened, the state hounded with especial harshness these 'workshoppers', as the black-marketeers became known. If they fell into the hands of the law the 'workshoppers' would be handed down far stiffer sentences than other law-breakers, even if they had stolen similar amounts from the state. The main danger here for the state was not so much the amount of lost revenue or production but the sturdy growth in the midst of the socialist economic system of something quite alien to it, namely free trade, working according to the laws of the nonexistent market. And what was worse – the workers in the 'underground workshops', even though they only took a very small share of the illicit gains, worked to the limit of their energies whilst their neighbours working to enrich the abstract 'state' tried to get away with as little effort as possible and produced not goods so much as fictitious production figures for the official statistics.

Naturally the only 'workshoppers' to get into trouble were those who had not managed to attract into their mafia net all the people on whom their security might depend, or those who had been part of the old mafia gangs that had gone under in internecine battles. These underground workshops operated in Azerbaijan both before and after Aliev's time. But the prosecutors only pursued people who had been in league with the ones that had been removed from power. From the outside, however, it looked like an uncompromising confrontation with the mafia. So one important point was omitted from the mass propaganda and also from the reports submitted to the Kremlin: the battle was not against the mafia but between one mafia and another. The overthrow of the first led to the enormous strengthening of the second. As always the losers were those in whose name and for whose benefit all this web of intrigue was

182

operated – those countless individuals languishing in poverty and deprived of civil rights, those who are grandiloquently referred to as 'the people'.

In the light of the foregoing one can understand why Aliev pounced so heavily on one particular high-placed official, levelling against him an accusation which rang true – that he was connected to the 'workshoppers' mafia. The official in question was the chief investigator of the Azerbaijan prosecution service, Ibragim Babaev. It appeared that not only had he been protecting 'workshoppers' from being taken to court, but he also had shares (several hundred thousand roubles worth) in the business and, in proportion to his investment and to other services he rendered, was enjoying his share of the profits.

It would be difficult to state with precision whether or not there was any sound basis to this accusation. That there *might* have been is unquestionable: there are plenty of instances of the participation of high-level lawyers in mafia gangs. But two factors give one pause. The first is that Babaev had been appointed by the previous pre-Aliev rulers and, as a result, did not join the Aliev gang. And secondly, Aliev did not simply interfere in the investigation and trial in the Babaev case, he personally requested that Babaev should be shot. Only shooting would do – any other sentence would have laid the judges themselves open to trouble, perhaps even the same fate that awaited Babaev. I have at my disposal written evidence from a member of the Supreme Court of Azerbaijan, Firudin Guseinov: 'The case of Babaev came to the Supreme Court, and I was ordered to hear it. I was warned by the president of the court Ismailov that Aliev had personally arranged for the sentence to be the shooting of Babaev and two other accused. I categorically refused to take a case in which the outcome had been decided in advance, the more so since I saw at once what a brutal violation of the criminal–professional code had been committed during the course of the investigation. Another member of the court – my namesake R. Guseinov – also refused to hear the case. But somebody was found to do it – a member of the court called Orudzhev, who very soon afterwards was made Minister of Justice. Just as soon I was dismissed from my job. I am lucky not to have been jailed.'

With unbelievable speed, the Supreme Court of Azerbaijan under Orudzhev delivered the verdict desired by Aliev. On appeal the

Babaev case went to the Supreme Court of the USSR. The flimsiness of the charges was obvious. The haste with which Babaev had been sentenced to death put them on the alert. The members of the Supreme Court of the USSR proposed in general to stop the proceedings and acquit Babaev on the grounds of insufficient evidence. The deputy president of the Supreme Court of the USSR Yevgeny Smolentsev (as of today the head of the Supreme Court) was more cautious: he questioned the sentence and proposed that there should be a new investigation and subsequently that the new evidence should be presented in court for a second time. A very modest and just court decision, the more so if one remembers that a man's life was at stake.

That really did it! Here is just one written deposition that I have at my disposal. The author is an official of the department of the Supreme Court of the USSR, doctor of law Oleg Temushkin.* This is what he said to me:

'One day I found myself on court business in the office of the president of the Supreme Court of the USSR, Lev Smirnov, when the red government telephone rang. I realized from the conversation that it was Geidar Aliev on the line. He told Smirnov that he had heard about the questioning of the sentence in the Babaev case, and was very worried about Smolentsev's action. He also said the shooting of Babaev "was in the general interest of the whole republic" and if the Supreme Court of the USSR interfered with it then "on their own heads be it". Aliev finished the conversation thus: "I hope that you have got my message, otherwise I shall have to be in touch with other quarters." Smirnov told me all this word for word after he had finished talking to Aliev on the telephone. It goes without saying that Aliev did not need to speak to "any other quarters": ignoring the will of his deputy and other members of the Supreme Court of the USSR, Smirnov there and then overruled Smolentsev's protest and

---

* Oleg Temushkin worked for many years at a senior level in the Soviet prosecution service, had the rank of State Counsellor of law third class (corresponding to the military rank of major general). Later he was transferred to the Supreme Court of the USSR where he works to this day. He became widely known for his participation in the trial of Sinyavsky and Daniel, where he acted as state prosecutor. Unfortunately, to this day he has not deemed it possible to distance himself from that disgraceful travesty of justice. However, he has done a lot of useful work for the democratization of the Soviet legal system, actively helping the rehabilitation of victims of the Stalin and Brezhnev terror, going into print and on television with severe criticism of the inhuman legal process and punitive court practices in the USSR.

obediently informed Aliev of his action. In Azerbaijan they did not hesitate: as soon as written confirmation arrived from Moscow Babaev was promptly executed. Effectively, it was murder.'

What provoked this mad action? Why was such a politically hysterical measure thought necessary for all to see? The vengefulness and evil nature of Aliev, for all his external softness and smiling face, was well known in Azerbaijan. But in this matter, these characteristics showed themselves in a completely unforgivable, blatantly obvious form.

Thanks to his official position Babaev had a good idea of the life led behind the scenes by the new mafia that was now to the fore and flourishing, as well as of the mafia that was leaving the stage. Thus he simply had to be replaced, and not only put safely into prison, but destroyed. All of the old gang would then learn an obvious lesson – anybody that could neither keep his mouth shut, nor forget that he ever knew anything he shouldn't, could expect a similar fate. Now at last had come the final and most decisive argument for squaring accounts with the prosecutor Mamedov. After all, Babaev had been one of his protégés; Mamedov had tried to save Babaev, first from arrest, then from being put on trial, and then from execution. Now they had to put a stop to his career, since he was the protector of an extremely dangerous state criminal and a member of a mafia clan that had stolen millions from the people.

Mamedov was dismissed from his post as prosecutor in ignominy and disgrace, despite the limp opposition of his friend Chief Prosecutor Rudenko. But it was not yet the end; the mafia is never satisfied with a job half done.

It is wrong to imagine that all these replacements, appointments and transfers were or indeed are made easily and simply: the 'outsider' removed and an 'insider' appointed. That is the general direction and the purpose of the new appointments is obvious, but in each and every case a multitude of forces have to be taken into account, such as the opposing interests among those that make the decisions. It is often necessary to arrive at the desired outcome by means of several moves rather than by one alone.

The mafia found itself unable to replace Babaev with someone 100 per cent their man, who would fully answer their requirements of a person in such a position. They had to be satisfied for the time being with a 'neutral' lawyer belonging to no group at all. His name was

Maksud Kuliev. It was supposed that he would bear in mind what forces he had to thank for his promotion and serve them obediently, being as aware as everybody else of local tradition in these matters. But Kuliev did not become a poodle. Instead of crushing the remains of the displaced mafia groups he went for those who were avidly taking over more and more positions of power. Yet behind these people stood a strong, widespread clan whose tentacles reached into all spheres of existence and all parts of the republic.

Very close relatives, and nobody else, monopolized the area of operations. To catalogue them all – or even a small part of them – is impossible. The situation was almost a parody of that in Romania, where not only Ceaucescu's close relatives but also distant ones occupied all the top positions. The Aliev brothers controlled extensive 'territories'. One brother, Gasan Aliev, became an academician in the field of geography. His brother Djalal, a biologist academician, controlled not only his own institute. A third, Agil Aliev, an economist by training, held complete sway in a medical institute and in the university. Gasan Aliev's son was the chief architect of Baku – all construction work in that city came under his control. A fourth brother, Gusein, who had worked as an ordinary photographer and picture editor on a local newspaper, was suddenly an 'outstanding artist of Azerbaijan', was awarded honorific titles and became lord and master in the art world. Aliev had sisters and all their husbands turned out to be ministers or generals. Aliev's wife (who was made a doctor of medicine) had a brother who was the minister for secondary and higher special education for the republic. Ask anybody in Azerbaijan what that means, if getting a university place will cost tens of thousands. And the minister controls not only student places but appointments to chairs, professorships – in fact all teaching posts in the republic!

I do not know what prompted Kuliev to take a look at the clan's activities – naïveté, saintly simplicity, lack of foresight, professional fanaticism? 'Take a look' is the appropriate expression since no sooner had he started going down that road than he was swept away by a tornado emanating from the office of the First Secretary of the Central Committee. That was fortunate for him. If he had remained any longer in the post and delved deeper into mafia affairs, he would have been dealt with far more harshly.

Now at last it really was Mamedov's turn. Although fired from his post, he had retained his party membership and was even a deputy of the republic's supreme soviet. That had been a tactical error on Aliev's part, although he later claimed it showed what a loyal, gentle and patient soul he was. Mamedov realized that his final punishment was at hand. He decided to anticipate events. At a regular sitting of the supreme soviet he suddenly ran up to the rostrum, without even awaiting the chairman's permission, and managed to tell some home truths before reptilian deputies drowned his words with whistling and foot-stamping. 'The state plan is a swindle, likewise the budget – also, of course, those reports of economic successes are a pack of lies, and ... ' It was on this last 'and' that he was bundled off the rostrum and his place taken one after the other by seventeen 'opponents' who angrily denounced 'the traitor and slanderer'. The weightiest accusation against Mamedov was levelled by the 'people's writer of Azerbaijan' Suleimen Ragimov, who asked Mamedov: 'Who are you fighting against, Gamboi? God sent us his Son in the form of Geidar Aliev. Are you then opposing God?' The transcript at this point records 'loud and long applause turning into a standing ovation'.

Mamedov was expelled from the party and a criminal charge was brought against him. It was the usual pattern: a campaigner against the mafia is revealed himself to be a mafioso – a bribe-taker and thief. 'Witnesses' against him were being got ready. Unlike Averbukh, he didn't shelter in hideaway flats but took up residence with his sister in Leningrad. Probably they could have located him if they had really wanted to. But Aliev did not institute a search. There was an unspoken agreement which suited him better. 'If you keep quiet, you'll be left in peace. If you don't, do not blame me for the consequences.' By this time Aliev feared no one and nothing. And Mamedov knew this and so kept quiet. Moreover, he came himself from a nomenklatura background and was perfectly aware of the rules of the game.

Why was Aliev by now afraid of nobody and nothing? The reason is that he had established personal contact with Brezhnev, who had found Aliev greatly to his liking. A significant turning point in the story of their 'brotherly love' was when Brezhnev came on a visit to Baku in 1978. It was the last leg of the trip on which Brezhnev detoured to Mineralnye Vody and met Gorbachev. In Baku generous gifts awaited the dear and honoured guest. The most costly one was not the golden ring with an unbelievably large solitaire diamond, nor the hand-woven Oriental carpet which on the rail journey home took up the whole government dining saloon. No, the most expensive was the portrait of Brezhnev executed by the well-known Azerbaijan artist Tair Salakhov. At some stage, long before Aliev's time, Tair Salakhov had painted Khrushchev's portrait and had obtained for it a sackful of precious stones from the republic's treasury, with which he then decorated his creation. But Khrushchev, a diligent student of the school of Stalinist asceticism, declined to accept the portrait. It languished for many years under lock and key. Now the jewels would come in handy. Salakhov unpicked them from the Khrushchev portrait and stuck them onto Brezhnev's portrait with the same effect on the sum total of its value.

Brezhnev did not turn the gift down. On the contrary, when receiving it he uttered a phrase that became widely known: 'Azerbaijan is making giant strides.' This phrase was reproduced everywhere, millions of times – on the front pages of newspapers or on the façades of buildings. Azerbaijan was indeed striding ahead, not stinting on expenditure of its gold and diamonds, and also of human life, as the shootings of political opponents went to show.

At the editorial offices of *Literaturnaya Gazeta* there was a constant flow of letters, anonymous more often than not, describing dramatic happenings in Azerbaijan: victimizations, savage reprisals, mysterious disappearances, blackmail, extortion, robbery, falsification and the unbridled ways of the political mafia which connives at thievery and extortion whilst at the same time sending thieves and extortioners to prison. It was noticeable that these letters had one thing in common. They had all been posted from outside the republic, from neighbouring Georgia or Dagestan. I was reliably informed that all letters addressed to official bodies in Moscow, as distinct from private individuals, were subjected in turn to inspection by the Azerbaijan party central committee, the MVD and others. A former Azerbaijan KGB officer, asking not to be named, told me at the end of 1988 that he himself had worked on the selective checking of letters and used to produce a digest on 'the public mood' for Aliev personally.

There was one anonymous letter from someone who had specially driven to Derbent in Dagestan to post it. He wrote of the murder of the Minister of Internal Affairs of Azerbaijan: a criminal act which he said had been the work of the mafia. We were already aware of this but knew none of the details. Our own correspondent in Azerbaijan was Emil Agaev, but in answer to all our enquiries he just answered that it was 'an act of a deranged lunatic and was of no news interest for the public'.

I decided to go down to Baku and find out for myself what was behind this bloody incident. Nothing seemed to stand in the way of my departure. In my pocket I already had the editor's written authorization along with the air ticket, but there had been a leak. On the eve of my going I was asked to see our first deputy editor-in-chief: 'Your assignment will have to be cancelled. There's been a call from the Central Committee. Comrade Aliev doesn't think it advisable for you to go. The situation in Azerbaijan is complex ...'

In our country everything is 'complex'. It always was, and still is, when you are getting close to unpleasant facts which the authorities do not want known. My only thought then was who had given the game away. Later I discovered it was our man in Baku. Perhaps it had been careless of me to have asked him to make my hotel reservations.

What had been going on to force Aliev to take such precautions? An officer called Muradov in the prison service at Shusha, a town in Nagorny Karabakh, had been posted there as a sort of disciplinary measure. He lived in the mess on his own, his wife, several children and elderly parents staying behind in their home town in the district of Kasum-Ismailova where they had their own house. Several times Muradov put in an application to be transferred to a post somewhere closer to his family but without result. Eventually the police authority relented and prepared the documentation for Muradov's transfer to the local militia in the little town where his family lived. All that was needed to complete the transfer order was the signature of the deputy minister, Guseinov. This should have been a mere formality. Guseinov asked Muradov to come and see him. Imagine, a deputy minister wanting to see a little fish of a policeman from godforsaken Shusha. They spoke alone and the minister refused the transfer.

A few days later Muradov flew back to Baku and went straight to Guseinov's offices. The orderly told him Guseinov was at that moment with the minister himself. Muradov went there and, ignoring the shouts of the officers on duty in the anteroom, burst into the minister's office. Without saying a word he drew his pistol and killed the minister outright plus some other generals that were in the room. Guseinov was not among them. He had left the room seconds earlier to go to the toilet. After the killing Muradov turned the pistol on himself.

In the pocket of his tunic they found a suicide note. In it Muradov related the conversation he had had with Guseinov, if one can properly call it a conversation. In short, the deputy minister had insisted on a bribe. In Azerbaijan everything is achieved on this basis, and nothing without it. Why then did this 'normal' demand by someone in a high position come as such a shock to Muradov? Because he saw the injustice of it. His position as a prison officer offered far greater opportunities for graft, taking bribes from prisoners' relatives, than did the policeman's job in an insignificant rural centre. Thus he was volunteering to exchange a better job for a worse one, but being asked into the bargain to pay for it. Where was the justice in that?

In this tragicomic sketch was reflected as clearly as in a pool the everyday reality of Azerbaijan, 'the striding giant'.

But the 'iron curtain' which had been dropped by Aliev himself in front of this trivial matter evoked amazement. I was the more amazed when I heard that Balygyan the prison governor had been arrested (it was a wild charge: that he had not immediately reported that Muradov had 'disappeared' from Shusha) and that from twelve volumes of investigative material only one had been sent to the judge – the rest had been hidden in a 'special' archive. This matter, trivial from a legal point of view, acquired an almost mystical secrecy and depths hidden to ordinary mortal eyes.

But there was nothing mystical or secret or deep about it. Everything was simple to the point of being primitive. Guseinov, one of the people closest to Aliev, was expecting promotion at that time – his name could not be associated with scandal of any kind. And he did indeed obtain a key post as head of a department of administrative affairs of the central committee of Azerbaijan; that is, according to the structure in those days, he became the official in charge of all courts and prosecutors in the republic, over the MVD and even the KGB, or at any rate on the same level as them. It was such a powerful position that even after the utter defeat of the Aliev clan, it remained almost impregnable. Even as these lines are being written,

S. Guseinov is working in the administrative department of the Presidium of the Supreme Soviet of Azerbaijan. As before, he has power at his disposal, even if it is somewhat less.

Semen Tsvigun was no longer around: he had put a bullet through his brain. But there was Andropov and there was Brezhnev – more than enough for Aliev and his circle to feel themselves all-powerful and protected from any danger. He was always going to Moscow. Moreover, he preferred, if there was no hurry, to go by train rather than by personal aircraft. His special government carriage, No. 5555, would be discreetly stationed in a siding in Moscow's Riga station when its master was expected. When arriving from Baku, it would be loaded with an unbelievable quantity of presents for 'useful people'. Furs, carpets, jewels, imported clothes, caviar, cognac, fruit – all of this was carefully collected and packed up to be delivered by couriers to the addresses indicated together with touching little messages from 'your most admiring G. A. Aliev'. The purpose was not purely admiration, but that the whole of his clan should thus strengthen their positions.

The golden hours of the clan came with the visit of Brezhnev to Baku just before his death. His doctors were against the senile old dictator undertaking this relatively tiring journey, but the insistence of Aliev and the extreme desire of Brezhnev to see the happy faces of the citizens awaiting his arrival and above all to get his hands on the material proofs of their unlimited affection won the day. With Brezhnev travelled his closest aide, Andrei Aleksandrov-Agentov, and his closest adviser, Leonid Zamyatin (later to be appointed ambassador to London).

The tragic farce of this nationwide celebration of the visit by one demigod to another is well remembered, and not only in the Soviet Union: pictures of this 'universal triumph' were relayed to television screens all over the world. It is well known too that a magnificent palace was specially built in Oriental style for Brezhnev's visit. Something less widely known is that Brezhnev was told in advance that after this palace had been blessed with his presence it was subsequently to be converted into a 'Museum to Comrade Brezhnev'. Rather as in North Korea, where every place where the 'great leader' Kim Il Sung has even once set foot is decorated with a commemorative plaque, Aliev wished to declare the dwelling whose walls had once had the honour of witnessing our 'great leader' as a holy place of pilgrimage. The death of the dictator prevented this idea from being carried out, and millions of roubles spent on the equipment of the palace went up in smoke. This was nothing out of the ordinary in the Soviet Union, either before or since. Now, the museum that never was is just a house for high-ranking visitors. But VIPs do not exactly hurry there any more, now that blood flows continuously and one dreadful occurrence succeeds another.

But in those days, in the autumn of 1982, it was long before these awful events – it was unthinkable that they should ever take place. The usual diamond ring awaited Brezhnev in Baku; this time it was not only an object of material value but a masterpiece of the jeweller's art. On the ring was set one enormous stone symbolizing Brezhnev the Sun King, and around it glittered fifteen smaller stones symbolizing the fifteen union republics like planets orbiting their sun. This masterpiece as a whole was called 'The Unbreakable Union of Republics of the Free'. When he received it and heard the recitation of the symbolism embodied in it, Brezhnev burst into tears.

These tears of tender emotion cost the republican treasury 226,000 roubles. The same Baku jewellery workshop also produced a bust of Brezhnev in white gold and a dagger studded with diamonds, to be bestowed on the hero of Malaya Zemlya by his Baku comrades-in-arms. As he received each of these gifts in turn the dying autocrat dissolved in tears. It was a shameful and very sad sight: the self-interested mockery of a dying lion became in essence the mockery of a ravaged and cheated people.

To say that the money for these 'presents' was lost from the treasury can only be true in a very conditional sense. The money came from the mafia – from what they had stolen, looted or taken in the form of bribes. Nobody has ever dared to check the financial documents of the jewellery workshop, the circumstances and methods of accounting. My efforts to gain access to the documents (they would be very interesting regardless of whether they were genuine or faked) were unsuccessful. But the director of the workshop, Tofik Aliev (no relation of Geidar Aliev), within a few months 'died suddenly'. The records disappeared.

Aliev himself now questions with disarming frankness whether there ever was such a ring. He asks in speeches, newspaper articles and interviews which he grants willingly to the Soviet and foreign press. The whole country saw on their television screens how Brezhnev admired it as he put it on his finger, how he cried with joy and thanked the 'father of the Azeri people' for their 'loyal friendship'. 'Show us documentary proof!' correctly demands the 'father', knowing very well that no one will ever come up with a document anywhere. No one. Ever. It is hardly likely that the single reliable witness – the inheritor of her father's wealth, Galina Brezhneva – would present the material evidence: the ring itself. If she were to take such a hasty step, the ring would have to be given back to the treasury as having been obtained by illegal means.

Astonishingly this Aliev-type argument was used by the deputy head of the KGB (until February 1991) Filipp Bobkov to justify the escape from punishment of his former colleague. Bobkov has given an interview to a recently founded 'independent' Moscow newspaper. In it he says: 'The KGB has no incriminating evidence against Aliev. If you could produce any document showing that Aliev took bribes ... Not a single such document has been produced ... '

It is not in the least surprising that the KGB has no 'incriminating evidence'. It has no authority or right to operate in respect of Politburo members. But 'evidence' of a bribe would anyway be a criminalistic novelty, as if in future bribe-takers are only going to be brought to court when one can produce a list they have kept of bribes taken, from whom, what for, when, etc.

During the short time that elapsed between Brezhnev's return from Baku and his death, the leader managed to pay a tsar's ransom to his 'friend and brother'. It cost him as little as it had Aliev, so they could continue to compete in generosity as long as they liked. Brezhnev proposed to promote Aliev from candidate to full membership of the Politburo.

Yes, it did not cost Aliev himself or Brezhnev a thing, but it did cost somebody something. As I was told in Baku in spring 1988 by two very well-informed representatives of the higher echelons of the Azeri intelligentsia close to Aliev: the mafia collected four million roubles to pay for this career move of Aliev's. This does not include the value of the ring and other gifts to Brezhnev. Millions were contributed in cash and in kind to various Moscow officials on whom depended the 'nod': to express the thought, forward the proposal, uphold the proposal and generally sing the praises of the future member and his unrepeatable personality in print, on television and in the cinema. That amount was only just enough – and if it had not been, they would have found more.

The agreement of other members of the Politburo was obtained; it just remained to await the next plenum of the Central Committee so that everything could be properly signed, sealed and delivered. But then the hand of God intervened. The dictator died. Andropov not only upheld his predecessor's previously-agreed decision but also transferred Aliev to Moscow – as first deputy prime minister.

This transfer, or promotion, evokes an ambivalent sensation. Undoubtedly Andropov saw in Aliev a long-standing and successful loyal man on whom he could rely whole-heartedly. But he was not so straightforward or as one-sided a politician as might be supposed by some. He had brains and cunning and far-sightedness. Perhaps it was the same sort of 'promotion' that, three years later, Gorbachev meted out to Grigory Romanov when he transferred him from Leningrad to Moscow? It deprived him of his most important support – his complaisant local cronies. He lost his total power over a territory, however small. He was no longer king of a small but unbelievably wealthy state – now he was just one of many 'first deputies' in the powerful 'centre'. He was not so much a winner as a loser*. And, of course, Aliev himself fully understood this. And, of course, the powerful mafia standing behind him understood that as well. But Aliev did not hesitate for long. If he had really wanted to, he could have insisted on having his own way and stayed in Azerbaijan. But he did not want to cross Andropov (in this he was right: Andropov then and there awarded him a second gold star of Socialist Labour). But able people learn early how to make a plus out of a minus.

At that time the Azeri mafia had worked out a detailed plan, astonishing both in its scale and simplicity. Aliev's acquisition of the title of 'full' member of the Politburo, his transfer to a high post in Moscow and lastly his proximity to Andropov and Chernenko, gave them a real hope of the possibility of realizing this grandiose scheme.

---

* Things were different for Yegor Ligachev whom Andropov also transferred, in his case from Tomsk to Moscow. Ligachev did not lose so much as gain. Instead of illusory regional power he obtained boundless power over all party workers in the country, which until very recently meant power over everyone and everything. Ligachev had long enjoyed a reputation as an enemy of corruption, a hater of any mafia groupings – Andropov needed him as an 'iron fist' to carry out the long-desired sorting out of the party apparatus.

At the onset of spring, millions of Soviet citizens head south to find sun, sea and fruit. The narrow beaches of the Black Sea coast – in the Caucasus and the Crimea – are filled with hordes of holidaymakers: the Soviet service industry is not equipped to provide them with tolerable human conditions. Meanwhile, the beaches of the Caspian Sea are just as good. Many kilometres of sandy beaches, a good seabed, reliably warm weather with a season lasting from April to November, curative mineral waters and mud, plenty of tourist sights, the proximity of picturesque mountain scenery, an abundance of vegetables and fruit – all of this adds up to the ideal conditions for a perfect holiday. Azerbaijan could easily have taken the load off the Crimea and the Caucasus by taking several million holidaymakers a year.

That was the brainwave which the Azeri government put to the Union government. A brainwave, it seems to me, of exceptional intelligence and absolutely justified – I say this without any irony. Baku suggested they establish a future spa complex with 'the status of an All-Union Curative Centre'. Aliev was going to press the idea in Moscow and get it incorporated into the next state plan.

On paper there was nothing particularly wrong with the plan. In fact it was completely worked out by the mafia, which had the highest hopes of this grandiose project and of the rich opportunities it would offer them.

The notorious 'all-union status' opened wide horizons for gigantically striding Azerbaijan. Enormous sums would be released from the state budget, including hard currency for purchases worth millions or billions. There would be the prospect of acquiring unobtainable building materials, equipment and so on. The mafia drooled in sweet anticipation of future income. However large the building project were to grow, it would never satisfy the tourist demand. In the Soviet Union demand always exceeds supply anywhere, for anything. These deficits made all kinds of speculation possible. Thousands upon thousands of fruit and vegetable producers who then as now would transport their produce thousands of miles to market would no longer need to expend effort and energy on that, because the holidaymakers would buy it all up on the spot for the same price. With justification, the mafia at all its many levels began to count the new billions they saw in this 'project of the century'.

195

But bureaucratic delay, without which nothing happens in the Soviet Union, played a nasty trick. Andropov left the scene, Chernenko came and went; then came perestroika and a fierce power struggle. Nobody now had time for the 'project of the century'. Other projects had seized the minds and hearts of the country.

Aliev had foreseen his approaching downfall. People of that type have a built-in seismograph which can sense the slightest movement in the ground. There was a flood of letters being sent to Moscow by people who had been crushed, trampled on and ditched by Aliev's regime. Nobody calculated their numbers – perhaps thousands. Mamed Mamedov, first secretary of the Kurdamir district party committee, had died 'suddenly' in a prison hospital. In a Siberian Gulag camp a wine cooperative director, Alisahib Abdulaev, had died 'suddenly'. Vakhid Ismailov, the first secretary of the district party committee at Zhdanovsk, had 'hanged himself' from a tree in his own garden. The list of people dying, hanging or shooting themselves, and of those who had fled or been exiled, could go on and on.

All the relations of the prosecutor Gamboi Mamedov who lived in Azerbaijan – twenty in all – suffered savage reprisals. They were thrown into prison, sacked from their jobs and evicted from their homes. In Shusha itself the house built by Mamedov's father was demolished. Here is an excerpt from a long letter sent to me from Stepanakert, the capital of Nagorny Karabakh, by Vladimir Akopyan:

'I have worked for many years in the militia. One day I was summoned by an officer, Colonel Muradov, who said: "We've been asked to undertake an urgent task by the first secretary of the district committee, Kevorkov, who had his orders from Aliev himself." We were required to go immediately to Shusha and find material at any price which would enable us to arrest the senior doctor of the local sanatorium. The person in question was Mansur Mamedov, a relation of the former prosecutor of Azerbaijan. We had one week to do the job. I tried all sorts of people: financiers, engineers, builders, doctors and inspector generals, but we could find no evidence of wrongdoing. I reported this to Muradov and he said, "Don't be stupid ... a senior doctor at a sanatorium and you can find nothing to pin on him?" The enraged Kevorkov ordered the district people's control commission to conduct a further "search" and within two days they "found" something. Mansur Mamedov was sacked from his job and arrested.'

A similar fate awaited everyone who not only tried to complain but tried to speak the truth or give early warning of alarming symptoms. No one was allowed to cast any sort of doubt on the already-established image of Azerbaijan flourishing and 'making giant strides'. The prosecutor of Sumgait stammered an account of the unsatisfactory situation in his town, where it was plain to see that rioting youngsters were under the control of the mafia, ready at any time obediently to carry out any task. The author of this statement was accused of calumny of the wonderful Sumgait workers, sacked from his job and deprived of the right to live in the town. There are any number of such instances, but I know too many to enumerate them.

Psychological pressures made themselves felt: Aliev suffered a heart attack actually sitting at his desk in his office. A perfect opportunity arose to pension off the invalid: for Gorbachev knew very well what Aliev really thought of him and of perestroika, although he continued to vote for him in the Politburo.

He went through two stages of retirement: to begin with he maintained his membership of the Politburo and the post of vice-premier. Then, instead, he was given the post of government consultant, remaining a member of the Central Committee and a deputy of the Supreme Soviet – with a flat in a block reserved for high party apparatchiks, a government dacha, a car which his driver at any hour of the day or night would bring to the front door and all the privileges of the nomenklatura. Only now is it possible to say something about him (and very far from everything) in our censored press. All my previous attempts to get something of this material printed in a newspaper suffered a categorical editorial 'nyet'. It was a vulgar departure from our normal standards when in 1981 our newspaper printed a widely publicized interview with Aliev under the pretentious headline: 'Let Justice Be Victorious'.

In this interview Aliev told how, in the ordinary people's interest, he had cracked down on corruption, deceit and every kind of fraud, and pursued bribe-takers. Several passages are astonishing in their severity. He announced, for instance, that the children of lawyers did not have the right to work as lawyers, and the children of party apparatchiks must not work as apparatchiks. His populist aim was obvious. Enough suffering had been caused by family clans. But since Aliev's strictures were at odds with the law and with human rights, nobody was interested in them. His strictures did not in the least hinder the children of lawyers from becoming party apparatchiks or the children of party apparatchiks from becoming lawyers. Demagogy remained demagogy, and reality remained reality. The only practical consequence of the interview (leaving aside the scandal which surrounded it) was the flat in Moscow which the woman journalist who had conducted the interview speedily – and jumping the queue – acquired. The mafia had kept faith with its own.

But now times have changed and eventually on 21 September 1988 in *Literaturnaya Gazeta* my article, 'Wild Applause', appeared, in which I told how a cult of semi-divinity had been created around Aliev in Azerbaijan, and how Mamedov had fallen a victim to his intrigues. Several republic, city and regional newspapers in Azerbaijan and Armenia reprinted the article. Within a few days, the postman brought sacks of readers' letters – heart-rending tales from victims who had themselves experienced the horrors of being hounded by the mafia. And a little while later, Aliev himself rang up.

Unfortunately, the conversation is not recorded on tape. Aliev's call took me by surprise. I have to reproduce it from notes which I took immediately after our telephone conversation.

Aliev: 'Why did you write that article? Who put you up to it?'

A. V.: 'I only cover what I decide needs writing about.'

Aliev: 'If you had had a talk with me you would have had a better impression of me. I have always hit it off with journalists and they go away happy. It could have been like that with you.'

A. V.: 'What do you mean by "hit it off"?'

Aliev: 'Come round and find out. You'll probably want to write a retraction of your article.'

No meeting took place. I declined to try to 'hit it off' with him, although other colleagues did. Just for publishing one miserable little article or a single favourable reference to the leader of gigantically striding Azerbaijan, they all (not only our lady reporter mentioned above) jumped the queue for flats, cars, promotion, commissions to write books and trips abroad. Aliev knew how to be a charming and cordial host, a good partner in conversation and patron of the Muses.

Not only was political feel at work here, but also his own personal inclinations and inner needs. His party comrades at the top took pleasure in the company of alcoholics, foul-mouthed swearers and womanizers. Aliev preferred a different crowd – composers, theatre directors, actors and artists. His friendly chats with Shostakovich sometimes went on past midnight. Not only 'court' toadies but genuinely talented people would go home after meeting him, captivated by his charm and friendly disposition. Aliev liked to go to painters' studios and offer them patronage and encouragement. He not only supported but pushed through the making of the film *Interrogation*, the first Soviet work in any medium that fiercely attacked corruption; there was nobody in the top leadership who fought corruption as hard as did Aliev. The world chess champion, Gary Kasparov, has much to be grateful to Aliev for. Born in Baku and having his home there (he barely escaped the anti-Armenian pogroms in 1988), Kasparov, as is well known, was subjected to harassment and discrimination by the central authorities who had put their money on his constant rival, that true party man and member of the central committee of the Communist Youth League, Anatoly Karpov. It is hard to say what would have happened to Kasparov had he not been able at the most critical moments to rely on Geidar Aliev's help and support. There is no paradox in all this. Cultural patronage has been demonstrated by the most brutal monarchs known to history. It is important to bear in mind the various facets of this many-sided character in order to understand the divergent attitudes towards him in Azerbaijan, and beyond the confines of that republic.

'There is no place for the tyrant Aliev in our land' was a slogan on the front of a house in Baku. On the opposite side of the road another said: 'Geidar Aliev is the father of our nation – come back and save us!'

Many of the place-names which have cropped up in this chapter are familiar to readers and viewers all over the world. Names such as Nagorny Karabakh, Stepanakert, Shusha or Sumgait are familiar in the context of very different events, which took place after Aliev had left Baku, and an end to which is not yet in sight. Yet there is no coincidence here – rather a deep-rooted organic connection.

The events in Nagorny Karabakh and the ensuing chain reaction have historic origins beyond the scope of this book. At the first outbreak of disturbances the whole Soviet press as one reported that they had been set off by the mafia. At the time it was already possible to admit the existence of the mafia; but to admit that the country, which Lenin had dubbed a prison of the peoples, had under the Bolsheviks turned into a country for butchery between the peoples – that was still out of the question.

Once again, as always with the Soviet political dictionary, they were juggling with concepts and the misleading substitution of one for another confused people, preventing them from seeing current events in their true light. A journalist put a question to Konstantin Maidanyuk, the special investigator from the Soviet Prosecutor General's office, who had been sent down to Karabakh immediately after the first shots were fired to find those guilty of the murders. He was asked whether he also insisted that the whole mess in Nagorny Karabakh was cooked up by the mafia. He replied that he did not, although it represented the received opinion. 'Can one imagine,' he asked, 'that local thieves and swindlers could organize tens of thousands of people into a political campaign just for the sake of possibly catching a goldfish in a murky pond? As far as I judge the situation, it's the opposite, because the usual links seem to have been severed.'

It is quite clear from this that for the Moscow investigator, 'mafia' means a cohesive and highly organized group of criminals, whereas in Soviet conditions the decisive mafia role is played by politicians, no less cohesive or well-organized, a grouping of 'servants of the state and public' who use criminal methods to preserve their jobs and their strongholds.

Whenever the fundamental interests of the ruling oligarchy were at stake, national differences evaporated. An Armenian, Boris Kevorkov, the party leader of Nagorny Karabakh, was the appointee of the Azeri leadership and carried out all Aliev's orders in his region, and was outstanding in his limitless loyalty to his protector. This so-called (in their language) 'friendship of the peoples' was in fact simply a mutual guarantee for politicians welded together by common interests. The whole world knows to what a catastrophe that led.

On the other hand, the Baku leadership certainly did not respect their Azeri brothers when their words or deeds in any way knocked those who were in power and wished to remain so. The example of

Gamboi Mamedov was not unique. The prosecutor of Sumgait and his colleagues in the city prosecution service frequently gave warning of the dangerous criminal situation in the city, of the social processes taking place there – partly because there was a build-up of a great number of unemployed youngsters, delinquents and drug addicts who could easily be exploited by any group for their own purposes. What, apart from thanks for important information, might be expected by way of a response? This was the response: the prosecutor of Sumgait was putting up a poor fight against hooliganism, spreading panic and provoking internecine conflict. While blood was flowing in Karabakh, and savage butchery was taking place in Sumgait, Aliev watched what was going on from his Moscow flat or dacha outside Moscow, where he was occupied, he said, with the upbringing of three grandchildren, with walks and reading the newspapers. Nor was his voice raised during the bestial pogroms on Armenians in Baku – that peak of Soviet internationalism. When the troops sent by Moscow entered the Azeri capital and started mercilessly killing the peaceful inhabitants, where there were no Armenians left and virtually no Russians, Geidar Aliev appeared again on the political scene. He went to the office of the Azeri permanent mission to the Soviet government and made his famous announcement of support of the Azeri People's Front, which up till then had blamed Aliev for the tragedy which had befallen the Azeri people. It had said so publicly on more than one occasion.

Everything was muddled, confused, interwoven – one fact seems to contradict another, paradoxes pile up and increase – the most likely sign of the activity of deeply hidden mafia forces, each of which was at work in its own self-interest, having long since abandoned any principle, ideas or even logic. It is totally obvious that a peaceful process of change was taking place in Azerbaijan, whatever clearly nationalistic character it had and however patient or democratic it might be, and that the replacement of one political group by another was inevitable.

This rotation of power is inevitable, and those who fall bring down previously well-established mafia connections with them. Put simply, other people with other connections are getting into the driving seat. For those on the way out, the mafiosi losing their positions but still incredibly strong, there remains only one hope: to stick it out, blow on the flame of internecine strife and pander to the most extremist forces, in order to hang on even piecemeal in posts which could protect the mafia's capacity to act. There was no real option (and moreover an unarguably effective one) except the incitement of nationalist feeling.

So, whether or not direct evidence will ever be found of Aliev and his circle's connections with the nationalist extremists, their vested interest in the support of them is self-evident. 'The worse, the better' – this is the only banner around which they could make a stand: only if things got even worse could perestroika be discredited completely together with Gorbachev personally in the eyes of the Azeri people. It was not the sudden explosion of patriotic feeling but cold calculation which caused Aliev to try his luck anew on the greater political arena. He had never tried particularly hard to get to the top in Moscow, understanding that he would never be number one, whereas to be number ten or even number four was not his style. It was better to be a demigod in Azerbaijan than a bigshot bureaucrat in Moscow. He had a chance to return to his position in his home territory – in conditions of semi-chaos and interracial strife. This was not only because the president of Azerbaijan, Ayaz Mutalibov, had been helped at the start of his career by Aliev. Principally it was because he was known to be supported by that part of the population which is either in some way linked to the mafia or dreams of a return to strong government, a concept they associate with him as a well-known and authoritative figure. Aliev in this sense has still not lost his previous standing.

An 80,000-strong crowd which turned out to greet him in his native Nakhichevan consisted then not only of the idly curious. It is not insignificant that the bust of Aliev positioned as befits the twice-over hero in his native land is always bedecked with flowers even in a time of fratricidal skirmishes. No attempts have been made to remove his busts in other cities in Azerbaijan, although there were no qualms about removing monuments to Lenin. A known segment of the working population of the republic still considers him a fighter against the mafia, and against the privileges of the elite. The image of God and Father, which he wanted to create in the eyes of the citizens, still has, it seems, its persuasive power. For many years Georgian taxi-drivers blatantly decorated their windscreens with portraits of Stalin. Similarly their colleagues in Nakhichevan drive around now with portraits of Geidar Aliev. This is not just local patriotism; it is a primitive and obvious form of protest against the chaos, anarchy and terror which has seized their native land and against the violence which no one seems able to stop.

One did not have to be a prophet to predict the stunning victory of Aliev in the elections to the supreme soviet of Azerbaijan and to the supreme soviet of the Nakhichevan Autonomous Republic. He stood in the town where he was born and where nearly everyone was either a relation or a friend or was obligated to him for their positions. Having become a deputy twice over, he is protected by his deputy's immunity and now no sanction threatens him, even if the KGB should suddenly find a list of his bribery receipts written in his own hand. The mafia needs his presence as a working politician: certain powers are rallying around him to give the mafia a chance to get their revenge, or at the very least a chance of immunity.

There is no point in speculating where Aliev's fate will lead him, either as a person or as a professional at work on the political scene. In any case, it is obvious that he is a very different case (and always has been) from the other old men of the Politburo whose departure marked the end of the Brezhnev era: Grishin, Romanov, Kunaev and Tikhonov. He stood out because of his energy, ambition, cunning and capacity to see ahead but not to swim with the tide. He possesses unmistakable signs of individuality, of which the known and unknown 'colleagues of Brezhnev' were totally bereft and for that reason fell into the political void the very day they were removed from their posts.

And one more thing should be taken into account when assessing the moves of the pieces on the Azeri chessboard. Even the economic mafia have no interest in turning their backs on the existing party structures – they exactly fit the Oriental–feudal traditions and mores which date from before history began and which remain entrenched in the republic.

Why does the call to rebel against a market economy and against the independent cooperatives, those 'leeches feeding off the body of the people', and against the notorious black-marketeers, find such a lively response in the local populace? The people's ignorance is taken advantage of, play is made of their real social problems and concerns. But who is throwing down the challenge? In whose interest could it be to prevent the normalization of the economy and the introduction of its objective laws into everyday life? Yes, the party apparatus, which would then lose all its political positions. But standing behind them is the mafia which would lose its economic power. A market economy would lead to honest competition, to the end of monopolies, to the need to work, to demonstrate skill, energy and initiative. Today's mafia under the existing administrative command system achieves its goals without making the slightest effort, without risk and without working, using stolen as opposed to bought or earned basic capital. It monopolizes vast assets stolen from the state. It does not fear competition and for that reason is indeed all-powerful. All-powerful, that is, as long as the state machine continues with its present party and administrative-economic institutions.

The mafia does not want perestroika. That is why Geidar Aliev, that demigod come down from heaven who has got a political second wind, is – as before – its support and its hope.

Chapter Nine

Dear Comrades....

I never thought that I would come across a picaresque novel in real life. This is the tale of the long career of an adventurer who enjoyed astonishing and total success in thumbing his nose at privilege and wealth. His story merits attention because it has a direct bearing on the theme of the Soviet mafia.

The hero of this non-fiction adventure story is a semi-literate man of advanced years (he is now over eighty, and the events I describe took place ten years ago). By the way, I am not sure that 'semi-literate' is an accurate description of someone who was once described by a witty lawyer as capable of making seven spelling mistakes in a six-letter word. This gifted individual, using the simplest possible means, controlled those things of most importance for a Soviet citizen: goods and services in short supply. This man's skill consisted in the following: he would introduce himself as either a minister or a party veteran, sometimes a 'great intelligence officer' in retirement. He would ask the managers of shops, those in charge of bulk stores, supplies or running restaurants and workshops (i.e. not party bosses but people who had influence over the everyday life of millions) for goods in wholesale quantities and would pay for them at firm government prices. You would have thought that the managers and bureaucrats would have dismissed this defenceless senile racketeer or handed him over to the militia, but they gave him everything he asked for without a murmur. In broad daylight in the centre of the capital Yuri Sokolov, the manager of the most important food shop in Moscow, which even now, three-quarters of a century after it was confiscated from its proprietor Eliseyev is still known by the latter's name, personally loaded a minibus with hundreds of tins of caviar and tens of kilos of delicatessen which were then taken to the 'great intelligence officer's' dacha outside Moscow for sale to speculators at ten times the price.

What was the influence which forced powerful people to obey the will of an ignorant old rascal? It was quite simple: photographs which he willingly gave them to see. This 'great intelligence officer' was captured in group photographs in informal poses and even in the embrace of a tipsy Brezhnev, a superciliously smiling Suslov, and Gromyko, pompously standing to stern attention. These snaps disarmed even the most stubborn and resolute: any desire of the 'bosom pal' of all the members of the Politburo had to be fulfilled without question.

The most astonishing thing was that these photographs were not some clumsy montage. They were genuine. To understand their provenance, one or two words about our hero:

Zakhar Dvoiris was a professional swindler who succeeded in living well without lifting a finger even during Stalin's time. He got out of being called up during the war, spending most of the war years in Siberia where, according to him, he was 'tracking down deserters'. It can easily be imagined what sort of 'deserters' he tracked down and how they might have paid him off for his noble contribution to society.

In Khrushchev's time fate had led him to a certain party relic. Their meeting played a decisive role in the future of the clever old rascal. The old relic was Fedor Petrov, an Old Bolshevik – one of very few whom Stalin's terror had passed by. He was once upon a time vice-premier of the puppet government of the 'Far East Republic', then he was in charge of all Soviet science and finally at the appropriate time slipped into a quiet harbour, editing encyclopedias. Under Khrushchev, he was the oldest of all the surviving Bolsheviks – a member since 1896 of a party founded in 1898! That's the sort of phenomenon that is only possible in our country. 'The oldest Bolshevik', he was called in our papers. In this capacity, with the status of honoured guest, he attended various party and other gatherings in the Kremlin and first Khrushchev and then Brezhnev very much liked having their photograph taken with this exhumed old fossil, barely able to stand on his own two feet, thereby demonstrating their direct link with the 'Lenin guard'.

It is no accident that I mention that Petrov could hardly stand unaided. He appeared everywhere leaning on the shoulder of his trusty Zakhar who, believe it or not, was thirty-three years younger than him. Thus Dvoiris invariably, like a pair of crutches, would appear with Petrov and would inevitably fall into the camera's field of vision. This is despite the well-known fact that no one can usually get past members of the 'Ninth' (the ninth department of the KGB in charge of security of the top leadership) – they cannot even get near any location where the leaders might be. And the Ninth could have found their own pair of in-house crutches for Petrov if need be.

It was these pictures, in which Dvoiris with one hand was holding up Petrov and with the other chummily leaning on Gromyko's shoulder or clinking glasses with Brezhnev, which opened every door for him. To begin with, these were the doors of middle managers through whom he established a standard of life which in Soviet circumstances was available otherwise only to the leadership. His two villas in the suburban Moscow settlement of Ilinskoye are reminiscent of pre-Revolutionary nobles' palaces, and equipped with ultra-modern electronic technology including automatic gates, an automatic alarm system and a special telephone line. For curiosity's sake I can reveal that a deputy minister of communications (equivalent to a Western minister of transport) gave him unheard-of permission to drive over level crossings when the barrier pole was in the lowered position; thus the crossing guard would have to stand saluting the passenger in the car as it hurtled across the path of an oncoming train.

Having insinuated himself into the Soviet party-administrative structure, Dvoiris did not only come to know but also saw with his own eyes to what extent all the apparatchiks and bosses were involved in illegal or simply criminal operations and how they feared discovery although they each had, it appeared, their own fairly effective protection. Demonstrating to them 'material proof' of his closeness to the very top leadership, Dvoiris on the one hand had sown in them the fear of angering such a bigshot as he appeared to be and on the other hand hinted at connections which could be useful to them. The risk of accidentally losing any part of their ill-gotten gains was in every way less than the risk of losing them all. For years on end the illiterate, puny old man held in his hands the most powerful mafia forces. There was no hope of anybody simply deciding to do away with him: his daring, licence and air of complete impregnability led all to assume that he was somehow connected with the 'relevant authorities'. I have no evidence whatever of this, but I assume that Dvoiris was a 'stool pigeon' of the KGB who with his help (possibly without his knowing it) was able to uncover the connections of various agents of the commercial mafia within the party and administrative apparatus and to follow how and to whom goods with which this mafia meekly furnished the swindler were distributed.

It is curious that the greater part of the goods went to corrupt officials who had no idea where Dvoiris had got them from. The absurdity was that the suppliers and the recipients were often in one and the same camp: a subject fit for the theatre of the absurd which, however, in Soviet circumstances is the ordinary and everyday reality.

There would perhaps be no point in going into this pretty picture of contemporary Moscow mores in such detail were it not for events which were revealed after Dvoiris's eventual downfall. He came to grief completely by accident, like a mountaineer who has conquered Everest without a slip, but who slips and breaks a leg on a bit of orange peel in the street. Confident in his impregnability, Dvoiris on holiday in Sochi had cheated a humble little tailor by not paying for a suit he had had made, legging it back to Moscow like a common-or-garden cheat. Although the tailor had been shown the snaps designed to inspire terror, he did not fear Dvoiris's threats because he was not a member of the mafia, he did not belong to the party apparatus and he had nothing to lose. He kicked up a fuss, to start with bringing a criminal charge of common theft, but the thread inexorably led further. Then the storm broke. The case against the tailor's client for a bill of 160 roubles suddenly drew into its proceedings the prosecution service of the Russian Federation. The investigation was entrusted to the senior investigator for particularly important matters in the republic, Zoye Sheikin, and was conducted in the utmost secrecy. That the investigation lasted for many months and that hundreds of witnesses were called in to give evidence, spoke volumes.

It emerged that among those involved in the affairs of the accused were ministers of the USSR and of the union republics, deputies in the Supreme Soviet of the USSR, members of the Central Committee. It is known for certain (a sensation in the early '80s) that the investigator summoned as a witness (and he even turned up) a Central Committee secretary, Yakov Ryalov, later Soviet ambassador to France.

There was probably no criminal (as distinct from political) case in the Brezhnev period that was surrounded with such secrecy. There was an impenetrable wall of silence around it. But now I do know where the threads were leading – to that ever-popular team we have met, namely Churbanov, Shcholokov and Brezhnev, but in this case also to Viktor Grishin, the boss of Moscow who was soon to become the crown prince and contender for the all-union throne. What I now know could only be guessed at then.

My interest in the Dvoiris case I owe to Sergei Mikhalkov, familiar to many not only as the father of two film directors (Nikita Mikhalkov and Andrei Konchalovsky) but also as the favourite poet of Stalin, Khrushchev, Brezhnev and Chernenko, as the author of the words of the Soviet national anthem and, lastly, as the chairman of the ill-famed Union of Writers of the Russian Federation. Early on he was just a friend of Dvoiris. Realizing that Mikhalkov had access to the highest levels, Dvoiris had made a point of making his acquaintance and with the help of the 'poet not averse to prose' pulled off a few profitable deals. Then, as usual, Dvoiris played dirty on his friend and began to apply blackmail and extortion. Over the years when they had been on friendly terms he had found something out about the poet that the poet preferred not to be aired in public. Mikhalkov took fright and cried for help. I was one of those he turned to: 'Make public mincemeat of that scoundrel,' he demanded.

This topic and the truth about it were of the greatest interest. It illustrated with utmost clarity the whole complex tangle of Soviet reality, in which one can cross from the tragic to the comic in only one step. I wrote up everything I found out about Dvoiris in two articles for *Literaturnaya Gazeta*. Included was a reference – more ironical than stinging – to the manager of Eliseyev's, Yuri Sokolov. The reaction to the mention of this name plunged even our editorial chiefs into a state of shock. One might have expected our hardened editor-in-chief, Alexander Chakovsky, a man who was thoroughly expert in party intrigues, not to be astonished by anything of this sort.

First there came a telegram signed by a dozen or so cosmonauts.

How could you possibly impugn, cried the heroes and double heroes, the good name of a wonderful man who always 'sees right' his regular and grateful customers? In those days the cosmonauts were still cocooned in an aura of romantic mystery and, as they were held in especial regard at the highest levels, the manager of the food store probably gave them everything they asked for. Their telegram afforded a smile but came as no surprise.

An hour later came another telegram with an identical text but signed by a group of high-ranking generals. On the morning of the day following the article there was a third telegram – from honoured artists in the world of culture. In the evening an armed official messenger brought an envelope, sealed with wax and the seal of the mayor of Moscow. Vladimir Popov expressed 'his sharp disagreement with the groundless criticism of a most successful Soviet tradesman, who has always been a reliable supplier to the staff of the Moscow city soviet'.

We had never had anything against the city soviet staff, but what invisible force could have made these evidently frightened and evidently stupid people mount such an attack on a newspaper – and and in so doing leave written evidence of its fear and stupidity? However, the person leading the attack left no written evidence. Viktor Grishin simply picked up the receiver of his Kremlin telephone and gave our editor-in-chief a dressing-down for his 'serious blunder'. Needless to say, he did not start going on about the special attention given by the store manager to members of the city party committee – this would have been too trifling an issue for such a senior political personality. A far greater matter of principle is what exercised him. 'Was it not rash,' he castigated the editor, 'to relay the unvarnished truth to Soviet readers? You write about caviar and other fish delicacies being supplied under the counter, but meanwhile the shelves of Moscow shops are empty.' (Compared to today's situation, his 'empty' was abundance.) 'You could set off disturbances. Do you want to be the cause of outbreaks of disorder?'

I cannot resist putting on record another occurrence a few months later because of the completely identical party reaction and the same phraseology, which allows one to understand what had been causing them concern.

Literaturnaya Gazeta published an article of mine, 'Spring Floods', in which I reported the death on a massive scale of cattle in the Vladimir oblast due to insufficient feed. Local managers had left it to rot while they pursued their own personal interests. The day the article appeared the editor-in-chief's government telephone was bombarded with hysterical calls. First party secretaries were phoning from all over the Union, Vladimir included. They all made the same protest, namely that my article could lead to food riots against the party leadership, even that this was our intention. By the end of that day there was a local call. It was Mikhail Zimlyanin, the Central Committee secretary responsible for ideology. Without beating about the bush he anathematized 'Spring Floods' and the fact of its appearance as 'the greatest political error'.

The editor-in-chief was terrified and called me to his office. He suggested that I myself should write a refutation for the following week's issue. Chakovsky was sympathetic enough to allow me 'not to use the strongest terms of abuse' against myself but added that the retraction should contain a 'categorical dissociation from any of the general conclusions'. At risk of perplexing my readers, but holding to the truth (what was, was) I admit that I agreed to do it. But I knew that if I were to write the disclaimer I could do it in such a way that our readers would understand 'between the lines' that we had been forced to publish it.

The next morning I took a draft text to Chakovsky whom I found in a splendid mood. He was holding a pencilled note and told me to look at it and tear it up, not showing it to anybody. Early that morning before I had arrived there had been a phone call from another party secretary, Mikhail Gorbachev, who had only just been appointed. As will be recalled, he had replaced Fyodor Kulakov as party secretary responsible for agriculture. Gorbachev had thanked the paper for its 'brave and hard-hitting piece' which, as he said, would help him in the task of putting right the serious failings in the area for which he had been made responsible.

By 'putting right failings', Gorbachev had in mind personnel replacements. That is indeed what he instituted: many regional party secretaries with responsibility for the agricultural sector, including the one in Vladimir, were fired.

I hope the reader will forgive me this digression enabling me to tell the story of the first time – if at one remove – Gorbachev gave me his support. Maybe he did not intend it, but this in turn enabled the paper to continue campaigning against the party mafia. We are now coming near to the unexpected denouement of our picaresque tale.

Nothing further came of Grishin's protest, and there was only one reason for that. We knew in general if not in detail that the KGB was keeping an eye on the investigation and, moreover, quietly controlling it. By unravelling more and more episodes the investigation was in a way helping Andropov in his duel with Shcholokov. Chakovsky, who was familiar with palace intrigues, considered that Andropov wielded the greater authority and we therefore decided not to react to any wiggings from Grishin.

Everybody expected a sensational trial. We could have made it sensational even if it were to be held behind closed doors, because we had already worked out a plan of how to get hold of news of its progress. And it could hardly have been a completely closed trial as there was no article in the legal code to warrant it.

However, no trial took place, either closed or open. Andropov had taken the usual course, finding a way of avoiding the courts but at the same time isolating the old Jew from the rest of society. Compliant psychiatrists immediately certified Dvoiris an incurable schizophrenic and had him put away in a psychiatric prison. Unlike those prisoners of conscience for whom the psychiatric hospital is an insult and a far more cruel punishment than ordinary prison or labour camp, Dvoiris was delighted at Andropov's decision. It meant that he would escape having his property confiscated and in effect it repudiated what had been in the newspapers. We would be seen as having weighed against a sick man rather than a criminal!

Through relatives Dvoiris sent me a letter inviting me to go and see him and jointly with him (!) work out a battle plan against the Kremlin mafia. He promised to reveal sensational things about Galina Brezhneva and her husband Churbanov, about Grishin and his part in the Moscow trading mafia. Moreover, he would tell me about the group that had cosily latched onto this mafia, living comfortably off its gifts. The group was large and consisted of well-known poets, playwrights, composers, actors, artists, theatre directors and other creators of treasures for the soul, possessors of the highest honours, of prizewinners' medals and other rubbish pompously called Orders of this or that. (It is clear that the Central Committee knew how well-informed Dvoiris was and that he intended to speak out, so together with the KGB they had preferred to 'spare' him a court trial.)

I made immediate plans to go to the Smolensk oblast to see Dvoiris. He had been sent there, given a room to himself and the job of supervision of the hospital's canteen. In order to get to see him I would need the permission of two ministers. Shcholokov categorically refused a signature and the Minister of Health of the USSR, Academician Boris Petrovsky, ticked me off for being insensitive towards a very sick man and for threatening to aggravate his condition purely for the sake of a 'journalistic sensation'. We shall not tolerate any 'monkeying about at the expense of the individual', he told me, trying to make me feel a barbarian and scoundrel.

Nevertheless, there was a sensation, even if a little later on. Immediately after Brezhnev died, Andropov instructed the KGB to hand over to the prosecution service the material that his former department of state had gathered on the activities of the Moscow mafia. The first person to be arrested as a result was Yuri Sokolov, the manager of Eliseyev's foodstore – the man who had so zealously taken care of the cosmonauts, generals and actors and had looked after the nomenklatura and gone to endless trouble for the staff at the Moscow city soviet. Alongside him in the dock were all the leading lights from that outfit which is the main control centre for the distribution in the capital of food and other goods in short supply. In the back of the shop, next to the manager's office, was a comfortable room where the table was laid round the clock with drinks and 'zakuski'. Not only did Grishin, Churbanov and other party bosses come here to rest their weary souls, it was here over whisky and black caviar that board meetings were held by the Moscow mafia, whose complete membership list remained a closely kept secret.

As always, in cases like this, the chain reaction gathered speed. One secret door opened after another – both in the literal and in the metaphorical sense. The trail of revelations led to the person in charge of managing trade for the whole of Moscow, Tregubov, and thereby to the Ministry of Trade of the Russian Federation. Here they distributed stocks of goods in short supply, here permissions were issued for the purchase – both wholesale and retail – of furniture, clothing and groceries, which on the black market were worth three, five or sometimes ten times more than state prices. The scheme was always the same: goods were transferred to wholesale buyers; they in turn raised the price and sold them on. The militia took their share of the trading profits, as well as prosecutors, judges and party and state bureaucrats. The threads of the capital's mafia led far from Moscow – to the Transcaucasus and Central Asia, but most importantly to somewhere nearer home, namely to Old Square in the centre of Moscow.

First it was the republic's deputy Minister for Trade – it was up to this rung of the nomenklatura ladder that investigators were authorized to penetrate. By arresting him, they had exhausted the possibility of digging further and deeper. A blow to the mafia had been dealt, but even Andropov did not intend to attempt to get at the top people involved. In the Politburo he still had alongside him the whole senile gathering, from Chernenko to Grishin, and, in Soviet circumstances, crushing them was not something to be achieved through the courts.

Nevertheless, it was possible to progress the investigation a bit further – if not upwards, then sideways. It seemed to me that a simple tactical step could help this: with the help of new medical expertise Dvoiris's responsibility for his actions could be questioned, thus enabling the investigation into his affairs to be re-opened and a case brought to court. It is clear that thereby new names and new episodes from the lives of highly-placed mafiosi would emerge. This idea appealed to some people in the Committee for Party Control, who in harness with the KGB were collecting 'dirt' on the Shcholokov clan. Nobody dared cross Arvid Pelshe, the aged president of the committee, who was hardly capable of moving and who would cover up the slightest hint of scandal. He would not 'slander the party' at any price; even so, his first deputy Ivan Gustov had, as it were, 'made soundings'. They even asked me to put together material which had been collected but not printed in the newspaper to make it available to 'competent comrades'. At which point everything came to a full stop. Andropov was already at death's door and nobody else rushed to take such a responsible decision on himself.

Meanwhile, an invisible trade where people's lives rather than money were at stake continued in the wings. Sokolov was being held at the Lefortovo prison in the wing administered by the KGB, not the MVD – but it is hardly likely that a kind of impenetrable 'Berlin Wall' was maintained between the various wings. Thus one way or another Sokolov was offered a deal on terms which he could only accept: he had no choice. His silence or his life. He was warned that a court would sentence him to be shot, but he should not be afraid: he would put in an appeal for clemency which would be granted. And then afterwards, not immediately of course, but soon – he would be quietly released and in prison camp, of course, he would not have been exposed to harsh conditions.

All this seemed perfectly plausible: Sokolov knew that trials of mafiosi lower down the scale had taken place on these terms, and there had not been a single occasion when the mafia had not kept its word. Sokolov's trial was mounted in great haste behind half-closed doors. The accused kept to his word: he did not name so much as one new name, did not mention so much as one new fact. Incidentally, he did not have the occasion to do so: the prosecutor in the trial made no effort to extend the scope of the charge and by dint of great effort succeeded in getting answers that were as laconic as possible to his questions and to questions for the defence.

As expected, the death sentence was pronounced, and the accused accepted it with unruffled calm. Within the accepted time limit, he lodged an appeal for clemency without taking too much trouble over the convincingness of his arguments or over the need to appear in the most favourable possible light in the eyes of the Presidium of the Supreme Soviet of the USSR, which has the rights of clemency in such cases. But his appeal was refused. The accused was informed of this half an hour before he was executed. He could only cry out as loudly as he liked that he had been deceived: the train had left the station – for ever.

However, his direct boss Nikolai Tregubov saved himself. He wrote personal letters from his prison cell to Grishin and the first deputy president of the Presidium of the Supreme Soviet of the USSR, Vasily Kuznetsov: 'I beg you for a face-to-face meeting. I must tell you something which I cannot possibly mention in court.' The hint was taken. Neither Grishin nor Kuznetsov came to see Tregubov in prison but contact was established and an agreement reached: his life in exchange for silence. As we know, such an agreement in no small way prevented the mafia from doing away with those who knew too much and accomplices who had fallen by the wayside. But Tregubov's trial was delayed, Gorbachev came to power and sentence was pronounced in autumn 1986. Grishin and his friends lost any real power, it became even more difficult to eliminate an unwanted friend with impunity. Thus both sides carried out their obligations. Tregubov got fifteen years and, maintaining deep silence, is serving them far from Moscow. How long will he keep silent? He is already past seventy. If he can succeed in overcoming the fear for his life, he could tell his story. In any case, he knows a great deal about a lot of people. And it is hardly an accident that the authorities in the prison and in Moscow carefully shield him from any contact with the outside world.

In previous chapters we have already pondered over the fact that the highest posts in the shadowy mafia cabinet were probably not occupied by members of the Politburo nor by ministers or secretaries of area party committees but by anonymous restaurateurs or 'bent' motor mechanics who were not trying to be appointed to official posts but whole-heartedly made use of those who did, holding members of the Politburo, area secretaries of the party and ministers under their wing, allowing them to flourish. This was suggested as a theory or hypothesis – a perfectly plausible one, but one that could not be confirmed by any hard examples. However, there is one sole example, a concrete one.

It was after Gorbachev had already come to power and perestroika had started that the prosecution service allowed itself to give the go-ahead for the arrest of a certain 'respected comrade', signs of whose criminal activity had been noticed long before. But some invisible power stayed the prosecutor's hand every time that he was ready to authorize the arrest. More than that: according to some sources there was talk about the role which the 'respected comrade' played in the 'shadow cabinet', other sources had information about the glittering successes he had achieved in the field of trade. While the earliest information remained in the secret safes of the relevant services, the latter indicators had absolutely concrete business consequences. First the 'respected comrade' was confirmed as a member of the board of the chief trade council (a very high position in the Soviet nomenklatura) and secondly was appointed, sorry, 'elected' (for in those times the word 'elected' could only be used in inverted commas) a deputy in the Moscow city soviet. However, I repeat that he did not aspire in the least to official responsibilities and posts: unofficial ones were quite sufficient for him.

The man's name was Mkhitsar Ambartsumyan, and he had a

humble post as director of a vegetable depot in a Moscow suburb. When towards the end of 1985 his arrest was made known, hardly anyone except those on the inside track attached any importance to it at all: directors of vegetable, fruit and suchlike depots (an idiotic creation of the planned system under which the producer of goods and his customer are separated by an intervening stage in the form of a state depot where, trading in statistics rather than food, it is possible to make millions in a year) always held and continue to hold pride of place in the criminal calendar. However, the official newspaper reports about the investigation, trial and sentence imposed on this run-of-the-mill 'depot manager' were inconsistent with his position, which speaks volumes about how far he was from being 'run-of-the-mill'.

I met Ambartsumyan once. In the Moscow House of Cinema they were celebrating the premiere of a new film, and one of its producers, a friend of mine, invited me to go up to the restaurant for a private get-together after the screening. At the abundantly laden dining table sat famous actors, writers and directors – and amongst them one more modest couple. The man looked important and much less than his sixty-five or sixty-seven years, and while he sat there smiling without joining in the jocular conversation around him, his whole presence and manner made it clear that at this celebration he was the most important person present. Some young people were constantly dancing around the place with their cameras and the observant would have noticed that every shot included this taciturn dignitary. Choosing a quiet moment I whispered a question to the perpetrator of this dreadful party. 'How can you not know who he is?' he replied with astonishment. 'It's Mkhitsar Ambartsumyan. He's known throughout Moscow. He's provided this lot.' Here my friend pointed grandly to the table groaning with food. 'If you want grapes or bananas ...' Of course I could have done with both, but grasping who it was who was 'known throughout Moscow' I was too proud to accept the implied offer.

The money which 'Mkhitsarchik' had at his disposal had accrued to him in the following way: Ambartsumyan himself in exchange for bribes would obtain deliveries of fruit from Transcaucasia and Central Asia which was surplus to the statistical returns. And through bribery and off the record, he imported exotic fruit such as oranges, bananas and pineapples. Next, shops which dreamt of such goods that brought in enormous returns when sold under the counter, had themselves to pay bribes to him. What he received was significantly more than what he gave, so that at the end of the day he was always left with a profit. Over the twenty-two years that he was occupied in this trade, his income consisted not of thousands but of millions. But in time something other than fruit became his most important source of revenue. Gathering his forces, and concentrating his basic capital, Ambartsumyan became a merchant not just of fruit but of appointments. Many key posts in the party and state apparatus were occupied by people he had recommended, pushed forward and guaranteed. For example, the post of trade instructor of the Central Committee cost 50,000–60,000 roubles; an instructor in a special position cost even more. His 'recommendations' cost a lot of money – those who desired them did not stint themselves. Involved in this many-runged system of trade in official posts were bureaucrats at various levels, but somewhere very high up they possibly did not even know by whom and why an 'esteemed comrade' was being pushed forward for this or that post when they were looking at documents on which were placed tens of signatures under the magic word 'agreed'. The officials were playing their games unaware that they were merely puppets in the hands of an uncrowned king.

In the opinion of lawyers involved in the investigation of this and other cases concerning accomplices of the Moscow mafia group, there were not tens but hundreds of officials who owed their positions to Ambartsumyan and his circle.* Among them were highly placed party workers, ministry officials and central government people. It is quite possible that by now they have ceased to hold their posts, but their going into retirement, if they have done so, is less connected with the uncovering of the real reason for their original appointments than a general shuffling of officials in the apparatus. Having hung on in the still-surviving nomenklatura, they continue to be active in the system, serving the mafia 'shadow cabinet' which has lost its

---

Vladimir Oleinik was convinced that Ambartsumyan, who was already past seventy, could give valuable evidence and name important names, thus saving his own skin. He himself filled out an application with his plea for clemency and persuaded the prosecutor of the Russian Federation Sergei Yemelyanov to support him. The prosecutor approved the application late at night, but the following morning Oleinik arrived at the prison to tell the accused and was told that during the night Ambartsumyan had been executed.

previous leader but which no doubt got another in his place. Who was he? We can only guess. How can we guess? How can he be found among the thousands of depot managers, storekeepers and barmen in Moscow – the more so if nobody wants to look ...

Did Grishin know who Ambartsumyan really was when he was shot at the very end of the Grishin regime in Moscow? Perhaps, perhaps ... Ambartsumyan did not betray anyone, although the example of Sokolov conclusively proved that it was not possible to rely on anything or anyone, that nobody was really interested in saving his life any longer. The 'protection group', i.e. the people at the top of the nomenklatura, had decided to sacrifice the 'Godfather'. Also, he still had his family and he knew that any word he spoke out of turn would cost them dear.

Vladimir Oleinik, the inspector in charge of major cases in the Russian Federation prosecution services (now a people's deputy of the Russian Federation), told me that in the case of Tregubov and Sokolov, and in the case of Ambartsumyan, the threads led to Grishin and that the investigation tried to have him summonsed as a witness. Contrary to correct legal practice, lawyers were prepared to interview him 'at home' and certify a list of questions and answers as some sort of 'official record' in order not to humiliate his standing as a member of the Politburo. But even for this seditious scheme, the investigators (who were themselves members of the party!) were threatened with the loss of their party cards, jobs and worse things ...*

It had been widely rumoured for many years that Grishin was not just a protector of the mafia but an active member of it, where he played a far from insignificant role. One very famous public figure, senior in the party and legal hierarchies, who asked to remain anonymous, assured me that this claim was well documented. As a man

---

* Should this come as any surprise? Viktor Grishin was kept informed of the course of the investigation several times a day: who had said what, what names had been mentioned, were the amounts of bribes known? Facts which emerged during the course of this 'secret' investigation were also brought to the attention of interested parties and Grishin issued an instruction 'not to let this business get out of control', 'don't be led on by the accused'. Relatives and friends of the mafia 'godfathers' worked where important information was collated, their nearest and dearest were in charge of sectors: the deputy general prosecutor, militia bosses and party leaders. In this way, the mafia got to know whether their placeman was playing a double game, whether the mafia was operating effectively in the inquiry or whether it needed to exert more pressure.

who was officially responsible for the scrutiny of investigative materials, my informant, in his own words, saw conclusive proof of the by no means merely platonic love affair which connected Grishin with the already unmasked mafia 'godfathers' and their HQ.

Although I would like to believe not only both my well-informed informant and authoritative lawyers who have told me the same thing, but also finally myself (because I carried out my own journalistic inquiries), I must however say that there is no conclusive evidence in support of this accusation. Far more important, it is undeniable that today's state and party government are patently unwilling to carry out a single-minded inquiry because they already have data, however tangential and contradictory, about the involvement in the mafia of this former member of the Politburo, for many years the boss of Moscow and unsuccessful heir apparent.

It would seem that it was only because of persistent rumours that an inquiry was finally held, because they affected the 'honour of the party'. If Grishin himself was a 'victim of slanderous rumours' put about by the press, perhaps he should have demanded legal redress to protect his 'good name' from slander. But all attempts by various investigators to carry out such an inquiry, not 'privately' but by the proper legal means, were firmly suppressed. The same Vladimir Oleinik who was referred to previously and who was working in the insupportable atmosphere of the prosecution service apparatus, was required to resign his post 'voluntarily'. Although the party often trumpets its lack of meddling in the supervision of the prosecution service and the administration of justice, all this as always is no more than a demagogic propaganda device: the Chief Prosecutor of the USSR would not dare bring a single case against a member of the Politburo, even an ex-member, without direct authorization from Old Square. Such authorization has never yet been given and I do not think it ever will be. Society, having had its fill of suffering from ubiquitous corruption, wishes to know the truth about its recent leaders. This is not a thirst for sensation, blood or revenge, but a natural desire by people who have lived under the yoke of all-powerful and ignorant rogues. If it were a question of just one of the former leaders, the new government could easily give him up to be destroyed, presenting him as the black sheep – a sad exception to the general rule. But since it is a question precisely of all (or nearly all) of the members of the previous administration of autocratic old men, their exposure would lead to only one possible and inescapable conclusion from a historical perspective, that is, of the criminal character of the party and the whole political system which enables criminals to make their way into positions of power and fanatically protects them from exposure. The saving of former leaders no longer of use to anyone, whether in the political or the personal sense, is in reality motivated by the instinct for self-protection, and not by concern for their predecessors. A system of mutual protection is at work . . .

Meanwhile, we have to be content with rumours, but they are like rivers: the further they get from the source, the more diffuse they are. They must be treated extremely cautiously. Many times I have heard about the close friendship of Viktor Grishin and Grigory Romanov – the former ruler of Leningrad, who, by a cruel irony of fate, bore the same surname as the dynasty of Russian tsars wiped out by the Bolsheviks. Incidentally, this friendship was no more than a legend. At particular moments and in various situations, the logic of political battle obliged them to join forces, for example to try to block Mikhail Gorbachev's route to the top, but these temporary tactical alliances did not prevent them from being in profound opposition with each other as they competed for influence, for precedence in the high leadership, for a place on the mausoleum on Red Square or on the presidium at some ceremonial occasion. Each of them had long considered himself the most suitable successor to the leadership and had tried in advance to elbow out his rival. Grishin was closer to Brezhnev not only from the geographical point of view but in spirit, and he did not tire of skilfully denigrating his party colleague. I state this in the interests of objective truth, not hiding, however, my equally tender feelings towards both Moscow and Leningrad bosses.

It was Grishin himself who persistently encouraged the rumours by his thoughtfully assenting silences and his meaningful sniggers, and as they swept the country, they had a particularly powerful influence on all who were fed up with the triumphant arrogance of these latter-day lords of life. I have in mind, for example, the notorious story about the wedding of either Romanov's son or his daughter (I cannot be more precise, because I want to give the most accurate impression of the rumours which were circulating: I have heard both versions). According to these rumours, the wedding reception was held in the Winter Palace using the royal dinner service from the collection in the Hermitage. This rumour is still widely believed to this very day. I heard the story as if it were unquestionably true from the lips of people closest to Grishin, who had worked for many years on his staff.

On the wave of glasnost, I decided to check out the going version of this story and to publish my findings in our newspaper. But the then first deputy to the editor-in-chief, Yuri Izyumov, firmly opposed the idea. To begin with I thought that it was because of the same old unwillingness of the apparatus to touch on the doings of former members of the Politburo. And then I remembered: Izyumov was very close to Grishin, having worked for years as his adviser on cultural affairs. He was simply protecting the interests of his former chief and repeating what was said in those circles. Nevertheless, by dint of cunning, I obtained permission from the editorial offices to investigate some quite other criminal activity in Leningrad and contacted two retired colonels in the legal service, former army investigators and prosecutors, who had carried out a very careful inquiry and established that the popular rumours had no foundation whatever in fact. This in no way rehabilitates Romanov in the most important sense, i.e. for belonging to the political mafia which thrived alongside the economic and criminal mafia. But the Hermitage episode most likely never took place – we are obliged to conclude thus, at least until someone is able to produce a piece of reliable evidence, however small.

The desire to get to the bottom of the direct involvement of the Brezhnev Politburo in corruption is in my view the natural consequence of that norm familiar to everybody and pervading all relationships both upwards and sideways; that is to say: 'I'll scratch your back if you scratch mine.'*

To the extent that nothing could be achieved without open bribery

---

* This desire, as far as can be judged from various sources, is by no means universal. This is how the once undisputed leader of the most democratic wing of the Gorbachev administration, Alexander Yakovlev, answered a question from a correspondent of *Moscow News* about his relations with Kunaev, Aliev, Romanov and others like them. 'I have experienced the deepest fellow-suffering for all those who ruled over us and were ruled before our time ... They were all victims.' My deep respect for Alexander Yakovlev requires me to refrain from making the comment I would like to on his magnanimous statement, so I shall only say that I feel not the slightest sympathy for those who were put in power by the Soviet mafia and who from their seats of power did not consider themselves victims either.

and that the unquenchable greed of Brezhnev together with his family and his circle was there for all to see, an impression was created close to the truth, that every government official – literally each one of them – was using his position to take bribes for providing any service. This ubiquitous corruption seemed to the public to take only one form, namely the obtaining of money or valuable gifts. Thus, there was only one kind of difference between members of the high oligarchy as far as the public imagination was concerned: some took more and some took less.

Nevertheless, there were subtle nuances depending on personal preferences and leanings. There is no evidence, even any unsubstantiated claims, of any criminal mercenary interest by Kosygin, Suslov or Andropov. This does not exonerate Kosygin from his unprincipled manipulation of Brezhnev or his hand in the economic ruination of the country, nor Suslov from ideological banditry nor Andropov from the destruction of innocent people and the persecution of so-called dissidents. It is just that each individual's guilt cannot be reduced to a stereotype.

Yet these stereotypes did not arise arbitrarily – they do have a sound basis in fact. They were established during the twenty years of the Brezhnev regime when the character of relationships both at the very top and at the very lowest levels were marked by certain compulsory rituals, any deviation from which would knock a man off the rails, label him an outsider and deprive him of any promotion. Expensive presents to one's boss, on the occasion of a holiday, an anniversary, a visit – or without any excuse at all – were given quite openly. It was impossible for an apparatchik to get on without them, whether it was a question of promotion or of just not getting thrown out.

There was one particularly notorious incident: the banning at the last minute of the very popular Soviet television programme *Vzglyad* ('View') on New Year's Eve 1989–90. It was officially, and confusingly, announced that this was for 'aesthetic reasons'. An amazing real-life drama occurred exactly a year later, on exactly the same day on the eve of 1991 when *Vzglyad* was cancelled again – this time for overtly political reasons. The broadcasters wanted to comment on the resignation of Eduard Shevardnadze. A year earlier these political reasons had been disguised as 'aesthetic' ones. Evidently, the bosses of Gosteleradio had felt unbearable concern for Soviet viewers who might be exposed to the 'unaesthetic' fat and flabby face of a tipsy Galina Brezhneva. I think, however, that the censors were more concerned with politics than aethetics; in the television interview the daughter of the deceased dictator spoke about presents which she was supposed to have received from Raisa Gorbacheva, who was thereby seeking to curry favour with the 'first family' in the Soviet Union and thus open her husband's career path to Moscow. Galina even showed onscreen an expensive necklace which was one of the supposed presents.

I said 'supposed' and am surprised at my own caution. Although I have no facts either for or against this story, I am ready to believe Galina. The shameful system of backscratching which had ingrained itself at the top simply obliged people to conduct their relationships within the party in this manner. Just as in polite society it is not done to go to a family party without a bunch of flowers for your hostess, so in 'polite' party circles it was not done to transfer from the provinces to Moscow without bringing presents. A high-ranking Muscovite visiting the capital of a republic also had to be given presents, in gratitude for his bestowing the honour of a short visit. So, if one admits the possibility that Raisa gave Galina presents, this was no more than the tribute required in an obnoxious ritual. This is by no means, of course, to say that either side came out of it smelling of roses. Nor did it come as a shock to me: it was an everyday run-of-the-mill occurrence of party life, no more and no less.

Great misgivings are aroused by the accusation that Yegor Ligachev received 30,000 roubles' worth (or 60,000 roubles' worth?) of bribes. I will leave aside the fact that the accusers had nothing to go on except the evidence mentioned on one sole occasion by Usmankhodzhaev, which he later repudiated. Nor am I talking about the dubiousness of that evidence where almost two dozen high-ranking apparatchiks were named as bribe-takers (the list is always arbitrary). The point was that all of them were people whom it was necessary to get branded as bribe-takers so that the Brezhnev 'bandocrats' could be knocked out with one blow. It was as if Usmankhodzhaev specially picked them out to besmirch them and get rid of them once and for all from the political arena.

But the main thing that makes me doubt the credibility of these accusations is the attempt of the inquiry to please conventional public opinion, which easily understands one traditional form of corruption: taking money. Corrupt officials were not all the same and some of them belonged to the mafia for other reasons than money. They benefited not in the form of useless millions in bank-notes rotting away in some casket hidden in the ground, nor did they get their kickbacks in the form of diamonds sparkling on rings or watches.

There is no evidence that Ligachev received a bundle of money and I do not think that any evidence that he did will ever be found. However, there is incontrovertible evidence that he supported many embezzlers and undoubtedly corrupt members of the nomenklatura, took active steps to shield them, sheltered them from exposure, arrest and trial and even used his position to interfere directly in the prosecutor's work and the due process of law. For people far from the reality of life in the Kremlin and endless party intrigues there is only one explanation for this: since he had defended mafiosi leaders, and dragged them out of the hole they had fallen into, it meant that he had an interest in doing so, because he would not have got involved for nothing and thereby risked being discredited and accused himself. I am always surprised by the persistent question 'Was he or was he not on the take?', when it is a question of one of the most highly-placed in the land taking part in the protection of mafiosi by shielding them from the due sanction of the law. In all legal systems in the world, including the Soviet one, helping a criminal, hiding him from police investigation and trial, not to mention direct interference in the course of justice, sheltering the accused from punishment, is accounted being an accessory to crime.

Membership of high-placed protectors in mafia groups is con-firmed by one fact alone: their participation in 'rescue operations'. The need to establish and maintain reliable people everywhere* also appears to be the most powerful motivating force which pushes

---

* Ligachev had hardly taken up his key position in the Kremlin leadership and command of party appointments than he transferred his chums to Moscow with him. They amazed his colleagues in the capital by their complete incompetence. From Tomsk he brought to the capital Vladimir Karnaukhov and put him in charge of a trade organization; he appointed the former director of the Tomsk psychiatric hospital Anatoly Potapov – a totally illiterate petty bureaucrat – Minister of Health of the Russian Federation. It is clear that they would not have given Ligachev any bribes – he simply needed faithful servants around him. Thank God the reign of one of these 'Vikings' was not a long one: Potapov did not get into the new Russian government. But Karnaukhov managed to keep his grip and even got promotion: he became the deputy president of the executive committee of the Moscow city soviet.

functionaries of a high level to commit the most illegal acts and makes them, regardless of pecuniary interest, first hostages of the mafia and then members of the whole united mafia network. Everyone plays his assigned role. The most graphic example of this was provided by the scandalous release from arrest of Viktor Smirnov, the former second secretary of the central committee of the Moldavian Communist Party who had previously been in charge of the special sector of the Central Committee responsible for the whole nomenklatura in Central Asia. When the campaign against 'Rashidovists' began, he was among the most severe critics, exposing the very echelons of officials which he himself had created – or, at the very least, had confirmed in their positions. Having been appointed the representative of Old Square in Moldavia, Smirnov also made some exposés there: his finest hour was bringing a case against the deputy prime minister of Moldavia, Vasily Vyshku, who was sacked, arrested and sentenced as one of the most active participants in the Moldavian mafia. While Smirnov crushed the mafia in Moldavia, investigators in Uzbekistan presented evidence of his links with the local mafia. There were nineteen proven episodes of bribe-taking.

A typical Soviet row exploded behind the scenes, as always, with the observance of conspiratorial secrecy. Behind firmly closed doors, the Kremlin cabinet decided the fate of their 'party comrade'. To start with, they agreed to an inquiry, then Smirnov quietly retired 'for health reasons'. Then after about three months the Chief Prosecutor of the USSR was eventually given the go-ahead to authorize his arrest. It is clear that for this to happen agreement was needed from no less than two or three members of the Politburo, or perhaps the agreement of the whole lot.

But the war continued after his arrest. The victims did not concede defeat and began actively to prepare their revenge. On 19 May 1989 a new investigative team replacing Telman Gdlyan and Nikolai Ivanov suddenly obtained instructions from the collegium of the prosecution service of the USSR 'to reinvestigate the validity of prosecution evidence' which had led to the arrest of Smirnov and the charge of his involvement in corruption. The investigators could interpret official terminology and understood bureaucratic euphemisms. But by 22 May Smirnov was free.

But! On 12 May I had already been in the office of a very senior official of the Supreme Court of the USSR. We were talking about

226

other things when the telephone rang. From the conversation I gathered that it was the head of the administrative department of the Central Committee, Alexander Pavlov. Up to the present time, the party official holding this post is senior to the Minister of Justice, above the Minister of the Interior, above the Chief Prosecutor and above the president of the Supreme Court and he would have stood above the president of the KGB if that person hadn't been a member of the Politburo. When he rang off, he remarked with evident pleasure but without going into any detail: 'Smirnov is going to be released within a few days.'

Timofei Osetrov, the former second secretary of the central committee of the Uzbek Communist Party, was also released from prison and graciously accepted the apology offered to him. Moreover, a court (it was too late to prevent the case because it had already reached the Supreme Court of the USSR) acquitted the former secretary of the Uzbek Communist Party, Reno Abdulaev.

All these releases and pardons had a uniquely important, fundamental significance for the mafia. The mafia had demonstrated its unshaken power and capacity to drag its people out of the sort of hole from which no one would otherwise escape. It had always been considered that someone who had been put in prison, the more so if he was a big party or state official – that sort of business was extremely difficult to cover up – was already doomed and beyond help. The best he could hope for was an indulgent sentence, tolerable conditions in a prison camp and early release. But a hasty rehabilitation with a public apology? It was very important for the mafia to show what they could achieve – this gave a signal to the others who had not yet got into trouble (i.e. the vast majority) to display fortitude and put their trust in the reality of timely promised help.

It could also be said that the mafia had overfulfilled their plan by taking a step unprecedented in all Soviet history: even the most indomitable fantasists could not have foreseen it. The freed Viktor Smirnov went almost straight from his prison cell to the Kremlin, to a plenum of the Central Committee, of which he remained a candidate member, and they kindly offered him the opportunity to speak from that authoritative platform so that he could stigmatize those 'who questioned honourable party worthies' and declare his triumph to the world. This was, of course, not only and not so much *his* triumph. It was a real triumph for the mafia.

Roy Medvedev, the head of the commission of the Supreme Soviet of the USSR investigating the work of Gdlyan's group, told me that the grounds for abandoning the cases against Smirnov and Osetrov* were more than suspect and that it was vital to return to the objective investigation of the evidence against them. But nobody went back to it. Nor, assuredly, will they.

The release of Smirnov dealt a crushing blow to the process of cleaning up corrupt officials in Moldavia, although the arrest of Smirnov was connected with his 'services' in Central Asia, particularly in Uzbekistan, rather than Moldavia. Nevertheless, this arrest provoked an attack on the mafia in Moldavia itself – the attack which Smirnov himself had invoked so furiously. Now the signal about the unshakability of the mafia was received not only by the mafiosi themselves but also by those who were determined to unmask them. A feeling of doom was quickly felt in the departments preparing and planning operations against them.

I received a letter from a faithful reader, Peter Dovgal, a former assistant in the prosecution service in the Moldavian town of Bendera. Regardless of his lowly position in the prosecution service, he had already tried in Brezhnev's time – obviously on a local level – to bring to book local officials who were bestowing whatever favours and services they had at their disposal in return for considerable sums. The mafia got him dismissed from the prosecution service. In advance of that he had made contact with a henchman of Ivan Bodyul – the 'king of Moldavia' – himself the first secretary of the central committee there. Who was this man Bodyul? He was a personal friend of Brezhnev, Chernenko and Shcholokov, and an unfailing participant in the revels and 'royal hunts' on their visitations to Moldavian soil.

The fate of Dovgal – that tiny wedge trying to cleave a rock – would have been utterly deplorable if Brezhnev had not recalled Bodyul to Moscow and subsequently been called himself to his fathers. With the arrival of Gorbachev, Dovgal and some of his

---

* Osetrov was freed after an expert group of 'independent' prosecutors had concluded that nothing could be proved in a court case and Osetrov had to be discharged. Thus, the mafia diverted all suspicion from themselves, accusing the investigators of unprofessionalism. That the investigators, like many representatives of other professions in the USSR, do not possess the necessary skill is not in doubt, but the release of Osetrov cannot be explained that way.

supporters decided to finish the job they had embarked upon, and began to request that Bodyul be called to criminal account along with his 'pocket prosecutor' Ivan Cheban, who was the head of the republic's prosecution service under Bodyul. He covered up all the mafia's activities and hounded those who pursued the mafia. The arrest of Smirnov aroused hopes that the case might get moving again.

But alas ... As Peter Dovgal wrote to me: 'The Moldavian mafia have got their second wind ... There are unceasing threats to get even with us for trying to uncover thieves and bribe-takers and, more important, to reveal all their links not only in Kishinev but also in Moscow ... Those who should be dealing with these matters in the MVD and the prosecution service have lost heart. They are constantly being interfered with, and transferred to other, allegedly more urgent, cases.'

It is likely that those who were 'interfering' all the time would easily counter this reproof by pointing to several large mafia groups uncovered recently in Moldavia: cases of embezzlement in bakeries, in wineries and bribery in the trade system ... But it is as if these are the normal 'wastage', losses which the mafia 'budgets' for, like any trading enterprise, akin to broken glass, torn cloth or food gone bad. These losses do not affect the whole structure or the inviolability of the ringleaders.

Even a man like the president of the Moldavian KGB, General Georgi Lavranchuk, whom it would be difficult to accuse of being exceptionally critical, admitted that 'our current crop of millionaires have powerful protectors'. They are the ones that we find it so difficult to get our hands on.

Quite recently in Moldavia a substantial operation was launched by the local mafia in cooperation with their Polish 'colleagues'. Of all the possible routes from Poland to Hungary, Romania and Bulgaria, Polish tourists preferred the one which goes through the Western Ukraine and Moldavia. They carried an enormous quantity of computers and other Western technology across the border, and then secretly released the goods onto the Soviet market. Every computer would bring the mafia more than 50,000 roubles in pure profit. This contraband trade, carried on with the connivance of customs officers in the pay of the mafia, embraced thousands of personal and industrial computers. A hunt after these smugglers at night in the high forests of the Carpathian mountains would make an exciting scene in a crime film.

But that detective-story material is not the point. What is important is that this vast and long-running international trade (the equipment was American, West German or Japanese – not Polish of course) was conducted with the participation of influential people in power working in close collaboration with each other. None of them was ever called to account, nor even named. And this is not some 'heritage from the accursed past' but a reality of today's so-called perestroika.

Is there any hope that a serious blow can be delivered at the main mafia centres? Hardly. Who would now be interested in that, when Moldavia and other republics are torn asunder by very different conflicts which could lead to global political changes with all the consequences thereof? Thus it is perhaps not far from the truth to suggest that the reawakening of nationalist feeling with its deep historic roots and potential for international overspill may in effect save the Soviet mafia and all those 'dear comrades' in its leadership, because public attention is diverted to those very difficult nationality problems. Yet it is hardly probable that in the context of the new structures coming into being the mafiosi will feel as easy and coordinated as they did through all those years in the 'indestructible union of republics of the free', the most favourable political environment there could ever be for them to flourish in.

Chapter Ten

Criminals in Power: What Next?

Every chapter of this book confirms that its principal characters are the leaders of republics or leaders of the country as a whole, people who for years and years have firmly maintained their positions at the top of the party and government pyramid. In this choice of characters one should not see any attempt on my part to satisfy the natural inquisitiveness of the normal citizen about the life of the elite above him. On the contrary it simply constitutes a sad statement of dismal reality, one which leads to an inevitable question. Was it a coincidence that literally everywhere from top to bottom those in positions of authority and power were criminals, directly or indirectly connected to the powerful and far-flung mafia network?

The answer is obvious. A phenomenon which has lasted unchanged for many, many years, and has reproduced itself widely, regardless of national or geographic variations and amongst different groups of people making up the whole pyramid, cannot be a chance phenomenon. Its roots are deeply embedded in the political culture which gave it birth and thus a change in the situation will only be brought about by a change in the whole system.

Whenever I told anyone, especially my friends or colleagues in the West, about the book I was working on, they always asked which mafia I was writing about – the political, the economic or the criminal. I understand the reason behind the question but am at the same time astonished at its naïveté. Breaking down a single entity into three components may perhaps be useful for the purposes of carrying out a scientific examination, but it takes one far away from Soviet reality. The complexity of the various connections, of who depends on whom, of where the interface between the elements lies – all this makes our Soviet mafia unique in its way. But not quite. Whenever military diktat or political adventurism have led to the establishment of analogous totalitarian regimes – the Brezhnev variant being the worst of the kind – in every case the result has been the emergence and growth of flourishing mafia groups, great and small, and it is quite impossible to distinguish within them a 'pure' politician from a 'pure' criminal.

Politicians' decisions, often dictated by populist, conspiratorial or demagogic considerations, or by personal ambition, rather than being forced on them by mafia interests, nevertheless always found a response in the mafia, which turned them to its own advantage. Perhaps the most convincing and graphic example of this is the notorious anti-alcohol campaign which marked the start of the short-lived but impressive career of Yegor Ligachev at the top. It is sad that this campaign was upheld and blessed by Mikhail Gorbachev who – alas – could not foresee its consequences any more than he could those of even more fateful political actions.

It is quite obvious that in proclaiming the terms of the 'war against alcoholism', this newly-appointed number two in the Kremlin was foisting on the whole country the habits of his forefathers, who were teetotal Old Believers. Ligachev was seeking popularity, and counted on finding understanding and support among the wide masses of working people. The country was indeed languishing in widespread drunkenness born of the hopelessness and deadening quality of ordinary life. Thousands of letters, especially from worried mothers, wives and children of alcoholics, were arriving at the Kremlin with pleas to 'do something'. For Ligachev, a man of (putting it politely) limited intelligence, 'doing something' meant only one thing in Soviet terms: prohibition and punishment for breach thereof. The human and economic losses from this decision, taken by ignorant people, are now well enough known: not only tens of billions of lost roubles (40 billion in direct losses, and several times more than that in indirect ones), but at least 18,000 deaths from the use of toxic substitutes for vodka, hundreds of thousands of cripples, a countless number of patients in psychiatric clinics ... Far from the number of alcoholics and drunkards diminishing, their numbers increased. Tens of thousands of hectares of vines were destroyed – horticultural genocide, because these particular species, created tens and sometimes hundreds of years ago, can no longer be recovered. Others will be grown, but those that were destroyed cannot be recreated, having disappeared under the executioner's hatchet.*

This tragically ignorant decision – the most widely trumpeted of perestroika – had no connection whatever with mafia affairs, but the mafia were thrilled with it. It is not so much that it adapted to it – it derived the maximum benefit from it. The price of a bottle of vodka on the black market immediately doubled, but this was enough for hundreds of millions of roubles (in the opinion of certain Soviet economists the numbers run into billions) to find their way into the hands of the trading mafia.

I can tell a curious story in this connection. I went to cover the story of a farewell party being thrown in a Moscow shop for the saleswoman in the wine department, who was leaving for her 'well-earned retirement'. I was amazed at the youthfulness of this pensioner, who was clearly no more than forty years of age. 'You're rather young to be retiring,' I joked gallantly. 'No, not at all,' she replied with disconcertingly bold directness, and explained to me that four years of the anti-alcohol law had enabled her to accumulate sufficient means to keep her grandchildren and 'perhaps even great-grandchildren' in comfort. To substantiate her claim, she led me into her tiny 'sanctuary' where portraits of Gorbachev and Ligachev hung. Crossing herself elaborately before them, as if they were icons, she added defiantly that every day she lit a candle to her benefactors and prayed to them. Her tipsy bravado was grotesque and I saw in her no evidence of guilt, only a brazen fearlessness together with a sense of her own superiority in the presence of the press.

But this does not mean that in the circumstances Ligachev carried out some sort of special errand on behalf of the mafia and forced through a decision profitable to them. It was just that the system is organized in such a way that it draws up to the top and puts in the driving seat incompetent drivers whose every step enriches neither the country nor the people, but the mafia structure. The enormous revenues of the trading mafia, obtained thanks to a measure decided on by ignoramuses, certainly brought no financial dividend to Liga-

---

*The director of the world-famous Massandra winery in the Crimea committed suicide, unable to withstand the blow to his life's work caused by the destruction of the vines developed during the last century to make wine for the Imperial family and for export to the whole European market.

233

chev, nor to those who supported and approved the decision. However, there were those who really made a fortune and they had their protectors, who in turn had theirs, and so on and so forth ... And all of them supported each other because the fate of each highly-placed circle depended on a lower echelon, and the lower depended on the higher. Ligachev was applauded and warmly approved of by those who were interested in the support of those who ... Thus a chain joined them all together, regardless of the fact that some members of the chain were fighting for power and others for money.

The acute reduction in the amount of vodka available for sale led to an unheard-of growth in the production of home-brew. The authorities take particularly severe revenge on violations of the state vodka monopoly, although their leader and teacher Vladimir Ilyich Lenin criticized the existence of such a monopoly under the tsar, calling it inhumane and oppressive.

The demand for home-brew gave rise in turn to a wild increase in the population's demand for sugar, the most important ingredient for producing it. At the plenum of the Supreme Court of the USSR I myself heard from the lips of the then Chief Prosecutor, Rekunkov, that in the Ukraine alone in 1986 the demand for sugar had increased by 24 per cent. This led to extra purchases of sugar from Cuba, paid for not only with armaments but also with oil and other goods.

Who was benefiting from this? Apart from the numberless exporters, arms traders and other international businessmen, it was the Soviet black-market traders once again, who began to supply sugar under the counter at inflated prices; it was militiamen, closing their eyes (not for free, of course) to the production of home-brew; it was the so-called 'people's control' called on to 'be vigilant' and 'mercilessly expose', but managing very successfully to protect the usual 'offenders'. And who lost out? As usual, it was the unhappy country.*

---

*On the question of vodka: a great quantity of it goes for export, at the wholesale price of one dollar a bottle. Overseas traders supply it to their customers at 8–12 dollars. But the vodka is made from grain bought from the USA and Canada. That means that we buy grain for dollars, then sell the vodka – and at the end of the whole operation we are left with nothing to show for it. We are simply throwing dollar bills into the wind. Of course, the most important reason for this absurdity is the incompetence of the 'competent bodies' which are miraculously unprofessional. But, as always in such cases, corrupt officials are feathering their nests by doing deals favourable to their Western partners, on the principle of 'mafiosi of the world unite!'

I somehow got involved in a stupid argument in a Moscow intellectual's house where politics are debated endlessly from morning till night, or, more accurately, from dusk to dawn. It was on the burning issue of which Soviet mafia is more powerful. 'The vodka mafia,' affirmed some. 'The fruit mafia,' insisted others. 'The transport mafia,' returned yet others. 'The hotel mafia,' I suggested for a laugh, remembering my unsuccessful attempt even to book a hotel room in advance for a French friend.

This really was a ridiculous debate, because the mafia is all-encompassing. However, its power seems to us the greater to the extent that its effect can be felt on our daily lives. If I cannot book a hotel room, then it is that mafia which is blocking my path and therefore it appears to me to be a particularly powerful one. If, at the same time, I am having no particular difficulty in getting fruit, then the fruit mafia does not seem to me such a nightmarish monster, whereas for millions of people yearning for years for a bunch of grapes or a lemon for our so beloved Russian tea, it is precisely the fruit mafia that seems the personification of evil. The fact is that they are all strong and powerful and – most importantly! – do not have a separate existence, being closely connected with each other, acting in concert and generally propping each other up. The trading mafia can only survive through the closest links and most harmonious coordination with the transport mafia: otherwise it would not obtain goods wagons and transport planes for the timely delivery of goods to the place where it can obtain the best price for them. Even a normal ticket for a passenger train or a scheduled flight is, as a result, difficult to obtain. The transport mafia in turn would not survive without the hotel mafia. Tens of hundreds of hotel rooms in Moscow, Leningrad and other places lie empty, whereas thousands of foreign visitors currently pouring into our country are turned away, 'No room! No room!' The hotel mafia ignores the opportunity to earn foreign currency, because foreign currency goes to the government, not to the director or the administrator of the hotel, and keeps rooms free for 'their customers' who can have them at a moment's notice. The Russian answer to the puzzled customer's question is always the same: 'Bron'.

The Russian word 'bron', which can best be translated as 'reserved', has in fact little in common with that word either in content or concept. The uniquely Soviet slang word 'bron' came into regular usage and is summoned up for its overtones of armour and secrecy, to inspire respect and fear in the man in the street. 'Bron' is a kind of invisible powerful force which has its paw on train and plane tickets, theatre tickets, hotel rooms – everything, in fact, that people want but which is, alas, unavailable to the ordinary citizen who does not belong to the mafia.

In order not so much the better to understand but to get a feel for what this notorious 'bron' means for a Soviet person, here is a popular joke: a member of the mafia is sitting in a prison cell crammed full of other prisoners. He asks the prison governor to transfer him to a nice, clean, single cell. 'There are none – they are all occupied,' the governor replies.

'You'll be well rewarded.'

'There are no free cells – where would I get an unoccupied cell from?'

'You will be extremely well rewarded.'

'I've told you – no!'

'What do you mean no, comrade governor? On the second floor, third from the left, there is a nice clean dry cell with nobody in it.'

'Have you gone out of your mind? That is reserved ['bron'] for the party Central Committee!'

Many Moscow hotel workers get a second monthly salary, which in some cases is several times more than their basic pay, from the mafia. It cannot be doubted which of the two salaries they earn by putting their back into it. The hotel mafia controls not only the allocation of rooms, but related services such as the daily rota of the prostitutes working the Intourist hotels for foreign currency.

Today, it seems, the only real reason for retaining the rule brought in years ago controlling the entry of Soviet citizens into hotels is the cut which the prostitutes pay the administration and the so-called 'doormen' (that is, the KGB operatives disguised in doormen's livery at the entrance to the hotel). Thus, until very recently, in order to get into the Moscow International Trade Centre (known as the Armand Hammer Centre and hotel), a prostitute had to pay 100 roubles. When the KGB suddenly changed all the doormen at once, the cut went up to 300 roubles. But this, of course, is not the ceiling . . .

Not long ago, the hotel mafia carried out a further change of personnel. The managing director of the Moscow Intourist hotel, a place widely known to foreign tourists, having displeased the mafia, was handed over to the prosecution service for taking bribes (which, of course, he had done). The man was sentenced to ten years in prison and a different 'respected comrade' was put in his place.

For entirely understandable reasons, the decisions taken at governmental level are subjected to the usual analysis (especially by overseas commentators) from a purely political (and till recently, also ideological) point of view; they interpret them by surveying the strategy and tactics of the government in the light of international affairs or the internal situation in the country. But in the Soviet Union more than anywhere else the so-called 'human factor' is at work, the influence of their personal interests on decision-makers as well as the interests of those who are their protectors.

Is it possible to doubt that Soviet support of the fascist, semi-fascist and openly criminal totalitarian regimes all around the world was caused not only by the military–political doctrine of the Brezhnev regime and its political heirs, but also by the personal interest of the numerous clans representing our military-industrial complex?

The bilateral agreements arrived at certainly anticipated the sending to the respective countries of an enormous number of 'advisers', experts and supervisors. The preparation, signing and realization of these agreements entailed short but frequent visits by all sorts of delegations. Of course, Libya is not England, and Syria is not Canada. However, for the modest aims cherished in their dreams by representatives at various levels of the military mafia, Tripoli and Damascus will both do perfectly well, and so will even worse places still.

And this is not only because any poor little Syrian shop can match up to the 'special section' of the Soviet central department store, but above all because every adviser and consultant was fully aware that he would return home groaning under the weight of 'presents' obtained immediately from two sources. From the 'natives' in gratitude for brotherly help, and from Soviet colleagues working there in gratitude for being set up with a cushy number and in the hope that they will not be recalled home too soon.

Thus, when reading deeply-considered and well-argued explanations of why the presence of Soviet 'specialists' was so indispensable in this or that African, Middle Eastern or Asiatic state, it is necessary to look further than Soviet global political strategy.

Soviet strategy is often motivated by particular personal or clan considerations. But we do not know which influential officials in the military-industrial complex or the external trade network received the necessary 'gift' or the essential 'recommendation', or who in a given part of the country is pursuing what interest or long-term plan.

A convincing example of this is provided by the former Polish leader Edward Gierek, who recounts in his memoirs the 'services' provided to the Polish people by the then Polish prime minister Peter Yaroshevich. Gierek recalls that when Yaroshevich was setting off for talks in Moscow, he always took with him for his Soviet bosses a barrel of vodka for one, and Warsaw fashions for another. It was these presents which determined to a great extent the agreements arrived at, although they were officially based on political, ideological and strategic considerations.

The decay of total corruption reached into every corner and every level without exception: mercenary and career interests exclude all others. Here before me lies an unpublished document, the confession of a KGB major of the reserve, Tigran Melkumyan. Officially his job was vice-consul in Beirut, whereas in reality he was a member of the Soviet KGB residency in the Lebanon, whose 'patch' was mainly the Armenian diaspora. This former member of Soviet intelligence, sacked because of a conflict with his boss, tells how he obtained coded instructions from Moscow Centre.

Sensational revelations of KGB secrets are not to be found in his memoirs. The coded instructions from his secret-service chiefs had nothing to do with spying. 'Send ten tins of olive oil by return,' says one decode. 'I am expecting a grandchild. Buy a musical potty. I saw them on sale in such-and-such a supermarket,' said another. 'Send it urgently.' And it was sent: a secret-service operative took this potty which played music when a child peed into it from Beirut to Moscow as a precious trophy. Moreover, the same man would come back with fresh 'requisitions'. Or, even more disgracefully, 'requisitions' would sometimes be conveyed through secret channels intended for the transmission of secure information.

Coded telegrams would come flying in from Moscow Centre, such as: 'Some VIPs are on their way to you. Lay on entertainment worthy of their status.' The visitors would not be on KGB business at all, but travelling on behalf of other organizations, such as the

Central Committee or the Academy of Sciences of the USSR. For some reason, in this instance, the head of Soviet intelligence had sent the telegram mentioning 'special entertainment'. The senior KGB resident in Beirut took his team to a top-secret meeting where the plan for the relevant operation was discussed: lunch at such-and-such a restaurant, dinner at another, then a bar, a strip show and the presentation of gifts. No one had their own money to pay for these luxuries; they had to use so-called 'operational' funds. Melkumyan estimates that in the Lebanon alone several tens of thousands of dollars would have been spent from intelligence funds for the 'suitable reception' of such officials as Yevgeny Primakov, then the director of the Institute of World Economics and International Relations, and later a member of Gorbachev's short-lived presidential council – since disbanded; Karen Brutents, deputy head of the international department of the Central Committee, and several other of their colleagues in the Lebanon alone. Most likely, they did not know about the coded instructions to provide them with a pleasant stay in Beirut, and the welcome they were provided with would not have seemed out of the ordinary: for members of the ruling elite were accustomed to exactly this sort of life, and would not have worried about who was paying for their pleasures, nor what they were using for money. In order somehow to make good the expenditure, all the cars in the Soviet embassy were reported destroyed in the Muslim–Christian battles in Beirut, whereas in fact they were sold to local inhabitants at knock-down prices. Part of the proceeds were diverted for personal needs, of course.

These events, recorded by a very junior Soviet KGB operative, could be categorized as merely an illustration of some sort of personal dishonesty, an 'unfortunate recruitment error' to use a Soviet cliché. But no, this is an illustration, albeit a comic one, of mafia activity, the level of its 'culture' and the scope of its interests. If someone bungled an instruction of this sort from the Centre, if he showed incompetence or unwillingness to oblige the cohesive and well-organized group who had put him in the job, he would immediately be pushed out of the well-oiled corruption machine – as, indeed, was the case with Tigran Melkumyan. The pretext was a typical mafia project: he was required to squander money by mafia benefactors higher up, then he was accused by his boss of wasting the money! Thus, the mafia takes its revenge on 'traitors' who get in their way.

In my opinion, this apparently trivial example gives an impression of how, having seized power, mafia forces are looting our once-wealthy country in large and small ways. It also lifts the veil on how these powers are expanding into the international arena, where everything is shrouded in secrecy, and the mafia likes nothing better than secrecy. They long to be abroad, not only so that they can live in a 'decent society' and in conditions unobtainable to the tens of millions of happy citizens enjoying all the benefits of victorious socialism, but also because there are tremendous opportunities available for obtaining foreign currency off the record. It is by no means accidental that close relations and scions of the highest party hierarchy for whom all doors are open according to taste and preferences, are provided not just with work abroad but also with intelligence work. I will name only the son and brother-in-law of Sharaf Rashidov, the son and brother-in-law of Geidar Aliev, who never made any bad moves in the course of their careers.

The activity of these embezzlers of state property in the international arena is a completely unexplored area, where deliberate obfuscation and the magic stamp 'secret' allow well-organized wrong-doers to mount every imaginable illegal operation. Unscrupulous political aims are quite often achieved by unscrupulous methods, thanks to which considerable amounts of money stick to sticky Soviet fingers and to those of their foreign partners. The light of glasnost has not yet penetrated into these regions.

The practice of opening dummy companies which quickly become the trading partners of Soviet foreign trade organizations and use the revenues from their operations to provide reliable finance to 'fraternal' Communist Parties is well known. There can be no formal objection to this: it is all legal! I do not know about Western tax inspectors, but for Soviet ones the doors of these operations are firmly closed: it is a trade (for which read: political) secret. How much money sticks to the fingers of the initiates to whom the 'secrets' are entrusted we will probably never know.

A grandiose operation along these lines shook Great Britain and the rest of the world to the foundations in 1990. I have in mind the scandalous story of the money from the Soviet miners collected in support of striking British miners. The Soviet press devoted a vanishingly small amount of space to this scandal, justifiably reckoning that none of its readers would believe anything in the way of justification of Soviet trade unions and other such 'social organizations'. We already know only too well how 'spontaneous' and 'voluntary' campaigns of solidarity are organized. In this case, no aid action could arise 'from below' because there was no possibility of it doing so. As the rouble is not convertible, the money collected would have represented for the British miners no more than a heap of paper. If, let us say, they had used the roubles to buy produce (there was such a thing in the Soviet Union in those days) nobody could have transported it to those in need. Finally, according to the law then in force, it was not possible even to establish any sort of centre to collect money, let alone spend it on something. But the situation would change totally if there was a decision by the Politburo or the secretariat of the Central Committee. At once a centre would be invented, foreign currency allocated and transport and people to take on the arrangements found.

This dramatic story is widely known, so I will just touch on aspects which concern the immediate theme of this book. The organization which purportedly sent the currency to British miners was not some specially created committee of solidarity acting under some kind of popular control, nor was it the Soviet Union of Miners, which is in any case not under the control of the workers but of the state. The union's structure and mechanisms are designed for quite other purposes and do not guarantee total secrecy. It was in fact a mysterious organization called the Soviet Peace Fund which sent the money. Its name and statutes alone, specifying its competence (or, more accurately, not specifying anything, because the words 'activity aimed at maintaining peace' could cover a multitude of sins), speak for themselves. Behind the cosmetic front provided by ex-chess champion of the world Anatoly Karpov and cosmonaut Svetlana Savitskaya are high-ranking officials appointed by the Central Committee.

In the autumn of 1990 I unsuccessfully tried to find out why the Peace Fund should suddenly be involved in bilateral transactions between two counterpart trade unions – Soviet and British. Why did Soviet miners' money have to be transferred to a secret bank account of this 'peace organization' not even controlled by the state union organizations? The present president of the Union of Soviet Miners, Vladimir Lunev, told me: 'It was considered more convenient to use the account of the Peace Fund.' Who did the considering and where the convenience lay, it is not difficult to guess.

Moreover, it is agreed by everyone who formally took part in this 'act of solidarity' that there is no documentation concerning any collection of Soviet roubles, nor their conversion into foreign currency, nor any transfer to the all-powerful representatives of British miners. Everything was done in the strictest secrecy, which is an inevitable prerequisite for any financial intrigue. I have been categorically refused any information concerning why the roubles were paid into the Peace Fund whereas the foreign currency (whoever provided it) was paid out and handed over to the West by the Central Council of Unions. Incidentally, the word 'West' also needs some further definition. According to the former president of the Union of Soviet Miners, Mikhail Srebny, 1.4 million US dollars were given to Arthur Scargill through the former international miners' union organization with its headquarters in Warsaw. Clearly, Warsaw then and Warsaw now are far from the same thing. Deep secrecy still surrounds the mechanism of the transfer of the money to the Polish capital: a cheque? In favour of whom? Drawn on which bank? Or was the money handed over in cash? How did the money get to Paris? I quote again from two statements made by Srebny from his interview with a journalist colleague of mine at *Literaturnaya Gazeta*, who met him at my request: 'There is no official record on how or where the money was handed over ... Who precisely paid over the money and how I cannot say ... There was never any confirmation from Scargill's side that the money had been received. Nor was there a receipt. Everything was done verbally.'

There is no doubt that money did arrive in Paris – all that side of this sinister story is well known to the Western reader. I am interested in looking at the affair from the Soviet end, as someone who is pretty well versed in what goes on over here. Under the pretence of some political (politician's?) confidentiality and with no documents available for impartial verification, operations are carried out involving colossal – in Soviet terms – foreign-currency sums. The transfer of these sums and the way they are spent is carried out without any accounting procedure, an unthinkable, absurd situation and inexplicable by any political yardstick.

Being faithful to immutable legal principles, I put the question which in these situations the lawmakers of ancient Rome were wont to ask: 'Cui prodest?' ('Who gains?')

It would take us too far off the track to consider the question of where the voluntary donations which come from abroad to the Soviet Union go and how they are spent. We are still waiting for an account of the fate of the money and goods which were collected in the West for the victims of the tragic earthquake in Armenia in December 1988. Is it not odd that, apart from an extraordinarily short and unspecific newspaper report without any documentary evidence to back it up, the world still does not know where the money went?

Occasional newspaper reports were glimpsed, saying that jackets and blankets sent for the Armenian victims had been spotted on market stalls in cities in other parts of the Soviet Union, selling like hot cakes at black-market prices. But these instances of petty pilfering of goods are not our main concern. More to the point, how was the foreign currency spent? Where is the public accountability for every pound and every dollar? There is no accountability and there will not be. The foreign currency in the majority of cases will already have been exchanged for 'equivalent' roubles, or, more precisely, for building materials, equipment and commodities valued at the official set price in roubles for the goods in question. Not all the currency, of course, but a very considerable amount. And who knows how many pounds or dollars – real ones, not imaginary 'convertible' roubles – fell by the wayside? It is easier for them to fall by the wayside because there is no international control over the spending of the money. Charity – the act of goodwill – somehow precludes mistrust on the part of the donor. This human scruple, entirely understandable and reasonable in the civilized world, provides the ideal conditions for professional crooks, people who are strangers to any sort of scruple. They count on it.

It could be objected that all this is no more than suspicion. But in an environment of secrecy and lack of accountability and given the dominance of tightly-knit mafia forces, such suspicions are inevitable, and are close to the truth. Otherwise why all the hushing up? After all, it is not a matter of military establishments or strategic secrets. So they should render proper account for every penny to the countries that sent the money, if only to distance themselves from the mafia and to encourage charitable acts from abroad if the need should arise again.

One can say without fear of contradiction that a large proportion of the goods and money sent by the West to help the impoverished

Soviet people fell into mafia hands. Timed for pre-holiday New Year shopping in late December 1990, the secondhand shops in many cities held large stocks – not just one or two of each item – of packaged food, clothing and other goods sent by generous well-wishers in Germany and other countries. This shows that this humanitarian aid was, and will be, exploited for the benefit of the reactionary forces directly or indirectly in league with the mafia. On the other hand, it does go a little way towards reducing the fraught tensions in our society and the accompanying danger of unexpected explosions. The West has its defences against military attack, the danger of which may now be receding, but it has little defence against the Soviet system. New Chernobyls threaten the West no less than the Soviet Union itself. Radiation does not distinguish between democrats and reactionaries. As long as the Soviet Union lasts – in its present shape or in a modified form – the mafia will remain in being, an element which one must inevitably take into account.

The whole world knew about the scandalous attempt of former East German Communists – they now call themselves Democratic Socialists – to salt away just over a hundred million Deutschmarks using dummy companies with foreign co-ownership. Leaving aside what was fully written up in the Western press, I will only draw attention to one aspect of the matter. An attempt to use foreign bank accounts in the name of fictitious Soviet organizations cannot be made unless 'recommended' in the proper fashion, that is, put plainly, without the all-clear from the Central Committee. This estimable outfit is the organizer-in-chief and 'curator' of so-called independent organizations registered outside the country and called upon to save and protect the multi-million capital that the party has stolen from the people. For this purpose, the party mafia is adjusting to the new circumstances and recruiting experts in Western business practice and drawing foreign partners into its orbit. This currently involves people from Cyprus, Venezuela, the Netherlands, Germany and Norway, such is the broad scope of the operation! According to the magazine *Der Spiegel* it was people in the KGB residence in Berlin who advised party leader Gregor Gysi on this way of protecting his fortune. The actual executors of this secret task may have been officers of the KGB, but it is clear that the decision was taken on Old Square in Moscow, which is in full control of these dummy companies. Only there could the decision have been taken to rescue former party comrades. Is it astonishing that, no sooner had the affair been disclosed, the Central Committee immediately dissociated itself from the matter? But by then it had successfully got its money out. The main point is that as the mafia went international the party went over from veiled connections with the mafia to a direct organizational control of mafia groups.

The link between the Soviet mafia and various criminal circles abroad is becoming just as much of a sign of the times as is the greater openness of Soviet society, the dismantling of the Iron Curtain and the relaxation of frontier controls. These political developments coincided with the need the mafia now had to realize the value of its accumulated and still-accumulating riches, to put their resources into active use. In a non-market economy there were no opportunities, their devalued roubles were turning to dust and even Soviet low-carat gold does not hold a stable value.

All channels through which the mafia has attempted to hang on to its capital connect one way or another with the international business world. These are the conversion of roubles into hard currency, drug trafficking and speculating in antiques.

To start with the latter, investment in antiques, especially church-plate, is a long-established practice though which the most far-sighted individuals have saved themselves from ruin. As already explained, that is why Soviet law, the militia and the courts have been coming down so disproportionately hard on private collectors. The mafia has taken up this method of materializing its profits using the possibilities it enjoys, through high-powered connections, of moving antiques over the Soviet frontier. Tens of thousands of icons, silver icon frames, other church objects dating back as much as four hundred years, pre-Revolutionary objects made of gold, silver and other precious metals and stones, works of art, graphic art, sculpture, carpets, tapestries, furniture from museums and palaces – all these things have gone abroad in vast quantities, returning to the mafia vast sums in convertible currency. The great majority of these operations, which by their sheer scale could not have been kept hidden from the eyes of the customs, were carried out using proper legal channels under the supervision or on the direct instructions of high-ranking officials.

Antique dealers operate as loners or small groups, and always have done, especially when they are émigrés just managing to scrape a living abroad. This is not the sort of thing I am talking about. I am talking about a colossal conveyor-belt loaded with the converted product of useless paper roubles stolen or given as bribes, using the medium of antiques – a conveyor-belt which exists with the connivance of the national protectors of the mafia and with the shady cooperation of foreign partners. The conveyor-belt could not operate without such additional participation. The mafia is associated with the theft of numerous pictures, antique valuables and medals.

Instances of such deliberate theft have become more and more common in the USSR. Great works of art are appearing in the West on an amazing scale. A well-managed and very well-organized, complex mechanism is at work, in which not only the militia and the customs are involved, but also very powerful state officials. Lone 'one-off' operators not belonging to the mafia are often caught – and the newspapers boast of these victories. But the conveyor-belt continues to work uninterrupted.

In spring 1990, the Soviet Ministry of the Interior received operational intelligence concerning a business meeting between Soviet and Western mafiosi called for June in Warsaw, to discuss plans for future cooperation in the conditions of the Soviet switch to a market economy. One of the main items on the agenda was the method of transferring Soviet antiques to the West.

The ministry sent its experts to Warsaw and a journalist went with them to write a unique newspaper article as yet another brilliant example of Soviet perestroika. But the delegation returned empty-handed. Either the tip-off had been wrong, or the mafia had changed their plans, possibly as a result of having discovered that their arrangements had been leaked.

Several months later, a senior militia officer who told me not to mention his name said that the international mafia meeting had taken place after all, not in Warsaw but in East Berlin. Fearing leaks, the meeting's organizers by previous arrangement had always said 'Warsaw' when they meant Berlin, even in innocent conversations between themselves and not just in coded correspondence. This little ruse had worked like a charm. Moreover, there is evidence that it worked for another reason: some – a very small number – highly-placed militia officers knew that for 'Warsaw' they should read 'Berlin', but they did not share this information with anyone.

Antiques continue to flood to the West. They can be seen at the most prestigious auctions, having passed through many inter-mediaries and with all traces of their provenance lost. If you exclude the odd isolated item, the mighty mafia is behind the sale of all these valuables. Perhaps not a single other aspect of criminal business is so professionally organized and carries such a small percentage of mishaps or losses. This fact alone bears witness to the high level of organization and the reliability of the protective mechanisms at all stages of operations. Western dealers interested in the illegal buying and resale of Russian antiques usually only come to grief when their Soviet partners are a one-man band, lone operators working at their own risk rather than as part of a mafia group. But, for entirely understandable reasons, it is very difficult to gain the mafia's trust and to get into business with them.

As far as the Soviet drug mafia is concerned, it is still at an early stage, if not exactly in its infancy. It is not comparable either in its scale or its scope with American or European equivalents. So far it is not possible to verify with any degree of accuracy the distribution of drugs inside the USSR. Up to very recent times, the existence of Soviet drug addicts was denied. Then, as an aspect of growing openness, there began to be reports citing deliberately and absurdly low figures. The inaccuracy of official statistics was evident from the following facts alone. The president of the KGB, Kryuchkov, in an interview in *Pravda* in August 1990, stated that it was estimated that there were 120,000 registered addicts in the country and earlier that same year, in March 1990, the Soviet Minister for Internal Affairs Vladimir Bakatin had given a similar figure: 130,000. Then, in September 1990, only a month after Kryuchkov's interview, the head of Soviet criminal investigations, General Nikolai Khromov, confirmed that 500,000 Soviet citizens were regular users of nar-cotics: thus, in under a month, so it seemed, the statistic had increased fourfold.

The mystery of the Soviet calculations is quite easily solved. We 'did not notice' (and it is quite easy for the unwary not to notice) one little word casually dropped in, as if by accident, by the president of the KGB. He was talking about 'registered' drug addicts! That is, about those on a special card index. As distinct from the card index of political undesirables, it is compiled extremely slowly and grudgingly. The powers that be do not want to admit that a murky flood is overwhelming the country. But even the figure given by

General Khromov does not reflect reality. Official experts, using their own independently derived (and thus more reliable) figures, confirm that in the middle of 1990 in the Soviet Union there were no less than four million people regularly using drugs and that the number is growing constantly. And they calculate that the militia and the customs seize no more than 20 per cent of all drugs in circulation, or about thirty tons.*

The West knows that tens, let alone hundreds, of tons of drugs cannot be put into circulation by one-man operators whether in the field of production or of sales. Only a powerful, well-organized underground concern could handle such volume business. Although fortunately we lag behind the USA in this, the profits from the drug trade are nevertheless large by our modest standards and are growing fast. According to Kryuchkov's official figures, they now amount to 14 billion roubles a year. The specialists who are more expertly informed than he is – although much more cautious in their con-clusions – suggest a figure of 30 billion roubles.

The market share accounted for by home-produced drugs is decreasing proportionately as the figure for importation grows. The principal supplier is North Korea, from which a vast quantity of opium is brought in, largely by Korean forestry workers who come to the Soviet Union on intergovernmental contracts. The other supplying countries are Afghanistan, Vietnam, Iran, Hungary and Romania. There is also transit traffic from Pakistan through the Soviet Union to Europe, likewise from Afghanistan and the countries of the Middle East and South-East Asia.

The great majority of these operations are partially or totally successful and are carried out with the help of the well-oiled mafia set-up which is designed according to all the rules of a professional conspiracy. That is to say, the system is clear-cut; the lower tiers are answerable to the next above, and, apart from one link man in each tier, no one knows of the existence of any of the others, either horizontally or vertically.

Border guards, customs officers and militia services are all involved, of course, and in the event of a slip-up they have 'their' people in the prosecution service, in the courts, and in the party and

---

* This tonnage is roughly accurate but whether it accounts for as much as 20 per cent of the whole trade in drugs is doubtful; 10 per cent might be nearer the mark.

the state apparatus. According to General Komissarov, a senior official in the Soviet Ministry of Internal Affairs, the militia, the KGB and the prosecution service ensure the success of every third operation. But since in practice the officials responsible usually cut unwelcome statistics by half, it would be reasonable to assume that they are successful in ensuring no less than two out of every three operations.

The same General Komissarov privately gave me a very convincing illustration. Criminal investigators set out on the trail of one conspiratorial group from the town of Liuberts near Moscow. Here are based the most dangerous youth gangs which terrorize Moscow – well-trained karate and self-defence experts armed with guns and knives. Almost all 'Liubers', as these gangs are known after the town they come from, are habitual drug addicts. The vast sums which they need to pay for their drugs drive them to more and more mercenary crimes. Having uncovered the links of gangster groups with the drug mafia, the militia prepared a trap for them, but soon the people leading the operation observed that their cover had been blown. Attention was switched to the search for those who had informed the mafia about the exercise being prepared against it.

Three were unmasked: the lieutenant colonel of militia from the Chief Administrative Division of Soviet Criminal Investigation, decorated for his successes in the battle against the mafia; a KGB major; and the man in charge of the very counter-conspiratorial service of the Ministry responsible for the recruitment of non-staff informers and agents and infiltrating them into the mafia structures. All of these people were working for the mafia rather than for the government. But is it possible to distinguish definitively between one and the other in any case – far less contrast them?

When all three of these unmasked men were sacked from their jobs, the prosecution service launched a criminal prosecution case against them. But some powerful secret hand intervened. The case was dropped, and the 'victims' – the accused – were found other appropriate work. The militia is not in a position to find out the identity of the powerful hand. Not that it will even look: its teeth are too weak to crack this particular nut.

If as a result of the economic reforms the rouble becomes convertible, if it has strong asset backing and a steady conversion rate, drugs will flood into the Soviet Union. This is the opinion of the American academic, James Finkelnauer, in an interview he gave to the news-paper *Komsomolskaya Pravda*, and his point of view is shared by Soviet specialists. I was talking to Colonel Alexander Gurov, the head of the department in the Ministry of the Interior set up recently to fight against organized crime. He also reckons that up till now there has not been a powerful organized drug mafia in the Soviet Union, but there is every prerequisite for its establishment and the potential convertibility of the rouble would provide the necessary financial base. It is precisely this potential risk which finally led the powers that be in the Soviet Union to take the decision to join Interpol.

Up to a certain time, billions of roubles of the mafia's revenues were kept buried in the ground or converted into low-grade gold which had a stable value on the internal market: rings, bracelets, pendants and earrings. It was absolutely useless to keep roubles – they had long since turned into pointless paper which could not buy anything; gold also vanished even for the mafia. Incidentally, it could be turned back into roubles but roubles only, because outside the boundaries of the Soviet Union and even more in the West, this particular sort of gold has no value. The mafia's chief and only aim became the acquisition of convertible foreign currency. In coming years this aim (the acquisition of foreign currency) will determine the new moves of the mafia and changes in the direction of its many-faceted activities.

There is quite a lot of evidence to suggest that the abolition of the monopoly of external trade, the establishment of joint ventures, the getting of foreign capital, the almost free foreign travel – all this gives the mafia the possibility of entering the market economy not from a standing start but already in possession of solid start-up capital accumulated as a result of many years' activity. Somehow its representatives are able to emerge from the woodwork, legalizing their business.

But ... It is very important to enter one caveat. I feel that I may have yielded on this key issue to a common temptation to use the word 'mafia' too carelessly. It is widely used in Soviet conversation, and in the Soviet media, to cover everyone including those who are making a living in a not entirely legal way as well as those operating in an entirely illegal way. It is precisely against the so-called 'black-marketeers' that the people's entirely spurious anger has been aroused, while the real mafia which gave birth to these 'black-marketeers', and is both inseparably attached to them and dependent on them – i.e. the political mafia – escapes from public scrutiny, remaining undamaged. It even becomes in the population's eyes the forward command in the battle against the hateful mafia.

The absurdity of the situation parallels the absurdity of the political system itself, within whose depths the situation has its roots.

And, in fact, both the political mafia and its offshoot, the economic mafia, in all its forms and manifestations, are by no means striving towards any sort of government-administrative changes or towards a normal market economy. These forces were able to reinforce themselves and blossom only in conditions of police socialism under which the seizure of power by ignorant criminals was first procured, followed by the enrichment of certain groups and clans at the people's expense, thanks to the universal deficit created by the System itself. The mechanisms of democracy have established other methods of filling senior positions in government, clearing the way to power for new people not selected by a nomenklatura in their own image and likeness; secondly, the market economy brings to the most intelligent, energetic and skilful in conditions of honest competition. Neither of these are wanted by the Soviet mafia, because they would quite simply lead to its demise. As in the rest of the world, these two new concepts of democracy and the market do not exclude the appearance of another mafia – the European or American kind – but they do force today's Soviet mafia either to transform or die. Because of this, the most important task before the mafia – which is still very powerful, having waived none of its rights, having lost none of its strongholds – is in every way to obstruct political change and economic reform.

That desperate battle against a market economy which is being fought before the eyes of the whole world is the battle of mafia forces for the preservation of its own strongholds. The tragicomic paradox consists in the fact that it is being conducted under the banner of a battle against the mafia! The mafia-populists cry, 'Down with the black economy!', playing on the most sensitive heart-strings of the people, but actually dreaming that the black economy should continue to exist, because only this promises them financial prosperity. It is not all quite so straightforward, however: many with whose hands and voices the mafia work genuinely want justice, and struggle

251

not to allow the mafia to 'launder' money obtained illegally. These people do not understand – they do not want to or cannot understand – who is manipulating them. In our society, we are faced with the phenomenon of the bare-faced thief literally shouting louder than anyone else, 'Stop thief!'

The same scenario is applied in our tragic and bloody nationalistic internecine conflicts – the most brutal of all internal conflicts in the Soviet state since the days of the civil war. The first official commentaries on the explosion in Nagorny Karabakh made one prick up one's ears because of their oversimplifications and evident divergence from the truth. The version approved at the top (or, more likely, invented at the top) was that the local mafia ('black-marketeers') had created difficulties in food supplies and this had sparked off the riots. But as Galina Starovoitova, people's deputy for an Armenian constituency in the Soviet Congress and a social scientist by background, correctly observed: 'In Ulster, you do not need a ration card to buy sausages, yet there is a continuing ethno-religious conflict which has been going on for years.' Very soon, another explanation for the escalation of intercommunal strife was added, one which was even more dangerously far from the truth. It fell from the lips of Mikhail Gorbachev who was in Yerevan after the earthquake answering journalists' questions in front of the cameras. He said the events in both Karabakh and Sumgait were the results of conspiracies among corrupt mafia elements to cover up their tracks. 'They should not think that we see nothing and know nothing,' said Gorbachev. 'We see everything.'

After these words, which gave the official press a hook upon which to hang an 'explanation' of the events which ran so counter to the traditional Soviet 'friendship of peoples', we awaited the discovery of these notorious 'black-marketeers' and their being brought to trial. But nothing of the sort happened anywhere. Not once! Neither in Sumgait, nor in Fergana, nor in Osh – nowhere. Meanwhile, this version was put out and widely disseminated to whomever necessary. The bait was taken, even by people far from the official ideology and well-known for their democratic standpoint. One popular journalist, a colleague and friend, without doubt an honest and decent man – for which reason I do not wish to name him – affirmed in print, clearly using the words of the officials at the Soviet Ministry of Internal Affairs, that 'Five months before the bloody events in

Fergana, many people knew that leaders of the criminal underworld had gone there.' What is this 'criminal underworld' exactly? Which of its 'leaders' went to Fergana? If so 'many people' knew about it, why were they not stopped? And, finally, where are these 'leaders of the criminal underworld' who provoked a bloody battle in Fergana and yet up to this day have not been arrested or brought to trial?

Moreover and furthermore: the version necessary to the powers-that-be has its sequel. The same journalist reported that a group of investigators from the Soviet prosecution service were already in Azerbaijan investigating the uncovering of local 'black-marketeers'. But the events in Fergana forced the Moscow investigators to slow down their work: the danger arose that the arrest of anyone from the Azeri mafia would be fraught with similarly tragic consequences.

It is no accident that I have dwelt in such detail on the version so stubbornly and purposefully implanted precisely through the hands of those very journalists whom the readers trust. This is quite a well-thought-out and effective diversionary tactic. It allows the mafia which really did provoke such alarming events to stand on one side and even appear in the role of unveilers of the provocateurs. I mean the 'partocracy' which has sacrificed a certain number of its members in the course of perestroika but has saved itself as an intact monolith unwilling to yield, determined to try and keep itself in power at any price. These disturbances were very convenient to them on the principle of 'the worse, the better', although during the Brezhnev stagnation, as they hint, there were no disturbances and could not have been. It is these forces who can maintain themselves in power only by representing themselves as peacemakers able to reconcile the warring factions.

Of course, that support which the old local mafia enjoys from the Kremlin is the most indicative evidence of the intricately-moving political intrigue which has cost the people dear in the shape of thousands of brutally terminated lives. In the very heat of the upheavals in the Kirghiz town of Osh, where fanatics stripped the skin off living people, put out each other's eyes and impaled each other, Alexandra Biryukova, a candidate member of the Politburo who had arrived in the republic's capital of Frunze for a meeting of the republic's Communist Party, made the following statement: 'I will speak completely frankly. I have the strong impression that the process of renewal [i.e. in Kirghizia] is growing in the right direction, on the road of perestroika and a healthy democracy.'

'A healthy democracy' in the opinion of the Moscow leadership exists everywhere where the powers-that-be retain their former control, even if people are being burned alive on bonfires. At the same time, in those regions where new parties have come to power, for instance in the Russian parliament or in the municipalities of Moscow or Leningrad – there, of course, according to the Kremlin version, the tune is being called by the 'black-marketeers'. Thus the political mafia and the various structures which keep it in power, such as the top army leadership, the KGB and the Ministry of Internal Affairs, are trying to deflect public opinion away from the direction whence the real danger of revenge threatens the country.

I would like to cite the authoritative evidence of a well-informed, fully competent person. This man is a senior Soviet KGB officer, Alexander Kichikhin. He was involved in another inter-ethnic conflict which has not reached the stage of bloody clashes – the public opposition to the desire of Soviet ethnic Germans to return to the Volga lands, now part of the Saratov region, whence they were exiled by Stalin during World War Two. This is what Alexander Kichikhin wrote in an open letter to President Gorbachev: 'Corrupt circles are trying to keep themselves in power locally, concealing industrial and administrative crimes, trying to hide behind the people whom they themselves have provoked, having themselves stoked the fire of inter-ethnic conflict. All this work is being done by leaders of the regional party committee and certain of the city soviets of the Communist Party'.

All the present inter-ethnic conflicts in the Soviet Union are erupting and spreading on these same lines, with various divergences due to specific regional factors. There is no other power which would have any vested interest in provoking these conflicts apart from the ruling mafia which can feel the earth trembling beneath its feet. And it must be admitted that they have been successful in achieving their desired aim – maybe not always, but more often than not.

The clearest example is provided by the situation in Azerbaijan. It is possible that in no other republic has the mafia succeeded in taking so many posts from top to bottom in the state and party apparatus, in trade, science, agriculture and culture. Perestroika, glasnost, the removal of Aliev and the arrival on the political scene of new social movements would have led inevitably to the demise of this mafia structure. And it was in this republic that the first pogroms took place, to begin with in Sumgait and then the bloodbath in Baku ... Moscow sent in the army and forces of the Ministry of the Interior to help the reeling 'partocracy'. Yes, a few people lost their jobs, but the mafia remains unshakably in power. And 'elections', under the same army control, allow the vast majority of the elected deputies' seats to be held on to by apparatchiks, and by the party-military-industrial nomenklatura originally placed there by Aliev himself or during his rule. This is the same mafia which was screaming loudest of all about the uncompromising battle with the mafia. And Aliev himself returns triumphantly to political life riding on a white horse like nothing so much as the Messiah of his people. Nowhere so clearly and with such certainty did the Soviet mafia show its nationalistic–patriotic colouring, its resilience and capacity defiantly to withstand all stormy winds of change.

But Azerbaijan, of course, is not an isolated example. It is merely the most striking and obvious one. Not a single one of those promised trials of the mafia has yet taken place. It can be said with certainty that they will not, at any rate for the foreseeable future.

At public literary meetings and at meetings with readers, I am often asked: 'How can the continued flourishing and indestructability of the mafia be explained? Is it that the mafia continues to support the present leadership and that they, like their predecessors, are part of the mafia structures themselves?'

Putting the question this way oversimplifies the real problem, by linking it to the possible or actual corruption of highly-placed people. The mafia is intact because it grew up with the system and has become an inseparable part of it, which means that the mafia will only collapse when the whole edifice, i.e. the system itself, collapses. Changes in personnel at the top of the party or the government in this sense have no significant effect on the essence of the system and its component parts. For this reason, any leader who supports the system is inescapably upholding the mafia as well, even if he is bursting with a sincere desire to finish it off. This is an objective and inescapable fact of political reality.

In *this* sense, as long as Gorbachev remains a defender of the present political system, he will *ipso facto* remain a defender of the mafia. If his constant declarations about the truth of the 'socialist choice' and 'ideals of October' turn out not to be just a tactical move in a careful strategy, not just tribute paid in threadbare oratorical terminology, but his real political position, this means that henceforth he will be putting a brake as hard as he can on the course of history, whatever his personal view of the mafia might be.

Anyone who imagines that relations today between the Soviet political leadership and the controllers of criminal funds are built on the simple principle of 'You scratch my back and I'll scratch yours' is profoundly mistaken. This is not only because roubles (like in Stalin's time, but for a different reason) have no value any longer; nor even because in today's circumstances it is more and more difficult to hide such a relationship. It is above all because the strategic and therefore the tactical tasks have changed. A vicious battle for power is in progress, and that alone is now determining the mutual relations between those who are directly or indirectly involved. Money itself is not the point at issue: money only has purchasing power for those in power, but they have no need for money, because power gives them all they want practically free. Those who are in power can buy many goods for 1,000 roubles, whereas the ordinary citizen can buy nothing for 100,000 roubles.

It might be thought that this would stimulate those in power to accumulate money, since it has real value in their hands. But of course this money would lose its value if they lost power. Added to which, their main objectives – comfort, services, travel, the dolce vita – on the whole are not available for money. The powers-that-be supply these commodities free. A place in the sun has become the most important and valuable currency. Those in power are not concerned so much with obtaining money but with the establishment of reliable sources of support. They do not so much take money as allow those who protect and support them to take it. It is especially for this reason that there will definitely be no trials of the mafia. But there will be trials of some petty thieves who have tripped up. They were always brought to trial – under Khrushchev and under Brezhnev and under Chernenko.

The manner in which today's economic mafia is joined to the political leadership is unbelievably simple. In contrast to the period of stagnation, this alliance is more decorous and less blatant. It exists, but it is as though it didn't. The real money-bags carry out any wishes of 'their' leaders, not even bothering to tell them how it is done. Many intervening ranks divide the political master and the economic contractor, thus the man at the top of the pyramid is not in direct contact with the individuals swarming about at his feet. But without these underlings, he is nothing – like someone who lives in the most luxurious mansion which nevertheless will collapse if the foundations do.

The most important thing is for each man on each successive step of this gigantic flight of stairs to know who is standing on the step below. That is, the man to whom he is indebted – who has repaid him a good turn, whether in cash or in kind. And he to the next man, and so forth. How exactly payments are effected, whether it is with millions, with gold, with diamonds, charm, blackmail through a tip-off or something else, whether it was easy or difficult, whether someone had to be killed, put in prison or married off to the simple-minded daughter of some great magnate – does not matter to anyone. So long as there is a result! Nobody thrusts 30,000, 70,000 or 100,000 roubles on individuals at the very highest level.

Everything happens quite differently. In a modern way. Let us suppose, for example, that Mr Big wants to build himself a new mansion among the ancestral pines on the legendarily beautiful promontory of Pitsunda. To do this he needs a plot – about ten hectares of land. But there really is no spare land available in Pitsunda. It already belongs to someone, or someone has a claim to it. The achievement of the task he has set himself requires contact with local councils, with the spa authorities, with the state security services, with the health authority, with an enormous quantity of services . . . Only someone who knows the real conditions in Abkhazia (for it is within this region that Pitsunda is situated) will understand what an unbelievable amount of money all this would cost.

And so the task is achieved. The land has been acquired. Mr Big's longed-for mansion is being built to add to all the existing ones – he does not know and does not wish to know how much it cost nor who paid for it. Can one report that Mr Big has 'got something' from someone? Ridiculous. Of course not. He has no idea how much has been spent and will never know. Otherwise he would no doubt have demanded an inquiry and severe measures. But nevertheless, he would know exactly who 'fixed it' for him at the highest level. And that person would know the man at a slightly lower level. And he etc. . . . Thus they are all knitted together. But who could be accused of what? And what can be proved, and to whom?

257

It seems to some people that the popular talk in the country about the dachas, cars, jewels and expensive dresses of the ruling elite is the result of a common man's interest in the rich in a beggared country. But it is not this. The interest itself of that very elite in such perks and valuables bears witness to their petty, common tastes, desires and ambitions. You do not have to be a great psychologist to understand how their thoughts are occupied in reality, to see how they frenziedly cling to those privileges condemned and hated by the people, seizing everything that can still be seized. The personal worth of the nomenklatura is the holy of holies, the most tremendous state secret. It was not so much the confiscation (or prospective confiscation) of a tiny portion of their wealth which troubled the 'partocracy' with regard to the activity of Telman Gdlyan's investigative team; it was more the unheard-of political blasphemy in his verbal and printed speeches which made 'the private life' of the nomenklatura, its income and circumstances, a topic of public discussion.

Specialists reckon that in the Soviet Union there are no less than 200,000 families each with a fortune of more than one million roubles. Among these, only 300–400 individuals are famous show-business stars, popular artists, composers and filmmakers who could – more or less legally – make this sort of money through their work. The rest are the nomenklatura and the so-called 'spivs', between which the boundary is so shifting as to be indistinguishable. And yet the main wealth of the nomenklatura – that which cannot be calculated in any monetary terms – is the luxury bestowed by belonging to the System and by being its favoured pets, according to rank (quite free of charge!). The model is an invention of genius, developed and perfected by Stalin; it has outlived both him and his political heirs, and still gives splendid service to those who curse Stalin and anathematize him.

It is quite obvious that the present social processes created by perestroika will inevitably lead to persons even in the very highest positions of responsibility giving up their 'government' dachas and the posts to which these dachas are attached as perks. Now a new epidemic is gathering force: the conversion of courtesy state dachas into a string of paid private ones. Still they want to keep them for themselves, whatever the circumstances. Ryzhkov's attempt to 'buy' his state villa standing in 1.5 hectares of woodland for 47,000 roubles is well-known. Thanks to a timely article in a newspaper, the attempt failed. But tens of marshals, hundreds of generals and thousands of apparatchiks not over-worried by their popularity ratings have managed to buy property. For 30,000–40,000 roubles, twelve- or fifteen-room multi-storey palaces have been 'sold' with a number of ancillary buildings on site, woodlands, lakes, swimming pools and so on. By comparison I can say that the simplest two-room country flat in which I live (and it took me seventeen years to get permission to buy it!), without an inch of land, not even enough for a flowerbed – cost me 22,000 roubles . . .

The offer to the new 'lords of life' of enormous free flats and dachas (the rent for them is merely a token amount), enabling them to jump the queue, rocked the country when the papers reported it, but in no way embarrassed the leaders of perestroika. As might have been expected, they turned out to be exactly the same as their predecessors, whom they had passionately accused of illegal use of privilege. A long list appeared in print of those in Gorbachev's team who had cynically obtained comfortable flats of 150–250 square metres – significantly bigger than is laid down by standing regu-lations – without queuing at all, at a time when millions of their fellow citizens had to go on living in basements and temporary accommodation after waiting for ten, fifteen or twenty years for any sort of decent housing. None of the 'new' people could strictly speaking be said to be different from the 'old' in this sense, dem-onstrating as they did a greedy and brazen disregard for the law and social justice.

It is particularly telling that these very excellent qualities were demonstrated by the official fighters against privilege – people, for instance, like Yevgeny Primakov, the president of the committee of the Supreme Soviet of the USSR, and others. Not one of those named in the press, out of the many dozens of new senior members of the nomenklatura who had seized spacious flats and dachas, wished to comment publicly on the accusations levelled against them. But when marshals and generals, who as recently as 1990 had thundered about the impermissibility of living it up at the tax-payers' expense, managed to appropriate fifteen- and twenty-room villas for them-selves worth hundreds of thousands and millions of roubles, it was called by Minister of Defence Dmitri Yazov (who had built himself a mini-Versailles) 'a campaign to discredit the Soviet army'. There is no reason to be surprised at this. The system has remained unchanged. Almost all the 'perestroikers' come from the same stable of party apparatchiks; their level of thinking, moral criteria, the secret dreams they nurse and their concepts of value are exactly the same as those of their deposed predecessors. They simply could not be otherwise. Let us notice in passing that neither of Brezhnev's two country 'residences', worth ten million roubles, have been used since 1986. But 245,000 roubles are spent every year on their maintenance (thirty people are on that particular payroll). Who are these 'residences' waiting for? New residents?

The question is far from rhetorical. The answer to it might be given already. The former dacha belonging to Ṣtalin near Moscow was remodelled at the end of 1990 as a 'working office' for the president of the USSR – the reconstruction cost the Central Committee (!) about 50 million roubles. What is so amazing is not just the craving for tasteless luxury, the primitive idea of showy window-dressing, grandeur and beauty. What is far more surprising is the total flouting of public opinion, and indifference to the reaction of 'our' people, whose welfare the president has declared to be his highest concern. Incidentally, it was not only their Soviet predecessors who suffered from this malady. The militant anti-monarchist head of the Provisional Government, Alexander Kerensky, could not think of anything nicer in the summer of 1917 than to move into the regal tranquillity of the Winter Palace. Thus idiotic traditions proceed from roots reaching far back into Russian history.

Why do I consider it so necessary to yield to the man in the street's mood and deal with this topic? Because the urge of the ruling classes in the end (and maybe not in the end?) to snatch whatever they can from the benefits bestowed on them by the System strips bare their real desires, though they may be camouflaged by political demagogy. And this makes psychologically understandable their pliability to mafia pressure, their inability to resist the riches which pass through their hands, their spiritual kinship with those who skilfully lure them into their traps. Let it not be forgotten that the nomenklatura consists almost entirely of little-educated, wholly uncultured and, most often of all, simply ignorant people, from the most humble, narrow-minded, limited backgrounds, nouveaux riches in the literal sense of the word. It is very difficult for them to renounce the beautiful lifestyle which they have achieved with no effort (leaving aside that which they put into their career intrigues), the marble, carpets, crystal chandeliers, luxury furniture – everything that Boris Yeltsin so effectively mocks in his memoirs with a smile understood by every reader.

Of course, it is now unthinkable for them to allow themselves the privileges of the Brezhnev era, which were then considered the norm but now seem like madness and black farce. It is difficult to believe that until relatively recently a private railway train was sent after a member of the Politburo to his holiday spa, with his personal cow and milkmaid, so that his milk supply could continue unchanged, his weakened digestive system having been damaged by the back-breaking demands of the duties of the party hierarchy. But up till now, there still remain in the new hierarchy such unheard-of privileges for an impoverished country, that the People's Deputy to the committee of the Supreme Soviet on privilege, Ella Pamfilova, resigned her party membership abruptly, having clashed with the present (not the former, the present) leadership face-to-face. Let me close this subject with an excerpt from an article by Alexander Solzhenitsyn, 'Rebuilding Russia': 'The corrupt ruling class – the many million party-state nomenklatura – is not capable of voluntarily renouncing any of the privileges they have seized. They have lived shamelessly for decades at the people's expense – and would like to continue to do so.'

The achievement of this aim requires definite organizational efforts because it is too late now for anything to be put right by the will of one man: the political situation has fundamentally changed. This was clearly and convincingly shown by the recent Twenty-Eighth Congress of the Communist Party. Although they renounced their 'leading role' provided for by Clause 6 of the constitution, the party is by no means prepared to part with this right in practice. To avoid fundamental democratic changes inside the party which would allow it to change into a parliamentary type of party, mafia powers set as their aim to select a team of delegates implacably dedicated to the maintenance of the status quo. This task was entrusted to Gennady Razumovsky, the secretary of the Central Committee in charge of official appointments (as already mentioned the successor not long ago of Medunov and Vorotnikov in the mafia capital of Krasnodar). He carried out his task magnificently: no less than

90 per cent of delegates were passionate opponents of democratic transformation. And they (more accurately, those of them who represented regional organizations of the Russian Federation), declared that they were a founding congress and secured the establishment of a Russian branch of the Communist Party, in direct contradiction of the statutes and constitution of the Communist Party of the Soviet Union, confirming as its leader Razumovsky's own successor in Krasnodar, Ivan Polozkov. He had succeeded in driving more than 300 cooperatives out of business there before being transferred to Moscow.

Let it be noted that this same Razumovsky performed one more priceless service, this time for the military mafia. It was under his leadership that on 20 December 1989 a conference of generals took place in the Central Committee, to review the situation which had arisen in connection with the formation of a union which called itself 'Shield'. This trade union was composed of younger, middle-ranking army officers with radical views – the democratic opposition to the 'hawks' – fighting for glasnost in the depths of the Soviet army and for democratic reforms within the army. Under Razumovsky's leadership the conference took the decision to dismiss from the army with twenty-four hours' notice anyone who joined Shield. Also, Razumovsky drew up a candidate list for the Supreme Soviet from the ranks of the military. We know what kind of delegation that was.

Did the mafia remain in Razumovsky's debt? In no way. They expressed their appreciation according to a previous agreement. Razumovsky obtained a 'cushy number' – the post of consul general in Shanghai, a post in the gift of the KGB nomenklatura guaranteeing what every apparatchik dreams of: an untroubled life abroad, free from political gladiatorial combat with a foreign-currency budget whose expenditure in practical terms is not subject to any kind of control. A wonderful, heavenly little corner – before a final departure on well-earned retirement.*

---

* 'Good deeds' are not forgotten: in that respect there is a tradition which has been carried on since Brezhnev's day. For instance, the former head of the Stavropol division of the KGB, General Sergei Tolkunov, regardless of his age (he is seventy-five) is still working in the central apparatus in Moscow, in the very senior position of head of the inspectorate of the KGB. But this possibly has a very simple explanation: no doubt the General knows a great deal ... Nor are the services of great party magnates forgotten, who have done much to save 'yesterday's men'. Practically all of them have quietly been found jobs as 'diplomats'. The former boss of Moldavia, Semen Grossu, at fifty-six (!) became a modest attaché at the Soviet

In his turn, Ivan Polozkov, fulfilling the instruction of those who appointed him to his high office as leader of a still somewhat illusory party, declared, as might have been expected, a decisive war against the mafia! Turning meaning on its head and making brilliant use of the slogans of 'social equality' instilled in us for nearly three quarters of a century, Polozkov made his presence felt on the political stage with an attack on cooperatives and above all on the state-cooperative joint venture ANT, which was developing one of the boldest and most progressive projects: the sale abroad of rusty old military equipment for scrap in return for an enormous quantity of goods sorely needed by the country from sausages to trousers, from washing powder to jam. Gorbachev and Ryzhkov were supporters of this 35-million-dollar project, so the blow was not only directed straight at them, but also at the planned transfer to a market economy and any idea of free and profitable trade.

Why? Because the mafia nomenklatura had already become used to the old centrally-planned and command-administrative economy which allowed it to continue both in power and in the money. The so-called 'wheeler-dealers' and underworld businessmen obtained their incomes direct from the hands of the bureaucratically organized powers-that-be and shared part of their dividends with them. The investment capital of the nomenklatura is the percentage due to the ranks of the bureaucracy. Without any of these things it would amount to a big fat nothing. A market economy is simply not needed by the party-administrative nomenklatura.

If it loses power, it loses its revenues because under a true market economy it will not be able to obtain anything. However, there is a well-known grain of truth in the demagogic cries of the 'banditocracy' which is the legitimate child of the state monopoly. Real opportunities will be provided in a market economy for the mafiosi, who have amassed considerable capital, to put it into a legal business – to 'launder dirty money', as the Polozkovites put it in their newspapers. This is an inevitable moral problem of perestroika, the price to be paid for the economic chaos which the political mafia has

embassy in Mexico; the secretary of the central committee of the Armenian party, Suren Arutunyan, became consul general in Casablanca; the chief of the ideology section of the Central Committee, Alexander Kapto, became the Soviet ambassador in Pyongyang. But those upon whom nothing depended and who did not possess 'valuable information' were retired immediately.

established over three quarters of a century in the country. If hopes of a market economy are not realized, this mafia will flourish even more, as it has managed to do for many decades already.

In essence the struggle of the forces of reaction and the partocracy against a market economy is a fight of the mafia for its place in the sun and its wealth – both what it already possesses, and what it expects to gain if it stays in power. The worst elements in the mafia, interested only in staying in power, are fighting with another part of the mafia which wants to work under new economic conditions, using the accumulated wealth which is currently merely a dead-weight round its neck. If a market is created after all, this second mafia will cease to be a mafia (not now, but later!) and will turn itself into a normal participant in the economic system.

But – will it change? The future will show who the winners are. Whatever happens, it is clear even now that the mafia will win.

Postscript

This book was written during year six of the restructuring process, which was supposed to relieve millions of Soviet people from fear of a blindly cruel and terrorizing state machine. It also inspired hope that the all-powerful political mafia would retreat before the forces of democracy, justice and legality. That hope had a realistic basis and I personally felt the distinct change taking place in society. In the pre-Gorbachev period enormous efforts of cunning and determination were required to beat the censorship and sometimes one's own editorial management, in order to get investigative journalism into print, even if oblique or, at times, allegorical in treatment. The position then completely changed and the censorship quietly went to ground, hiding under a new name, trying to avoid drawing attention to itself. Our editors now could not wait to be brought investigative pieces for publication, because that makes the paper popular and increases circulation.

I too succumbed to the joyful euphoria that infected the public as a whole, but before long an ice-cold shower brought me back to stern reality.

Returning to the newspaper after my summer vacation in 1989, I met a colleague of long standing who works on the letters page. First making sure nobody was observing us he took me to the end of an empty corridor and said sotto voce: 'Take this, read and destroy.' He was taking a risk because the letter he had for me was one which should have been despatched by our 'special department' straight to the KGB. This would have happened had the author of the letter not written 'personal' on the envelope. Before I read the letter itself,

I noticed that the author, who no doubt wrote under a pseudonym, had typewritten it but only sent me a carbon, the third or fourth by the look of it. I recalled lectures on criminology at university, and that identifying a typewriter is virtually impossible from the third carbon onwards. So the writer must be a pro!

'Dear Comrade Vaksberg,

'As a devoted reader of your trenchant articles on legal questions I consider it my duty to warn you of the danger hovering over you and your family. I myself have worked for twenty years in close proximity to the organs of power and I am well acquainted with their ways, and not by hearsay. Your pieces do not leave our chiefs indifferent to your person; they keep a complete file on you. Our chief was lying when at the Supreme Soviet in answer to one of the deputies he said that we no longer operate telephone surveillance, do not read people's letters nor break into flats when the owners are away. It continues to be done on the quiet by specialists of our Special Technical Department.

'Our leaders are deliberately destabilizing the country because perestroika and democratization are against their interests. Everything is being done to provoke the people into crying, as one: "Let us have strong government back." We have people working for us in every organization, and not only in those critical of the government. We 'hook' these people by letting them off petty crimes such as foreign-currency fiddles or illegal street-trading, after which they conscientiously carry out our bidding. Through such people it is possible to get the public worked up and through them we can keep an eye on various groups. It was not for nothing that Gumbaridze [KGB head in Georgia, later first secretary of the party central committee in Georgia] moved up to the top position in the republic after the infamous savagery perpetrated in April 1989 by the army on peaceful demonstrators in Tbilisi. Millions of citizens are on our books. It is not true that all the records on the victims of the terror in the thirties have disappeared. Every single person that passed through our hands is on record in our data centres.

'We operate now as we always have, except that we have adopted a lower profile and changed our tactics. We have stopped taking protective measures against our customers but just gather information on them which will enable us to put them to work for us when the right moment comes. Everybody here curses the reforms on the quiet [no longer "on the quiet"!] and expects the fall of democracy, and it will happen sooner than you think. And the army is behind us too.

'The only thing which might save us is a complete disbanding of the KGB – apart from the 1st, 2nd and 9th Departments [i.e. intelligence, counter-intelligence and the VIP protection group]. Let them get on with their business. Only then will you have some guarantee that in return for your "lampoonery", as our people call it, you will not have to wear your trousers out on Butyrka's or Lefortovo's prison benches [both famous jails with special sections for KGB 'clients'].

Meanwhile, be on your guard and take care. With my deepest respect for you and your work.
V. N. Voloshin
Lawyer'

One might assume that the KGB would welcome the unmasking of highly-placed mafiosi – after all it is their job, the more so as it is in line with the oft-declared policy of the new leadership, which instructed the organs of state security to support the policy and to put it into effect. So why on earth are they looking to gather evidence against their would-be allies in the campaign against that mafia, a campaign which was launched with such energy by their former chief, Yuri Andropov?

The answer is becoming increasingly clear, namely that the head of the KGB was not campaigning against the mafia so much as against a potential rival in the struggle for power. Any actual attempt to harm the mafia would mean harming the System itself and neither Andropov nor his successors or their colleagues wished to do that at all. The people in the ruling political mafia, which controls all the commanding heights, change from time to time and will continue to do so. But the mafia remains essentially unchanged, preserving its smooth, well-organized structures. Standing on guard for them are all the main elements of the System, and this will continue. Thus, somebody who offers, within the permitted limits, small doses of watered-down criticism of ex-mafiosi grandees after they have been thrown overboard and are of no further use to anybody, is a friend and ally of the regime because he is helping its noble image. On the

267

other hand, those that go further and draw general conclusions are enemies of the regime. Today this is more so than ever before, because due to glasnost there is a far greater possibility than in the so-called years of inertia of fundamentally exposing the system which has given rise to the invincible mafia and, moreover, become part and parcel of it.

This is the explanation for the reanimation of the ongoing faultless tactics of the mafia protectors behind the scenes. They are attempting to split the ranks of those fighting the mafia, to cast aspersions on them and to instil distrust among them. The KGB's rumour machine, which for decades has operated so successfully, is working as hard as ever to provoke conflict between people who share the same views, setting them against each other and thereby depreciating the value of any exposure of the mafia arising out of their investigations.

Here is just one example. It concerns a person already mentioned in this book, Anatoly Churganov, an implacable opponent of Medunov and his clan, and one who has paid for his unbreakable devotion to the truth with six years in the Gulag. Churganov was addressing one of the mass meetings in Leningrad and was suddenly attacked as he began his prison-camp reminiscences. Some unknown person shouted: 'Informer! Agent!' and the whole audience immediately reacted like dry brushwood to a spark. Churganov tried to ask for the evidence but the crowd wouldn't allow him to speak. Similar accusations were hurled at others investigating the mafia, people beyond reproach, who for years had stuck honourably to the task and had suffered for it.

Bringing discredit on anti-mafia campaigners is easy; one simply accuses them of being linked to the KGB. There is a countless number both of established informers and of 'volunteers' – almost anybody you meet could be one. Such accusations will be believed a priori by everybody, now that the curse of informerism has been on our great land for three-quarters of a century. Nobody can insure himself against the all-seeing eye of the secret service, or against its cruelty and its guile. In the minds of millions there is no greater evil than being party to the activity of the secret services. For this reason the quickest way to get rid of an investigator's unwanted attentions is to launch a rumour that he has secret-police connections. In those circumstances who cares about the concept of the presumption of innocence? About the need for proof and justification of all charges?

To whom should the proof be demonstrated? Where and how? There is no sure way of dealing with rumours, which is why it can be easy and productive to use them. In its fight for survival the mafia chooses weapons on the same level as its own 'moral' principles: rumours, fantasies, terror and blackmail.

Now I am no longer so astonished by the curses and threats that I hear with increasing regularity. Since I installed a telephone answering machine, the number of my 'well-wishers' wanting to unburden their feelings has grown and grown. I usually wipe their messages immediately but I decided to keep one for posterity, so to speak, and here it is, recorded only a few days ago:

'You son of a bitch, whore, dandruff-ridden yid, bite your filthy tongue or you'll regret it and too late. Stop pouring out pigswill in your stinking Zionist paper and belt up if you want to stay alive. I heard you in your lecture at the Library of Foreign Literature filling honest Russians with a lot of shit about the mafia. The mafia is you, you filthy Jews. Don't you touch the party, keep your hands off our motherland. And if there *is* any stealing going on, as you say, then it is the Jews that are being robbed, and rightly so. As I said, keep your filthy hands off the party and off the motherland – not yours, ours – otherwise you'll end up hanging like rotten carrion. Do I make myself clear or should I repeat it all once more? If . . . '

At this point the recording ended, as it had overrun the time on the tape. So far the unknown voice has not repeated its call.

Everything is as to be expected. The mafia is alive and well, and fights on in the knowledge that it can count on the power of the ruling apparatus and on the stupidity of the citizens, bamboozled as they have been by the System. Fortunately, however, more and more people have seen through it.

At that meeting in the foreign literature library mentioned by the anonymous telephone-caller, I was asked whether I lived in fear. I shall answer the question in the same way as I did to that audience. I made my choice and made it a long time ago, and there is no way for me to retreat now.

I shall finish with words from Corneille, although the idea behind them must have been expressed by many authors: 'Faites votre devoir et laissez faire aux dieux.'*

'Do your duty, and leave the future to the gods.'

*Pierre Corneille (1606–84), *Horace*, II, viii.

269

Index